STUDIES IN CHRISTIAN HISTORY AND THOUGHT

Martyrdom from Exegesis in Hippolytus

An Early Church Presbyter's *Commentary on Daniel*

A full listing of titles in this series
appears at the end of this book

STUDIES IN CHRISTIAN HISTORY AND THOUGHT

Martyrdom from Exegesis in Hippolytus

An Early Church Presbyter's *Commentary on Daniel*

W. Brian Shelton

WIPF & STOCK · Eugene, Oregon

Wipf and Stock Publishers
199 W 8th Ave, Suite 3
Eugene, OR 97401

Martyrdom from Exegesis in Hippolytus
An Early Church Presbyter's Commentary on Daniel
By Shelton, W. Brian
Copyright©2008 Paternoster
ISBN 13: 978-1-60608-311-6
Publication date 12/5/2008
Previously published by Paternoster, 2008

This Edition published by Wipf and Stock Publishers by arrangement with Paternoster

Series Preface

This series, *Studies in Christian History and Thought,* complements the specialist series of *Studies in Evangelical History and Thought* and *Studies in Baptist History and Thought* for which Paternoster is becoming increasingly well known by offering works that cover the wider field of Christian history and thought. It encompasses accounts of Christian witness at various periods, studies of individual Christians and movements, and works which concern the relations of church and society through history, and the history of Christian thought.

The series includes monographs, revised dissertations and theses, and collections of papers by individuals and groups. As well as 'free standing' volumes, works on particular running themes are being commissioned; authors will be engaged for these from around the world and from a variety of Christian traditions.

A high academic standard combined with lively writing will commend the volumes in this series both to scholars and to a wider readership.

Series Editors

Alan P.F. Sell, Visiting Professor at Acadia University Divinity College, Nova Scotia, Canada

David Bebbington, Professor of History, University of Stirling, Stirling, Scotland, UK

Clyde Binfield, Professor Emeritus in History, University of Sheffield, UK

Gerald Bray, Anglican Professor of Divinity, Beeson Divinity School, Samford University, Birmingham, Alabama, USA

Grayson Carter, Associate Professor of Church History, Fuller Theological Seminary SW, Phoenix, Arizona, USA

To my wife Sally, whose love and support under girded this work and an entire graduate career. Although Hippolytus and historical biblical exegesis meant little to her, she patiently endured my task with sacrifice, sympathy, and encouragement. She has proved Solomon's words accurate: "An excellent wife is the crown of her husband."

Contents

Acknowledgements

The author would like to express appreciation to Father Kenneth Steinhauser for his enduring support of this doctoral project; to Robert Lee Williams for his kind and thorough editorial suggestions and backing of the book; to Anthony Cross and Jeremy Mudditt for typesetting and administrative support; and to Paternoster, for the decision to include this book in the Christian History and Thought Series.

Brian Shelton
Toccoa Falls College
October 2007

CHAPTER 1

Confronting Martyrdom in Exegesis

Hippolytus is one of the most significant figures of the ancient church. This revered churchman was a productive writer, pioneer exegete, and champion of Christian orthodoxy. Jean Daniélou depicts his importance: "Among the young men whom Irenaeus taught.... Hippolytus came to be his great successor as the foremost figure of Greek Christianity in the West."[1] Centuries after his death, the West seemed to overlook him as a person while a legacy of writings and theological influence followed him.

This book will consider one particular exegetical work of Hippolytus, his *Commentary on Daniel*. Written about 204 CE during a time of severe Roman persecution against the church, the commentary applies the text of Daniel in a way that offered encouragement and theological credibility to the martyrs witnessed by the church. This book explores how Hippolytus' crafting of this work was influenced by a complex tradition of martyrdom, biblical exegesis, and eschatology, as well as a passion for a rigorous and sacrificial Christian life. This book also factors in how the Book of Daniel figured prominently in the early church in understanding these experiences because of its tales of perseverance under persecution, as well as its confidence of God's control over foreign nations that oppress his people, and a future hope of deliverance. It is no surprise that an early Christian presbyter would adopt this text to encourage a persecuted church, given the commentary's tendency toward the elevation of martyrs and its eschatological consciousness.[2] This book evidences this phenomenon of establishing martyrdom from exegesis.

---

[1] Jean Daniélou, *Gospel Message and Hellenistic Culture*, vol. 2, *A History of Early Christian Doctrine Before the Council of Nicaea* (Philadelphia: Westminster Press, 1973), 143.

[2] Daniel's themes of sovereignty and eschatology go hand-in-hand with the resolution of experienced martyrdom and persecution—a fundamental principle applied in this book. The early church employed the text for purposes of encouragement, and this is evident in articles such as John G. Gammie, "A Journey Through Danielic Spaces: The Book of Daniel in the Theology and Piety of the Christian Community," *Interpretation* 39 (1985): 144-56, and Ulrich Kellerman, "Das Danielbuch und die Märtyrertheologie der Auferstehung," in *Die Entstehung der Jüdischen Martyrologie* (New York: E. J. Brill, 1989), 51-75.

Hippolytus holds a place of preeminence among the patristic exegetes and his significance deserves recognition that this book offers. He is like Irenaeus and Justin in literal exegetical method, but extends the scope of his exegesis to never-before-explored fields of scripture. Hippolytus is recognized as a transitional figure in the early church for several reasons. (1) He was the first orthodox writer to create an expansive commentary on a single book of scripture, the first of which scholars believe was his *Commentary on Daniel*. (2) He used the Old Testament as his text, especially Daniel, Song of Songs, and the Pentateuch, while the early patristic preference was for New Testament material. (3) He demonstrated a theological emphasis on scripture that was more Christological than it was eschatological (like Irenaeus) or apologetic (like Justin). Hultgren has suggested that figures such as Hippolytus lived during a time of transition focusing on "more urgent and fundamental tasks of defining the scope and limits of what Christianity was to become."[3] An example was the church's need to confront the pressing issue of martyrdom that led to Hippolytus' reading of the Book of Daniel and his application of the text for his persecuted readers.

A Martyrdom Motif in the *Commentary on Daniel*

Hippolytus is long associated with early Christian liturgy through the work *Apostolic Tradition*. Here is safeguarded a record of Roman church order and liturgy from the late second century. Hippolytus' reputation is so linked with this book of church order, it might surprise some that he even contributed to the martyrological ideology of his era. Scholars have not exploited many of this church father's contributions to early Christianity, prompting this book's exploration of the unusual emphasis on martyrdom that emerges from Hippolytus' exegesis of Daniel. By evidencing a martyrdom motif in the commentary, this project also demonstrates the anxiety of Roman persecution in the early church and the early Christian hope of salvation that came in the scriptures.

Announcing Theory and Method

Chapter 2 establishes the provenance of the commentary as one of persecution. The question of martyrdom and the social harassment against the church constantly emerges as he comments on the scriptural text in this work. This theme of martyrdom is consistent with the events of persecution that surrounded it, the personal life of its author, and the theological traditions of martyrdom, suffering, and eschatology that preceded it. Hippolytus' exegesis in

---

[3] Arland J. Hultgren and Steven A. Haggmark, eds., *The Earliest Christian Heretics: Readings from their Opponents* (Minneapolis: Fortress Press, 1996), 2.

the commentary becomes an interpretive tool that unlocks numerous theological issues of concern to the early church, and the issue of suffering persecution repeatedly in his reading of Daniel.

The relationship between the Roman Empire and the Christian church in the early third century CE was one of major confrontation. In 202,[4] Emperor Septimius Severus (r. 193-211) initiated severe persecution against the church for its failure to join the empire in worshipping the Unconquered Sun, *Sol Invictus*. Christian noncompliance prompted the emperor to issue an additional edict that outlawed all new conversions to Christianity.[5] The result was a large number of martyrs within the Christian church.

As a presbyter, Hippolytus had to deal with the problems confronting a persecuted church such as fear of capture, hardships of secrecy, and stigma of apostasy, in addition to questions about God's providence and the divine purposes of their suffering. This pressure would have been intensified if his provenance was around Rome. Chapter 3 brings out the martyrological material of the *Commentary on Daniel*. Here, Hippolytus suggested that these disastrous events were in fact divinely approved, setting in motion an era of persecution that was announced in a prophetic way in Daniel. Hippolytus interpreted the symbols, visions, and narratives so that the meaning of scripture would bolster the faith of a persecuted and beleaguered church. He tried to build their confidence by the godly examples of faithfulness in the book and by justifying the large number of Christian martyrs they saw. Here especially this book establishes a martyrdom motif in Hippolytus' *Commentary on Daniel*, a phenomenon overlooked by past scholarly studies. Thus, chapter 3 is the most important chapter of the book in many ways. This martyrdom motif evidenced here functioned paraenetically to encourage his own congregations through his interpretation of the Book of Daniel, and the motif's points deserve close examination to see how they shaped the original reading of this book.

Hippolytus finds distinct parallels between the events under Babylonian kings and under Severus, so the presbyter used the text of Daniel to strengthen the Christians of his day to confront their harsh persecutions. The text effortlessly lends itself to his purposes with its examples of persecution that

---

[4] This becomes the basis for dating the commentary. Scholars vary about the year of its writing; most say 202, 204, or 205, while McCollough suggests 211 without explanation. C. Thomas McCollough, "Daniel," *Encyclopedia of Early Christianity*, ed. Everett Ferguson, 1st ed. (New York: Garland Publishing, 1990).

[5] Persecution under Severus was most severe in Africa, but the early church left vivid descriptions of anti-Christian violence in Rome, Corinth, Antioch, and Cappadocia. Although Hippolytus himself evidences such a decree, T. D. Barnes contends that there was no formal edict. Scholars almost unanimously agree that it was a time of severe persecution rather than support Barnes' denial of a formal edict. T. D. Barnes, "Legislation Against the Jews," *Journal of Religious Studies* 58 (1968): 41. For an analysis of the effect of the edict on the church, see pp. 40-43 below.

empathize with the church's current social situation, enabling him to offer a faith vision that would enable them to interpret contemporary events and to gain resolve in suffering for their faith. The Danielic characters become models of faithful suffering, they represent the antagonists amidst persecuted protagonists on the stage of history, and the prophecies are interpreted in light of Roman persecution. He stops short of claiming that the prophecies in Daniel are a direct prophecy of his contemporary persecutions, but their similarities give Hippolytus an effective forum to guide Christians to a correct response to the threat of martyrdom. The aim of his exegesis and his commentary are pastoral as he exhorts them to be willing to die for their faith. The historical novelty that comes with Hippolytus writing a pioneering commentary on scripture—when hardly any other orthodox writer had done so—is part of the mystery that surrounds the commentary and consequently this book's investigation of the work. Part of Hippolytus' exegetical rationale discussed here reinforces this book's overall thesis, that the text of Daniel lends itself to a presbyter who wants to lead his congregation in study of the scriptures while providing a forum to confront the reality of martyrdom and persecution of God's people. The explanation of the particular motivation for Hippolytus to engage in a commentary project can be found below at "Hippolytus' Novel Exegetical Task" in chapter 4.

Many of Hippolytus' apocalyptic treatises and commentaries evidence a similar milieu of martyrdom; they contain strong overtones of martyrdom with pastoral encouragement to persecuted Christians. On occasion, these will be reference to show similar points elsewhere in the Hippolytan corpus. However the martyrdom motif is not clearer and in a sense purer than in his *Commentary on Daniel*. Reminiscent of later patristic works that were written to encourage Christians facing persecution, this commentary posits and stresses a theology of martyrdom similar to Tertullian's *To the Martyrs,* Origen's *Exhortation to Martyrdom*, Cyprian's *To Fortunatus,* and Pseudo-Cyprian's *Glory of Martyrdom*. Unlike these works, Hippolytus contextualizes his exhortations to persecuted Christians in a commentary on scripture. This is part of what makes this study so interesting. Some examples here illustrate in an introductory way.

Finally, chapter 5 offers a synthesis of all the material. Theological inheritances, historical milieu, pastoral intentions, and a reading of Daniel enable Hippolytus to exhort a suffering and beleaguered church to be willing to die for Christ. This synthesis also functions as a quick summary of the entire work for a person wanting an abbreviated reading.

A final comment on organization deserves explanation. One might expect a study of Hippolytus' exegetical methodology, found in chapter 4, to precede the exegetical data that is reported in chapter 3. The reason for this delay is the need to examine the martyrdom motif in the commentary and to capture its effect, and then to allow this data to inform our study of his exegesis and his novel exegetical task in writing such a commentary. Hippolytus' writing style, his passionate flavor, his inheritance from Jewish and early patristic exegetes, his view of Scripture and the biblical "letter," his use of allegory and typology, and the place of faith in literary reading finally comes together in chapter 4. With this order of chapters, our study of methodology can employ examples from the exegetical data without spoiling the effect of a commentary-wide martyrdom motif, presented on its own in chapter 3.

Historic Importance of the Commentary

According to historians, this work comes to us as the oldest continuous, orthodox Christian commentary on any book of scripture. The current debate on what defines "orthodoxy" and "heresy" in earliest Christian centuries has challenged long held assumptions about these categories, but we can still speak of a basic, consistent catholic theology in the tradition of the apostles over against Gnostic interpretations of scripture. The Gnostic author Heracleon wrote a commentary on the gospel of John preserved only in Origen's *Commentary on John*, and the Gnostic understanding and use of scripture are challenged.[6] Heracleon's work on John may be the oldest continuous commentary of any book of scripture, but its heretical tendencies surely precluded its success. Thus, Hippolytus' commentaries become the oldest of this special type of work to have a successful, long-term influence on the church.[7] The Gnostic teacher Ptolemy also wrote a brief exegetical commentary on the prologue to John's gospel in the late second century, but it is not a running commentary on a complete book of scripture.

Hippolytus' *Commentary on Daniel* has broader significance than just the martyrdom motif, and the work deserves closer examination because of its significance for our understanding of the early church. As a running commentary on any book of scripture, this work is among the first extant of its type of a unique genre. It is thus a treasure for examining early Christian theology and history, and a sample of its features will help the reader understand a range of interest that this genre can serve. In the case of history, this commentary reflects how the church understands itself in relation to divine interaction in history. For instance, Hippolytus is the first to see contemporary Rome as the referent of the fourth kingdom of the beasts (Dan. 7:2-12); this is "the kingdom which is now in power," namely "the kingdom of the Romans" which persecutes God's people.[8]

---

[6] For an analysis of this work, see Bart D. Ehrman, "Heracleon and the 'Western' Textual Tradition," *New Testament Studies* 40 (1994): 161-179.

[7] For an exact discussion on why Hippolytus would engage in such a pioneering commentary task, see "Hippolytus' Novel Exegetical Task," pp. 111-115 below.

[8] *Commentary on Daniel*, IV.8.1-2. Quotations from the *Commentary on Daniel* are from the Greek version found in Hippolytus, *Kommentar zu Daniel*, trans. Georg Nathanael Bonwetsch (Berlin: Akadamie Verlag, 2000) and Hippolytus, *Commentaire sur Daniel*, vol. 14, Sources Chrétiennes, trans. Maurice Lefèvre, Introduction by

Furthermore, this commentary furnishes important insights into the church's view of scripture, such as her responsibility to discern prophecy and her leaders' duty to apply the Bible's precepts to the lives of believers. Hippolytus thoughtfully weds the two principles of interpretation and application along the lines of perseverance and suffering, as when he interprets the foods consumed by the faithful, persecuted Jews in Daniel 1:12 as a type of Christian grace: "These are not earthly meats that give to men their beauty and strength, but the grace of God bestowed by the Word."[9] The commentary also illustrates how apocalyptic literature functioned to encourage the church in the face of impending persecution, as its themes of transcending death, the dualism of good and evil kingdoms, and the rewards of immortality all combined to offer theological sympathy to the suffering church.

Besides these important theological contributions, the commentary also contains many small details that are unique among early Christian writings. For example, the work contains the oldest recorded citation for the dating of Christmas.[10] It also contains an important historical description of the Montanist phenomenon.[11] These details are passing incidences stemming from Hippolytus' careful commentary and interpretation of the text. So thorough are the interpretations in this commentary, that, before Origen, we can only speak of Hippolytus of Rome as the first Christian exegete. Simonetti remarks that with this work:

> Catholic exegesis, restricted so far to controversial, catechetical or doctrinal purposes, at last frees itself from these fetters and become an independent literary genre, with works devoted exclusively to the interpretation, if not yet of an entire book of the Bible, of fairly extensive passages.[12]

This ancient commentary, therefore, uniquely uses an Old Testament book to advance a Christian theology of martyrdom in the early church. The severe persecutions by the Roman Empire in the early third century led Hippolytus to endow his exegesis of Daniel with a martyrdom motif to persuade Christians to

---

Gustave Bardy (Paris: Éditions du Cerf, 1947). Whenever these two works differ in the Greek text, preference is given to the more recent Bonswetsch edition version while the commentary chapter and verse reference continues in the tradition of the Sources Chrétiennes version. These are the only two versions of the complete commentary text. The translations in this monograph are by the current author. For a brief analysis of the manuscript material, see pp. 73-77 below.

[9] *Commentary on Daniel*, I.11.4.

[10] *Commentary on Daniel*, IV.23.

[11] *Commentary on Daniel*, IV.19-20.

[12] Manlio Simonetti, *Biblical Interpretation in the Early Church: An Historical Introduction to Patristic Exegesis*, trans. John A. Hughes (Edinburgh: T & T Clark, 1994), 27.

suffer for the sake of Christ. In the commentary, he exegetically elevated the appeal of martyrdom in the minds of his readers in order to promote a spirit of resolve to suffer for the faith. Through his interpretation of the biblical text, Hippolytus proposed a higher calling to persecuted Christians in his day: to submit themselves to God, to trust his providence unto death, to participate in God's plan of history, and to transcend spiritually over the physically oppressive Roman Empire. This book's investigation will demonstrate unmistakable credence of such an interpretation—an observation that scholarship has not adequately substantiated or explored.

As author of this unique and valuable commentary, Hippolytus is also one of the stranger figures of the ancient church. His biography is shrouded in historical ambiguity. Writings by his contemporaries preserved little biographical data about him and the historians in the two centuries after him were not altogether clear about the details of his life. They did, however, attribute many works to him, and from their biographical sketches and his list of works, scholars have reconstructed an understanding of a life characterized by orthodoxy, biblical exegesis, ordained leadership, schism, liturgical observance, and theological discourse. Both a study of this church father among the patristic writers, and a survey of the particular concerns among nineteenth and twentieth century scholars, is in order.

Hippolytus within Scholarship

The scholarship on Hippolytus in the last century has centered on issues of his historical identity and his writings. There has been much discussion about whether his ecclesiastical office was Roman or Eastern, whether he was a schismatic claimant to the bishop's see or merely the leader of a small dissident theological group, and what constitutes his exact corpus of works. After a brief survey of the patristic evidence on Hippolytus, I will engage the recent scholarship about these issues before establishing the foundation for this martyrdom motif. Study surrounding the historical Hippolytus is important but not crucial to this book's treatment of his exegesis. A martyrdom motif in the commentary clearly establishes a provenance of religious persecution, and such a milieu is not uncommon in the early third century Roman empire. However, theories surrounding an Eastern Hippolytus deserve brief attention.

The Patristic Evidence

The patristic testimony on Hippolytus of Rome is scarce but still informative. Sadowski has quipped, "We are in the unusual position of knowing more about the life of Hippolytus than any of the church fathers did."[13] An examination and

---

[13] Frank Sadowski, ed., *The Church Fathers on the Bible: Selected Readings* (New

assessment of the ancient sources will be given below in a section on scholarly trends. This section provides the patristic data on the historical Hippolytus and the next section assess the scholarly trends in understanding this data.

The oldest biographical reference to Hippolytus is found in Eusebius of Caesarea. The great historian mentions several things concerning his ecclesiastical service and his literary works, but seems uncertain about his exact office and clearly omits its location. Eusebius reports about Hippolytus next to his report about Beryllus, in a way that seems confusing:

> There flourished many learned men in the Church at that time, whose letters to each other have been preserved and are easily accessible..... We have been able to gather from that library material for our present work. Among these Beryllus has left us, besides letters and treatises, various elegant works. He was bishop of Bostra in Arabia. Likewise also Hippolytus, who presided over another church, has left writings.[14]

It is peculiar that Eusebius fails to mention the exact location of Hippolytus and his exact ecclesiastical position. The term προεστώς means to "be head of, rule, direct" over a church but is not a technical term for a specific office in antiquity.[15] This church historian generally uses the term ἐπίσκοπον to denote the office of bishop, but uses προεστώς to describe Hippolytus.[16]

Eusebius mentions some of the works of Hippolytus, but among his omissions is the *Commentary on Daniel*.[17] This association with Bostra in

---

York: Alba House, 1987), 253.

[14] ὡσαύτως δὲ καὶ Ἱππόλυτος, ἑτέρας που καὶ αὐτὸς προεστὼς ἐκκλησίας. Eusebius, *Ecclesiastical History* VI.20.2 (cf. VI.22.1ff.). In both of these entries, Eusebius mentions a library where the writings may be found. In VI.20, he mentions the Jerusalem library founded by Alexander, bishop of Jerusalem 212-250; in VI.22, he references the library at Alexandria. The locations of the works do not necessarily offer insight into their provenance. For scholarship on the credibility of Eusebius, see Michael J. Hollerich, "Religion and Politics in the Writings of Eusebius: Reassessing the First 'Court Theologian,'" *Church History* 59 (1990): 309-25.

[15] William Arndt, Walter Bauer, F. Wilbur Gingrich, and Frederick W. Danker, *A Greek-English Lexicon of the New Testament and Other Early Christian Literature* (Chicago: University of Chicago Press, 1979).

[16] For a discussion of the terminology and offices, see Allen Brent, *Hippolytus and the Roman Church of the Third Century: Communities in Tension before the Emergence of a Monarch-Bishop*, vol. XXXI, Texts and Studies of Early Christian Life and Language Series, ed. J. Den Boeft et al. (New York: E.J. Brill, 1995), 475-501.

[17] "At that time Hippolytus, besides many other treatises, wrote a work on the Passover. He gives in this a chronological table, and presents a certain paschal canon of sixteen years, bringing the time down to the first year of the Emperor Alexander. Of his other writings the following have reached us: *On the Hexaemeron, On the Works after the Hexaemeron, Against Marcion, On the Song of Songs, On Portions of Ezekiel, On the*

Arabia leads some scholars to consider this Hippolytan citation as a reference to a different figure than a second Hippolytus citation in VI.22 which contains a list of his works. Meanwhile, a third Eusebian passage in VI.46.5 links Hippolytus as a courier between Rome and Dionysius in Alexandria. J.A. Cerrato rightly recognizes that scrutiny centers on the intention of Eusebius in these accounts, but might be second guessing to insist that he "purposely avoids connecting the three" because of uncertainty about the number of possible writers named Hippolytus.[18]

In his *Lives of Illustrious Men* from the late fourth century, Jerome provides the first patristic reference to Hippolytus' work *Commentary on Daniel*, as well as a reference to commentaries on Song of Solomon, Genesis, Zechariah, Psalms, Isaiah, Revelation, Proverbs, and Ecclesiastes.[19] He records the influence of Hippolytus' writings, reporting that the prolific writing career of Hippolytus inspired Ambrosius to encourage Origen to write commentaries on the scriptures in "emulation of Hippolytus." Jerome is admittedly unclear about the location of Hippolytus' see, but specifically states his office:

> Hippolytus, bishop of some church (the name of the city I have not been able to learn) wrote *A reckoning of the Paschal feast and chronological tables* which he worked out up to the first year of the Emperor Alexander. He also discussed the cycle of sixteen years, which the Greeks called εὐκκαιδεκαετηρίδα and gave the cue to Eusebius, who composed on the same Paschal feast a cycle of nineteen years, that is εὐννεακαιδεκαετηρίδα.[20]

His inability to connect this church father with any city is odd, given the otherwise familiar report of this historical character. It is pure speculation on Cerrato's part that Jerome and Eusebius drew from a common source focusing on Origen, with Jerome following the source more closely in order to explain the extra-Eusebian material.[21] Allen Brent seems more convincing when he attributes confusion to Eusebius and Jerome about Hippolytus' see because of his competition with Callistus as the bishop of Rome. This was "part of a development of a church order in a state of flux" that was beyond their

---

Passover, Against All the Heresies; and you can find many other works preserved by many." Eusebius, *Ecclesiastical History*, VI.22.1-2.

[18] J. A. Cerrato, *Hippolytus between East and West: The Commentaries and the Provenance of the Corpus*, Oxford Theological Monographs Series (Oxford: University Press, 2002), 43. His overall treatment of Eusebius on Hippolytus is the most technical to date; see Cerrato, *Hippolytus between East and West*, 26-44.

[19] Jerome, *Lives of Illustrious Men*, LXI.

[20] Jerome, *Lives of Illustrious Men*, LXI.

[21] Cerrato, *Hippolytus between East and West*, 38. For Jerome, Cerrato establishes a "non-provenance tradition," 68. Again, Cerrato's analysis of Jerome is the most technical within scholarship; see 45-68.

comprehension.[22]

In the ninth century, Photius uniquely calls him a disciple of Irenaeus, according to Hippolytus' own claim.[23] This reveals an important western milieu of Hippolytus. Other ancient writers agree with Photius by remaining silent on his see while calling him both "bishop and martyr."[24] Hagiographic writings reveal twenty-three occurrences of Hippolytus as bishop including details of his office, its location, a schism, and his reinstatement to the church, with a date ranging from Alexander Severus (r. 222-234) to Claudius II (r. 268-270).[25] Prudentius helps identify the geography of Hippolytus' see, as he narrates how the emperor "at that time was afflicting Christian heroes by Tiber's mouth," the exact location of the harbor at Portus.[26] The claim of Prudentius thus clearly provides a third century Roman provenance to the writings of Hippolytus.

When speaking specifically, all of these early church writers usually always located Hippolytus' office at Rome. Only Gelasius of Rome makes a definite contribution prior to the medieval period for an Eastern Hippolytus prior to the medieval period. This bishop (d. 496) refers to Hippolytus, "bishop and martyr of the capital city of the Arabians." The citation involves association with a work *Contra Noetum* in which scholars have find little consensus about its correspondence to the rest of the Hippolytan corpus and stands as a lone voice of explicit, early claim to an Eastern see.[27]

Meanwhile, the *Chronicon Paschale* reports that Hippolytus was "bishop" of Portus near Rome. Apollinaris of Laodicea excerpts the Daniel commentary, referring to its author, "Hippolytus, the most holy bishop of Rome." About 405 CE, Prudentius recorded in his *Crown of Martyrdom* epic that Hippolytus was one "who had at one time as a presbyter attached himself to the schism of Novatus."[28] However, Prudentius' report is clearly anachronistic, as Novatus

---

[22] Allen Brent, "Hippolytus' See," *Studia Patristica* 24 (1993): 37. This theory is discussed more below in "Trends in Hippolytan Scholarship," pp. 11-20.

[23] Photius, *Bibliotheca*, codex 121, trans. N. G. Wilson (London: Duckworth, 1994).

[24] Ebed-Jesu, *Catalogus* 7; Theodoret, *Dialogue* 1 et passim; Photius, *Bibliotheca* 202; so David G. Dunbar, "The Eschatology of Hippolytus of Rome" (Ph.D. diss., Drew University, 1979), 3.

[25] Dunbar, "The Eschatology of Hippolytus," 4.

[26] Prudentius, *Crowns of Martyrdom*, vol. XI, trans. H. J. Thompson (London: William Heinemann, 1969), 306-7, especially n.b.

[27] Cerrato, *Hippolytus between East and West*, 72-75. I do not find Cerrato's claim that Theodoret's comments to an unnamed provenance as establishing "his opinion of an eastern author." Cerrato, *Hippolytus between East and West*, 71. However, his assessment of the sources on pp. 26-93 remains the most technical and best researched to date.

[28] *Qui quondam scisma Novati presbyter attigerat nostra sequenda negans.* Prudentius, 306-7. It seems obvious that Prudentius used the records of Damasus for this, who called him a "presbyter in scisma semper mansisse Novati." A. Ferrua, *Epigrammata*

was a mid-third century churchman who did not cause a schism until twenty-five years after Hippolytus' death. Their similarity is obvious for Prudentius, as both vigorously opposed ecclesiastical forgiveness for those "lapsing" under persecution by denying their faith in Christ. Novatian's rigorous policy and schism date from the Decian persecutions of 250-51 with a rival episcopate in 254. The later bishop Damasus associated Hippolytus either with Novatian's unforgiving policies for the lapsed or else with a formal dissension and schism within the church.

This claim has lead scholars to believe that Hippolytus may have built a schismatic community competitive with the papacy similar to what Novatian would later do. An old catalogue of popes, the *Catalogus Liberianus* (c. 354 CE), reports that Hippolytus was banished about 235 CE with the Roman bishop Pontianus to the island of Sardinia. The former was buried in the cemetery of Callistus, but Hippolytus on the *Via Tiburtina*.[29] The next section shows how this has lead historical scholars to believe that Hippolytus was reconciled with the bishop of Rome in a way that resulted in his restoration to the community of faith, and consequential veneration for martyrdom. It is worthy recognizing that whenever the patristic tradition speaks of Hippolytus' see, it almost always points to Rome. Our turn to modern scholarship shows some skepticism about only one, Western Hippolytus.

Trends in Hippolytan Scholarship

A dramatic sixteenth century archeological discovery provided a lengthy corpus of Hippolytus' works and has confirmed theories that he held an episcopate appointment that was in or around Rome. This find has become a launching point for the modern study of the historical Hippolytus. Beginning with the find, this next part surveys the scholarly treatment of the presbyter, his provenance, and his corpus of works that will finalize our understanding the author of the commentary.

The ancient *Catalogus Liberianus* claims two different burial places of the two bishops exiled together, Pontianus and Hippolytus. It was in the cemetery on the *Via Tiburtina* that a mutilated statue of Hippolytus was discovered in

---

Damasiana (Pontificia Instituto di Archeologia Christiana 35, Rome: 1942): 169-73. Brent points out that the catalogue later provides a list of those reconciled from among the Novatian schismatics; despite his certain reconciliation with Rome, his name is unmentioned, corroborating the anachronism. Allen Brent, "Hippolytus' See," 37; *idem*, "Was Hippolytus a Schismatic?" *Vigiliae Christianae* 49 (1995): 234-38. For a critical discussion of Damasus' intentions by reflecting on the burial evidence, see Brent, *Hippolytus and the Roman Church*, 368-95.

[29] This is the road to Tivoli in central Italy, near the basilica of St. Lawrence. Philip Schaff, *History of the Christian Church*, vol. II, *Ante-Nicene Christianity AD 100-325* (Grand Rapids: Eerdmans Publishing, 1966), 761.

1551, described as "a venerable man clothed with the Greek pallium and Roman toga, seated in a bishop's chair."[30] Its discoverer, the Renaissance antiquarian Pirro Ligorio (1500-1583) noticed that its head was a replacement. Most authorities figure the statue was a second-century work reused and "reheaded" with Hippolytus' head by his followers. [31] The significance of this statue is the list of works on its side that are attributed to Hippolytus, but one listing has received the most attention: κατὰ πασῶν αἱρέεων ἔλεγχηος, commonly known as the *Elenchos*, or *On the All*. It was recognized as part of a larger work, *Philosophoumena*, of such significance that it deserves further explanation.

In 1842, there was a discovery of a complete text of *The Refutation of All Heresies*, or *Philosophoumena* (228-33), which was previously attributed to Origen.[32] In the late nineteenth century, John Döllinger identified Hippolytus as author of the work and brought scholarly attention to this (then) neglected church father. Döllinger was the first to begin reconstructing Hippolytus' life through the autobiographical details contained there. The author of *Philosophoumena* presents himself as an opponent to the moral and theological duplicity of certain Roman bishops. In this discourse, the author lays claim to priestly membership and to being a teacher, and perhaps even to a bishop office in the church.[33] Döllinger popularized the theory that Hippolytus was no mere

---

[30] Schaff, *History of the Christian Church*, 762. Hereafter, I will refer to this important find as the "Ligorian statue." Today, the statue sits outside the entrance to the Vatican Library.

[31] Scholars suspect that the statue was originally designed for a different purpose. Everett Ferguson's encyclopedia entry typifies this position, "Hippolytus," *Encyclopedia of Early Christianity*, 427. Schaff suggests that the statue may have been a Roman senator. For a thorough analysis of the statue and the discovery completed with photographic plates, see Brent, *Hippolytus and the Roman Church*, 3-50; for the logic of a middle third century sculpting, see Schaff, *History of the Christian Church*, 761, n.3.

[32] Scholars traditionally held that either Origen or the presbyter Caius was the author. Books 1-3 of the work had long been assigned to Origen when Minos Minoides discovered the corresponding books 4-10 on Mount Athos. The Ligorian statue revealed a work entitled *On the All*, a phrase opening the tenth chapter of *Philosophoumena*, Περί τοῦ παντός. The original title seems to be κατὰ πασῶν αἱρέεων ἔλεγχηος, so that the work it is sometimes referred to as *Elenchos*, or *On the All*. Döllinger, Schaff, and most scholars hold the authorship of Hippolytus. Origen is disqualified because of difference of style, theology, and the internal claim to authorship by one of apostolic succession. Although Photius suggested that Caius wrote a work so entitled and was bishop of Rome, he is disqualified because of his anti-Chiliast and his anti-Montanism tendencies, as well as his rejection of Johannine authorship of Revelation. Hippolytus was the opposite on all three issues, showing at least some sympathy with the Montanist movement. For additional scholarly analysis and lesser theories of authorship, see Schaff, *History of the Christian Church*, 762ff., n.3.

[33] *Philosophoumena* I.proem; Dunbar, "Eschatology," 8, n.1. The *Philosophoumena*

Roman presbyter, but that he claimed to be the legitimate bishop in Rome. He first proposed Hippolytus to be an "antipope" (*Gegenpapst*).[34] This was based on his accusations brought against Callistus, bishop of Rome from 217-222. His charges concerned several theological errors; most notably the bishop's tendency toward Sabellianism and his ecclesiastical forgiveness of moral laxity, based on the hagiographic record of Hippolytus' schism and reconciliation.[35]

After Döllinger, Adhémar D'Ales wrote a comprehensive work on the theology of Hippolytus in light of the controversy with Callistus and the newly available *Philosophoumena* that remains an instructive tool for Hippolytus' theology.[36] In 1947, Pierre Nautin challenged the authorship of Hippolytus' anti-heretical work *Philosophoumena*, now called *The Refutation of All Heresies*, and profoundly impacted Hippolytan scholarship with his book, *Hippolyte et Josipe*. Dissatisfied with the popular view about the life and corpus of Hippolytus, he engaged in a critical study of some of his works and concluded that *The Refutation of all Heresies* was not by Hippolytus, but one named Josephus.[37] Josephus was a Roman presbyter who became an antipope, Nautin claims, but Hippolytus was an Eastern bishop who authored several works in the corpus. This literary study stands as the first critical analysis about the historicity of Hippolytus of Rome. Its impact was so great that Dunbar describes its effect: "Nautin's study fell upon the world of patristic scholarship like a fox among chickens—there was loud squawks of protest and many feathers were ruffled."[38]

Scholars have repeatedly challenged Nautin's thesis on the whole, while his theory of multiple authorship to the Hippolytan corpus continues. Bernard Botte has accused the approach as too easily constructing a theory based on the mention of the name "Josephus," and he offers several other reasons to not

---

uses the term ἀρχιερατεία, high priest to describe its author. Eusebius generally uses ἐπίσκοπον to denote the office of bishop, but uses προεστώς to describe Hippolytus. For a discussion of the terminology and offices, see Brent, *Hippolytus and the Roman Church*, 475-501. Brent argues that Hippolytus presided over several congregations as προεστώς constructing the Roman church. This is the favored title for Brent, *Hippolytus and the Roman Church*, 476, n.27.

[34] John J. Ignatius von Döllinger, *Hippolytus and Callistus*, trans. Alfred Plummer (Edinburgh: T & T Clark, 1876). Bonwetsch prefers the term *illegaler Bischofsitz*. Brent, "Hippolytus' See," 32.

[35] The criticisms of Callistus are contained throughout *Philosophoumena* IX and revisited in X.23.

[36] Adhémar D'Alès, *La théologie de Saint Hippolyte* (Paris: G. Beauchesne, 1906). D'Alès provides historical, theological, and exegetical insights into Hippolytus' work on a level that remained prominent until recently.

[37] Pierre Nautin, *Hippolyte et Josipe: Contribution à l'histoire de la littérature chrétienne du troisième siècle* (Paris: Editions du Cerf, 1947).

[38] Dunbar, "The Eschatology of Hippolytus," 17.

reduce the works to these exact two authors.[39] Vincenzo Loi modified Nautin's theory by imagining two authors who were both named Hippolytus. The Western Hippolytus authored the *Apostolic Tradition*, the liturgical works, and those with a Western flavor, while the other, Eastern Hippolytus, authored the exegetical works and some anti-heretical works.[40] Josef Frickel resisted Loi by conceding *Contra Noetum* as unauthentic while arguing that the remainder belonged to Hippolytus of Rome.[41] Clemens von Scholten offered additional arguments solidifying the unity of authorship that still persuades many scholars.[42] David Dunbar has added to the opposition by critiquing Nautin on his easy dismissal of the internal literary evidence, statue evidence, and further criticism of the "simplicity" of the theory.[43] Dunbar accepts the traditional picture of the life and works of Hippolytus, and confirms his model by the continuity of his eschatological works. Scholars Burton Scott Easton, Gregory Dix, and Bernard Botte continue to argue for Hippolytus of Rome as a single figure who could have authored the entire corpus, while most scholars of the *Apostolic Tradition* maintain an association with the historical figure around Rome while preferring to attribute this work to an earlier tradition or a later attribution to Hippolytus.[44]

Since Nautin, scholars have tried to define the contributing authors of the Hippolytan corpus but have failed to reach a consensus. Against much patristic testimony, some have tried to divide the corpus into an Eastern bishop and a Roman presbyter. It seems that on the one hand, the eschatology witnessed in his many surviving dogmatic and exegetical works is highly apocalyptic and predictive. This differs from his *The Refutation of all Heresies*, on the other

---

[39] Bernard Botte, "Note sur l'auteur du *De universo* attribué à saint Hippolyte," *Recherches de théologie ancienne et médiévale* 18 (1951): 5-18.

[40] Vincenzo Loi, "La problematica storico-letteraria su Ippolytus di Roma," *Ricerche su Ippolito*, Studia Ephemeridis Augustinianum 13 (Rome: Institutum Patristicum Augustinianum, 1977): 9-16. For an exact list of Loi's categories as authentic and unauthentic works, see Beate Regina Suchla, "Hippolytus," *Dictionary of Early Christian Literature*, ed. Siegmar Döpp and Wilhelm Geerlings, trans. Matthew O' Connell (Crossroad Publishing, NY, 1998), 287.

[41] Josef Frickel, *Das Dunkel um Hippolyt von Rom Ein Lösungsversuch: die Schriften Elenchos und Conra Nöetum* (Grazer Theologische Studien, 1988).

[42] Clemens von Scholten, "Hippolyt II (von Rom)," *Rivista di archeologia cristiana* 15 (1938): 492-551, especially 503ff. See also Clemens von Scholten, review of J.A. Cerrato, *Hippolytus between East and West: The Commentaries and the Provenance of the Corpus*, *Vigiliae Christianae* 59 (2005): 85-92.

[43] See Dunbar, "The Eschatology of Hippolytus," 18-51.

[44] John H. Baldovin, "Hippolytus and the *Apostolic Tradition*: Recent Research and Commentary," *Theological Studies* 64 (2003): 520-42. Baldovin himself is not even convinced that the work is Roman in milieu or even early-third century. Such a position would be among the most extreme dissipation of the historic understanding of Hippolytus and the *Apostolic Tradition*. Baldovin, 542.

hand, which exhibits a more "realized" eschatology. Scholars often use categories like "certainly," "probably", and "probably not" to describe the originality of works attributed to Hippolytus.[45] A list of at least forty works may still be attributed to Hippolytus based both on manuscript discoveries in recent decades and patristic testimony. The *Commentary on Daniel* is almost unanimously attributed to Hippolytus, or at least to a figure named Hippolytus who authored the collection of exegetical works.

The most extensive examination of these issues is Allen Brent's *Hippolytus and the Roman Church of the Third Century: Communities in Tension before the Emergence of a Monarch-Bishop.*[46] Brent believes that the works in the Hippolytan corpus are not of a single author, or of two authors sharing the same name, but of a multiple authors representing a group of followers of Hippolytus of Rome. In fact, Brent prefers to understand that Hippolytus' followers enhanced his list of works, "If the statue is the symbol of a community rather than an individual, we need not limit necessarily the number of authors to only two."[47] Brent laments that the patristic and statue evidence has come to over-

---

[45] Suchla, "Hippolytus," 287; Nautin, "Hippolytus," 383-85. For the sake of analysis, Brent categorizes the works as those ascribed to Hippolytus independent of the Ligorian statue versus those known only by the statue in Allen Brent, "Ligorio's Reconstruction of Hippolytus' Statue and the Recovery of the Hippolytan Corpus," *Medieval Codicology, Iconography, Literature, and Translation: Studies for Keith Val Sinclair*, ed. Peter Rolfe Monks and D. D. R. Owen (Leiden: E. J. Brill. 1994), 3-7.

[46] Allen Brent, *Hippolytus and the Roman Church*; for bibliographic data see p. 8, n.16 above.

[47] Brent, "Ligorio's Reconstruction of Hippolytus' Statue," 2, n.4. Brent's fundamental evidence for a community's expansion of the Hippolytan corpus lies in a series of connections that begins with an unclear identity of the original gender of the Ligorian statue. Brent, *Hippolytus and the Roman Church*, 50-144, 259, 539-40. Guarducci's archeological analysis of the Ligorian find identifies the body of the statue of Hippolytus to be that of a woman, and further posits that it resembles the *grande dame* of Epicurianism, Themista of Lampsacus. Since the Epicureans depersonalized Themista to a symbolic figure of Wisdom, Brent assesses that a community of Hippolytus' followers created a similar allegorical representation of the historical man. Brent then supposes that the list of works on the statue functioned not to preserve the writings of Hippolytus but as "a means of establishing distinctive social identity and ethos of such communities." Brent, *Hippolytus and the Roman Church*, 109. In order to create their own identity as followers of Hippolytus, they added to his corpus of writings. The location of the statue and the fractionalized Roman Christian community by the mid-third century allegedly supports this theory. From all of this reconstruction, Brent can then dismiss a single author of the list of works in Patristic writings and the list on the statue and create a community that would embellish his corpus. Ultimately, Brent succeeds only when he separates his theory of authorship from the statue evidence. Brent, *Hippolytus and the Roman Church*, 300. See also Allen Brent, "St. Hippolytus, Biblical Exegete, Roman Bishop, and Martyr," *St. Vladimir's Theological Quarterly* 48

inform scholars' theories about Hippolytus' corpus, stressing literary evidence instead to suggest that not all are Hippolytan.[48]

Josef Frickel believes that the silence of Eusebius on the matter of Hippolytus' office and its location is due to an uncomfortable cognitive dissonance. He proposes that the documents in front of Eusebius at the writing of *Ecclesiastical History* report both schism and reconciliation, and Eusebius' embarrassment of Hippolytus' schism prompted intentional vagueness.[49] However, Manlio Simonetti has argued that his vagueness is due to a deficiency in personal details, accompanied by some confusion about two authors named Hippolytus—one Roman and one oriental.[50] Unconvinced that either scholar accurately grasps the dilemma for Eusebius, Allen Brent argues instead that Eusebius lacked a "conceptual framework in which Church Order was discussed in the fourth century to cope adequately with the state of affairs in the second."[51] Working from a more developed church framework, Eusebius and Jerome could not understand how Hippolytus might be a Roman presbyter or bishop in the time that Callistus was named in the bishop lists, especially when concepts such as "schism," "legal bishop," and "antipope" could not yet be properly applied. Brent attributes confusion to the patristic authors about Hippolytus' see because the conflict with Callistus was "part of a development of a church order in a state of flux."[52] In Brent's words, "Damasus reflected the same perplexity in his anachronistic description of Hippolytus as a Novatian presbyter, even though, like Eusebius, he had available the facts of the original situation which he could not interpret and so self-consciously constructed an explanatory legend."[53] Brent maintains confusion by Bishop Damasus when he anachronistically calls Hippolytus a Novatian based on Eusebius' confusion about a shift in terminology and concepts. Concerning Hippolytus as a schismatic, Brent understands the historical record to report that Hippolytus was genuinely reconciled to both the theology of the successors of Callistus and the concept of a monarchial ecclesial order. "Hippolytus consented to one Episcopal monarch over the presiding presbyters of the fractionalized Roman community."[54]

As source critic and historian, J. A. Cerrato has offered an analysis of part of Hippolytus' corpus to conclude a probable Eastern milieu of the commentary author. His study is critical of the traditional Roman hypothesis, especially in

---

(2004): 207-31.

[48] Brent, "Ligorio's Reconstruction of Hippolytus' Statue," 1-10.

[49] Frickel, *Das Dunkel um Hippolyt von Rom*; so Brent, "Hippolytus' See," 28.

[50] Manlio Simonetti, *Ricerche su Ippolito*; so Brent, "Hippolytus' See," 28.

[51] Brent, "Hippolytus' See," 29.

[52] Brent, "Hippolytus' See," 37.

[53] Brent, "Hippolytus' See," 36. If Brent is correct, we might say that Damasus was as confused as Eusebius and Jerome, but responded not with silence but conjecture.

[54] Brent, "Was Hippolytus a Schismatic?," 237.

light of external manuscript data that has evolved since Döllinger's original Roman theory for a unified Hippolytan corpus. His source-tendency treatment of the Daniel commentary is accurately detailed and his summary of the work is thorough.[55] Cerrato likewise shows how the authorship of the *Apostolic Tradition* is not easily proven, and he prefers to attribute it to the legacy of the Western Hippolytus figure.[56] However, just as the data favoring a Western Hippolytus is not as thorough as scholars would like, so the theory of two Hippolyti proposed by Cerrato is not yet convincing, either. The verdict is still out on whether a single figure and prolific writer authored the majority of the corpus attributed to Hippolytus or not.[57] Scholars like Whealey still argue for a unified Hippolytan corpus and against theories of two Hippolyti, as seen in his recently study that seeks the authorship of Pseudo-Justin's *De Resurrectione*.[58] On a positive note, Cerrato's contribution to Hippolytus studies includes a challenge to the many assumptions that have served traditional scholars; he rightly remarks that "the self-assurance with which they have spoken of his community of origin is unfortunate."[59]

Besides the scholarly interest in the historical Hippolytus and the identification of his corpus, there are some studies focusing on his other aspects of his writings. Half of the works attributed to Hippolytus were dedicated to scriptural interpretation, and many consider his scriptural writings to be his best. "Like Origen he was first an exegete, brilliant if not as profound as Origen."[60] Scholars have offered some treatment of the exegetical contribution of Hippolytus' works. Jean Daniélou emphasizes Hippolytus' contribution by noting that he "developed the literary genre of continuous commentaries on particular sections of the Scriptures" without positing that this church father necessarily created it.[61] Daniélou considers the strength of Hippolytus' exegetical method to be his Christological interpretation of the Daniel text, a

---

[55] Cerrato, *Hippolytus between East and West*, 134-37, 162-63.

[56] J. A. Cerrato, "The Association of the Name Hippolytus with a Church Order Now Know as *The Apostolic Tradition*," *St. Vladimir's Theological Quarterly* 48 (2004): 179-94.

[57] See my review of Cerrato, *Hippolytus between East and West: The Commentaries and the Provenance of the Corpus* in *Journal of Early Christian Studies* 12 (2004): 361-362. Three other reviews that in some way challenge Cerrato's case for Easternness are Graham Gould, *Journal of Theological Studies* 54 (2003): 312-14; Alistair Stewart-Sykes, *St. Vladimir's Theological Quarterly* 49 (2006): 353-355; and Allen Brent, *Journal of Ecclesiastical History* 55 (2004): 342-43.

[58] A. Whealey, "Pseudo-Justin's *De Resurrectione*: Athenagorus or Hippolytus?" *Vigiliae Christianae* 60 (2006): 420-30

[59] Cerrato, "The Association of the Name Hippolytus," 179.

[60] Patrick J. Hamell, *Handbook of Patrology: A Concise, Authoritative Guide to the Life and Works of the Fathers of the Church* (New York: Alba House, 1968), 82.

[61] Daniélou, *Gospel Message and Hellenistic Culture*, 261.

point seen in the martyrdom motif with its application to the ancient church. Scholars' analyses on the topic of persecution in the commentary are always cursory, however. Demetrios Trakatellis provides some more attention to the matter, setting forth the thesis that "Hippolytus introduced distinctive martyrological motifs in his exegesis."[62] Trakatellis has done an analysis of the content and style of the Hippolytus' *Commentary on Daniel*. He sees Hippolytus' style of exegesis in the commentary as similar to the "fighting exegesis" method, *logos agonistikos*, used by John Chrysostom. This rhetoric reveals a sense of conflict that Hippolytus has against theological opponents, especially heretics, pagans, and Jews. Trakatellis provides some helpful insights into the exegesis of Hippolytus in the commentary, such as the exegetical method, the use of scripture, and the focus of martyrdom in the commentary.[63] However, his work is quite limited with respect to a martyrdom motif, however, and his effort simply provides justification for a larger project.

There are few studies on Hippolytus' exegetical works and very few scholars have given special attention to his *Commentary on Daniel*. The problem with the scholarship on this ancient commentary's theme of martyrdom is that it has offered either a limited or a misunderstood treatment of it. All scholars agree that martyrdom was a fundamental component of the early church and a symbol of the triumph of Christianity over the empire, so that martyrdom's success in church history is immortal. In the mid-third century, Cyprian indicated the importance of martyrdom to Christianity:

> Let us not imagine that what is to come will be easy. The struggle that threatens will be hard and fierce, and soldiers of Christ must prepare themselves for it with incorruptible faith and unshakable firmness. If we daily drink the cup of the blood of Christ, it is in order to be ready to shed our blood for Christ as well.[64]

However, few scholars have recognized the topic of martyrdom as a theme with its own merits in this particular ancient biblical commentary. Manlio Simonetti comments: "The commentary concretizes the biblical text on the theme of martyrdom." [65] W. H. C. Frend remarks: "He pointed to the existing persecution of the saints as foreshadowing future (apocalyptic) strife." [66] Still,

---

[62] Trakatellis prefers to see Hippolytus as an apologist and "fighting rhetorician." Demetrios Trakatellis, "ΛΟΓΟΣ ΑΓΟΝΙΣΤΙΚΟΣ: Hippolytus' Commentary on Daniel," *Religious Propaganda and Missionary Competition in the New Testament World: Essays Honoring Dieter Georgi*, ed. Lukas Bormann, Kelly del Tredici, and Angela Standhartinger (New York: E. J. Brill, 1994), 537.

[63] Trakatellis, "ΛΟΓΟΣ ΑΓΟΝΙΣΤΙΚΟΣ," 527-550.

[64] Cyprian, *Letters* (1-81), vol. 51, *The Fathers of the Church*, trans. Rose Bernard Donna (Washington, D.C.: The Catholic University of America Press, 1964), 6:2.

[65] Simonetti, *Biblical Interpretation*, 28.

[66] W. H. C. Frend, *Martyrdom and Persecution in the Early Church: A Study of a*

these who recognize the theme in the commentary have not investigated it closely.

Some scholars do not even admit that martyrdom is a primary theme in the commentary. While Sten Hidal recognizes the motif, he remarks, "There is no consistent picture of the book as a whole belonging to a situation of martyrdom."[67] Hidal contrasts the themes of apocalypse and final persecution in the Daniel commentaries by Hippolytus and Theodoret of Cyrrhus, revealing a Christocentric development in the church's use of apocalyptic texts. However, no one from Theodoret to Hidal thoroughly has investigated the important role of martyrdom in Hippolytus' commentary.

The explicit or subtle expectation of martyrdom as a tool of rhetoric in the church fathers has received little attention, but is not altogether ignored.[68] For example, Lacey Baldwin Smith notes, "Quite consciously the early Christian fathers were articulating a psychology of martyrdom [in their writings]. That suited the troubled souls and anxious minds of late antiquity."[69] Gammie reflects on the impact of the Book of Daniel on the theology and worldview of Christians in the early church.[70] He captures the themes of sovereignty and eschatological expectation characteristic of the book's apocalyptic genre, but does not investigate its contribution to the church's theology of martyrdom. His profile of Hippolytus' *Commentary on Daniel* is not thorough, and he overlooks many valuable contributions that the work offers the history of interpretation. Despite its theological importance, the theme of martyrdom in this very important patristic commentary remains overlooked by scholars. There has been no thorough monograph discussing how Hippolytus interpreted

---

Conflict from the Maccabees to Donatus (New York: New York University Press, 1967), 241.

[67] Sten Hidal, "Apocalypse, Persecution and Exegesis," *In the Last Days: On Jewish and Christian Apocalyptic and its Period* (Aarhus, Denmark: Aarhus University Press, 1994), 50.

[68] The scholarship on martyrdom and persecution in the early church is vast, but the most comprehensive historical work remains Frend, *Martyrdom and Persecution*. For a briefer survey, see the entry by Robert Lee Williams, "Persecution," in *Encyclopedia of Early Christianity*. For a more insightful but less well-known reading of the history of persecution, see Robin Lane Fox, *Pagans and Christians: Religion and The Religious Life From the Second to the Fourth Century A.D., When the Gods of Olympus Lost Their Dominion and Christianity, with the Conversion of Constantine, Triumphed in the Mediterranean World* (New York: Alfred A. Knopf, 1987), 419-492. Additionally, Ivo Lesbaupin's work *Blessed Are the Persecuted: Christian Life in the Roman Empire, A.D. 64-313*, trans. Robert R. Barr (Maryknoll, NY: Orbis Books, 1987) offers a pithy overview of the impact of persecution on the early church.

[69] Lacey Baldwin Smith, *Fools, Martyrs, Traitors: The Story of Martyrdom in the Western World* (New York: Alfred A. Knopf, 1997), 95.

[70] John G. Gammie, "A Journal Through Danielic Spaces," 144-56.

the text in order to promote and encourage martyrdom.

The eschatology of Hippolytus is somewhat popular and is regularly treated in patristic eschatologies.[71] David Dunbar has analyzed the eschatological treatises and exegetical works of Hippolytus in order to construct a thorough portrait of his related theology.[72] This church father is unique because he is the first in a long tradition of millennialism to desert notions of an imminent *parousia* until a significantly later time.[73] The early church quickly attributed end-time prophecy to the text of the Book of Daniel, but there is disagreement among scholars as to how Hippolytus saw the current persecutions foreshadowed in Daniel's prophecies. For example, Simonetti and Hidal emphasize that his interpretation of some symbols in Daniel referred to the current Roman Empire.[74] Dunbar is confident, however, that these interpretations merely "provide a focus and guide" to some future kingdom's persecutions.[75] Constantine Tsirpanlis has contrasted the different details of eschatology in the works of Irenaeus, Justin, Hippolytus, and Tertullian, showing how our subject's theology is consistent with Irenaeus in many respects, but is also unique among the fathers.[76] Hippolytus' theology of last

---

[71] The most comprehensive analysis of patristic eschatology is Brian E. Daley, *The Hope of the Early Church: A Handbook of Patristic Eschatology* (Cambridge: Cambridge University Press, 1991). Another helpful analysis of Hippolytus' eschatology is contained in Charles E. Hill, *Regnum Caelorum: Patterns of Millennial Thought in Early Christianity*, 2d ed. (Grand Rapids: Eerdmans, 2001). The interpretation of Antiochus as the coming Antichrist in the church bears on this monograph, and its historical development is provided by William H. Shea, "Early Development of the Antiochus Epiphanes Interpretation," in *Symposium on Daniel: Introductory and Exegetical Studies*, ed. Frank B. Holbrook, vol. 2, Daniel and Revelation Committee Series (Washington, D. C.: Biblical Research Institute, 1986).

[72] His comprehensive work of Hippolytus' theology is David G. Dunbar, "The Eschatology of Hippolytus." See also Dunbar, "The Delay of the *Parousia* in Hippolytus," *Vigiliae Christianae* 37 (1983): 313-327 and "Hippolytus of Rome and the Eschatological Exegesis of the Early Church," *Westminster Theological Journal* 45 (1983): 322-39.

[73] Brent declares it "unthinkable" that a patristic author in a milieu of persecution would disassociate their current events from the Great Tribulation as Hippolytus does in *Commentary on Daniel*, IV.17-18. This is because Brent would prefer to establish multiple authorship of the Hippolytan corpus by the hand of Hippolytus' followers after his death. Brent, *Hippolytus and the Roman Church*, 278-80. However, if this martyrdom motif drives the commentary, then the "unthinkable" finds explanation when Hippolytus tries to turn Christians' focus from the return of Christ toward the persecution at hand, not expecting the parousia to be their hope of deliverance, but letting the rewards in the next life be their recompense.

[74] Simonetti, *Biblical Interpretation*, 28; Hidal, 50.

[75] Dunbar, "Eschatological Exegesis," 338.

[76] Constantine Tsirpanlis, "The Antichrist and the End of the World in Irenaeus, Justin,

things will prove important when considering his exhortation to martyrdom. His eschatology guards against any false hope in an immediate rescue, making his postponement of the parousia a point of departure from Irenaean eschatology.

Finally, scholarship has failed to explain adequately why Hippolytus first chose an Old Testament text for the purpose of Christian exhortation. One of the initial hermeneutical problems for the Christian church was how the Jewish scriptures related to the New Testament.[77] Many fathers either ignored or rejected the Old Testament, or employed it for Christocentric prophecy alone, or over-allegorized the text. Hippolytus occasionally allegorized the Old Testament, but in his *Commentary on Daniel*, he daringly interpreted most of this Jewish text in a historical-literal fashion.[78] Hippolytus wed the Old Testament text with contemporary Christian circumstances and events in a fashion that was unique among the fathers. His mysterious choice of the Hebrew and Aramaic Daniel, his complicated eschatology, and his rigorous devotion to Christianity collaborate to create a historic and intriguing commentary.

Foundation for a Martyrdom Motif

To advance our study of the martyrdom motif in the milieu requires understanding the community in which Hippolytus is writing. In this section, the scholarly research about the historical components of his life, person, and works will be integrated to reconstruct the historical character that crafted the *Commentary on Daniel*. Important for us is the location of Hippolytus'

Hippolytus, and Tertullian," *Patristic and Byzantine Review* 9 (1990): 5-17.

[77] Allegory marked much of the exegetical activity in the fathers in an effort to redeem the Old Testament from obscurity or dubiousness. For a discussion of these and other developments, see James N. S. Alexander, "The Interpretation of Scripture in the Ante-Nicene Period: A Brief Conspectus," *Interpretation* 12 (1958): 272-80. For an overview of patristic historical biblical exegesis, see Denis Farkasflvy, "Interpretation of the Bible," in *Encyclopedia of Early Christianity*. A recent, concise work on the entire field of patristic exegesis is Simonetti, *Biblical Interpretation*, while the most thorough work is that of Charles Kannengiesser, *Handbook of Patristic Exegesis: The Bible in Ancient Christianity*, 2 vols. (Boston: Brill, 2004).

[78] Among the resources on Jewish biblical exegesis, of particular interest is Reinhard Bodenmann, *Naissance d'une exégèse: Daniel dans l'eglise ancienne de trois premiers siècles*, Beiträge zur Geschichte der biblischen Exegese 28 (Tübingen: Mohr, 1986). For the exegetical influence of Judaism on the early church, see Richard Longenecker, *Biblical Exegesis in the Apostolic Period* (Grand Rapids: Eerdmans, 1975) and the collection of essays contained in Fredrick E. Greenspahn, *Scripture in the Jewish and Christian Traditions: Authority, Interpretation, and Relevance* (Nashville: Abingdon Press, 1982).

ecclesiastical office and the contributions that the schism makes to our understanding of Hippolytus' character and ambitions. This is important for knowing Hippolytus' personal context for his writing of the commentary.

Establishing a Roman Episcopate

The title "presbyter" is appropriate for Hippolytus, given the period of ecclesiastical development of the church at the beginning of the third century. His role was probably akin to that of Irenaeus found in Jeffrey Sobosan's study of the role of presbyter in *Against Heresies*.[79] Such an elder was a teacher in the tradition of the apostles, a minister to the congregation but not necessarily a bishop, and a leader in the Christian community with special administrative concerns. As particular communities arose, it would be important to have one person "assigned the task of preserving the faith, teaching it and making sure to defend it against error."[80] Hippolytus would serve in this special capacity, guarding and exhorting his congregations in the faith.

Such a task is affirmed in the *Apostolic Tradition*, in which the prayer for the consecration of a presbyter is that God may "impart to him the spirit of grace and counsel, 'that he might share' in the presbyterate 'and govern' Thy people in a pure heart."[81] On the other hand, the title "bishop" would also be appropriate for Hippolytus, given that his historical influence in the early third century Roman church seems to warrant this higher office. The record of schism in which he oversees church congregations, the legacy of his leadership in Rome, and the discrepancy of defining these offices during this period of ecclesiastical development allow for the use of label "bishop." Such an office is no less a task of shepherding, as the *Apostolic Tradition* records in its prayer for the consecration of a bishop. It entreats that he would "feed thy holy flock and serve as Thine high priest, that he may minister blamelessly."[82] These labels are confirmed by Alastair Campbell's descriptions of the offices.[83] The extent of his authority could range from a single to several congregations, and then from formal, authoritative shepherding to informal advising as church elder. Such a pastoral role corresponds to the paraenetic nature of the commentary.

A close geographical, historical, literary, and theological association between Irenaeus and Hippolytus lays the foundation for a Western, especially

---

[79] Jeffrey G. Soboson, "The Role of the Presbyter," *Scottish Journal of Theology* 27 (May 1974): 129-46. His treatment includes the New Testament standard for presbyter and bishop as well as the historical application of it. For a thorough treatment of the office of elder, particularly in the subapostolic era, see R. Alastair Campbell, *The Elders: Seniority within Earliest Christianity* (New York: T&T Clark, 1994).

[80] Sobosan, 146.

[81] Hippoltyus, *Apostolic Tradition*, viii.

[82] Hippolytus, *Apostolic Tradition*, viii.

[83] Campbell, *The Elders*, 234.

Roman, milieu. Photius records Hippolytus' claim about receiving instruction under Irenaeus of Lyons—a detail supported by the proximity of southern Gaul to his own Roman milieu. The theological proclivities and literary works shared between them support this relationship masterfully. For example, Irenaeus' *Against Heresies* (c. 180 CE) remains the most informative source of heresies in the early church, making us privy to the Gnostic dilemma of the late second century throughout the empire. This unique work is not unlike a later work, *The Refutation of all Heresies*, long thought authored by Origen but identified as Hippolytan. Similarities between this anti-heretical work and that of Irenaeus, *Against Heresies* are striking as they catalogue and often share entries of the numerous unorthodox doctrines, individuals, and movements in the Roman Empire at their respective times. Additionally, listed among Hippolytus' works is an earlier polemical work *Syntagma* or *Against Thirty-two Heresies* (c. 215), different from the other anti-heretical work. This work seems to be a synopsis of the teachings of Irenaeus, as its heresies and style of writing are quite similar.

In addition to the common anti-heretical character of Hippolytus and Irenaeus, there are very comparable eschatological outlooks.[84] The problem of the continuing delay of the *parousia* confronted Christians through the time of Hippolytus, although with Irenaeus the church began to formulate a more precise expectation of the events at the end of time rather than a mere imminent expectation.[85] Although at times tentative, both provide detailed comments from biblical exegesis about the events that will precede the end of the world. Hippolytus agrees with him about an upcoming tyrant, the persecution of the church in the end, material reconstruction of Jerusalem and its Temple, and the rule of a tyrant from Rome. Resurrection of the saints and millennial rule of Christ are synonymous between these fathers, and they agree that a clear name of the Antichrist has not been declared.[86] Perhaps Gnosticism's disconnect between this world's deeds and the future, as well as its alteration of the hope of resurrection of the body among Christians, prompted similar eschatological thought between these two church fathers.

Additionally, a high view of martyrdom characterized the religious and ecclesiastical environment of Irenaeus and Hippolytus (explored below in ch. 2). If we assume Hippolytan inheritance of Irenaean theology, we cannot ignore a powerful tradition of martyrdom, underscored by Ignatius and Polycarp,

---

[84] A summary of their views can be found in Daley, *The Hope of the Early Church*, 28-32 (Irenaeus) and 38-41 (Hippolytus), and Constantine Tsirplanis, "The Antichrist and the End of the World in Irenaeus, Justin, Hippolytus, and Tertullian" in *Patristic and Byzantine Review*, 5-17.

[85] Irenaeus, *Against Heresies*, V.25-36.

[86] Irenaeus, *Against Heresies*, V.30. However, Hippolytus prefers the name *Latinus* "Latin man" as most applicable to his political and social circumstances as well as to the number 666. *Treatise on Christ and the Antichrist*, V.215.

passed down to Irenaeus[87] and influencing Hippolytus. Perhaps the Eastern influence, training, and sense of continuity with these theological ancestors prompted Hippolytus to write in Greek—the last Roman father to do so, when contemporaries like Tertullian and Minucius Felix already were composing theological treatises in Latin. Without claiming any geographical see for Hippolytus, Quasten believes him not to be a native Roman, because of his familiarity with Greek philosophy, religion, and language. Instead, he is convinced of an Eastern nativity and rearing, preferring a possible education at Alexandria. [88] It is noteworthy that whenever the patristic tradition speaks of Hippolytus' see, it points to Rome with only minor interpretive contention.[89]

The apparent return of Hippolytus' martyred remains to Rome offers much credence to a Roman presbytery. The *Catalogus* is explicit about his exile as it reports that as a "presbyter" Hippolytus was banished to Sardinia with the Roman bishop Pontianus about 235.[90] It also says that the bodies of both were recalled and deposited by Fabian (236-250) on the same day, August 13, in different cemeteries. While Pontianus was placed in the cemetery of Callistus, Hippolytus was buried on the *Via Tiburtina* where the Ligorian statue of him was discovered. The legacy and canonization that the church later provided him suggests that he was reconciled with the church and restored as a confessor, probably in his exile with Pontianus.[91] Prudentius reports how he was martyred, but like many of the accounts of the *Crown of Martyrs*, some scholars are skeptical of its authenticity.[92] However, the high esteem of the martyrs within

---

[87] Eusebius records Irenaeus' early association with martyrdom in *Ecclesiastical History* V.4, where the martyrs (witnesses) recommended Irenaeus to the bishop at Rome, associating his candidacy for bishop of Lyons with the faithfulness of those decapitated, devoured by beasts, and dying in prison. Tradition maintains Irenaeus' own martyrdom under Severus, and this event may have even preceded and thus shaped Hippolytus' high view of martyrdom.

[88] Johannes Quasten, *Patrology*, vol. II (Utrecht-Antwerp: Spectrum Publishers, 1966), 163. Quasten's and other scholarly analyses on the linguist issue are further expounded at pp. 72-73 below.

[89] Cerrato, *Hippolytus between East and West*, 26-93.

[90] Schaff, *History of the Christian Church*, 759.

[91] Schaff, *History of the Christian Church*, 759; Sadowski, *The Church Fathers on the Bible*, 255. Schaff suggests that he died specifically in the mines of Sardinia.

[92] Prudentius, *Crowns of Martyrdom*, vol. XI. A drawing in the *Catalogus* probably enhanced his epic story, as it represents Hippolytus as being torn to pieces by wild horses. The name Hippolytus Ἱππόλυτος means "loosened horse," yet we cannot explain how a person's name seems to prescribe their mode of death. Perhaps the legend of his martyrdom would alter his name after death, thus "renaming" him according to the popular legend of his martyrdom. Or, perhaps his persecutors would see it as terrible irony to execute him in the fashion associated with his name or his namesake. Such a death is reminiscent of the ancient Greek legend of Hippolytus, son of Theseus. H. J. Thompson argues that Damasus himself admits basing his comments about his

the church may have contributed to the unexpected reconciliation he experienced.

While in exile, Hippolytus was probably reconciled to the bishop of Rome that was successor to Callistus, and after martyrdom, his body was honorably brought back to that city. This is the best explanation for his restoration to fellowship and consequential universal sainthood. Historians think it probable that Hippolytus abandoned his protest before his death, laying down any schismatic office and returning into fellowship with Rome, because of the fact Roman bishop Fabian recalled both bodies and provided solemn burial. Pope Damasus honored him with a tomb inscription that suggests favorable status with the church. Thus, Hippolytus is a fascinating example of a bishop who was both excommunicated and later sainted by the Church.

Finally, the discovery of the Ligorian statue with its list of works by a Roman presbyter offers additional credence to a Roman milieu, and it also evidences the ancient tradition about the return of his body and burial at Rome. On this one point, the argument of Brent remains interesting but insufficient to establish so easily a post-Hippolytan community that would prescribe works to a Roman presbyter belonging to another, especially an Eastern father.[93] Although the details about Hippolytus' reconciliation with the Roman church and about his death remain unclear, there are no facts contrary to this legend of his martyrdom or to his resolution with Pontianus while in exile that ought to make us think otherwise. The tradition and commemoration around Rome clearly establishes a legacy there that is unrivaled in other locations.

Thus, the historical record of Eusebius and Jerome, Prudentius' record of the emperor's persecution on the Tiber, Photius' assertion about his having a protégé association with Irenaeus, Hippolytus' burial site on a *via* of Rome, the discovery of a statue commemorating his contribution by his followers, his imperial banishment alongside the Roman bishop and the overall strong association with the Roman church among Patristic writers bear out a Roman livelihood. In fact, his constant conflict with the bishop of Rome and the evidence of schism almost necessitates an ecclesiastical leadership appointment in this geographical area. This next section will consider insights to Hippolytus' character and ideals from his conflict and schism in the Roman church. The issue of those who lapsed under persecution will be of particular importance, both as a source of conflict with bishop Callistus and as a potential error of

---

martyrdom on an oral tradition that he does not guarantee: *Haec audita refert Damasus; probat omni Christus.* Prudentius, *Crowns of Martyrdom*, vol. XI, trans. H. J. Thompson (London: William Heinemann, 1969), 304-5, n.a. For a critical discussion of Damasus' intentions of a reflection of the burial evidence, see Brent, *Hippolytus and the Roman Church*, 368-95.

[93] This ought not to diminish the invaluable contribution Brent has made toward understanding the historical Hippolytus and the critical insights into the corpus of works attributed to Hippolytus.

faith addressed in the *Commentary on Daniel*.

Character Insights from the Schism

The works of Hippolytus have a passionate flavor. As Trakatellis has demonstrated, his "fighting" and theological antagonism toward established theological opponents characterize his writings. Hippolytus' zeal for orthodoxy and his eye for error can be seen among the polemical works attributed to him: *Against the Greeks, Against Plato, Against the Jews, Against Marcion, Concerning Charismata, Against Caius, Against Noetus*, and *Against Artemon*. A close examination of a schismatic incident involving Hippolytus reinforces our understanding of his idealistic exhortation to Christian martyrdom. A personality so passionate about suffering for the faith, so moved to prepare and exhort his congregations toward martyrdom, would later passionately oppose ecclesiastical authority that would try to undo his work.

Scholars agree in recognizing some schismatic event in which the Roman presbyter Hippolytus and his followers opposed Callistus, bishop of Rome. There is certainly a corrective due to the use of the anachronistic term "antipope" in the literature, and also due to the connotations of the term "schism" between Hippolytus' churches and the established Roman church. Scholars have reconstructed the details of the conflict mostly from the historical allusions to Hippolytus as a Novatian[94] and the personal passion against Callistus in *The Refutation of All Heresies*.[95] These two factors combine to make a convincing case that a real division occurred between Hippolytus and his church community on the one side, and Roman ecclesiastical authority on

---

[94] Pope Damasus and Prudentius make odd references to Hippolytus' schism based on the old catalogue of popes, *Catalogus Liberianus* (circa 354). In their writings, both of these two refer to him as a Novatian, a follower of Novatian who established a rival bishopric in 254 CE. He desired a "pure" church that expelled those in the church who "lapsed" under persecution by denying their faith in order to survive. Hippolytus shares this same ideal (thus this monograph), and provides a case against Pope Callistus' leniency on repentant apostates in *Philosophoumena*.

[95] Gérard Vallée's use of the *Philosophoumena* as the source for the disputation raises questions about the historical accuracy of a polemic work. Vallée has argued that although we should not expect to gain the exact truth of the heretic or a ready-made account of historical interaction between opposing groups, a clear portrait of the system that the heresiologist would *like* to portray can be uncovered. In this case, we can see Hippolytus' theory of what ought to characterize the ecclesiastical leader of the church. Vallée says, "The essential content and motive of such polemics might emerge in a fuller light; for what each heresiologist sadly misses in the combated doctrines is very likely to stand close to what he holds to be the backbone of Christianity." Gérard Vallée, *A Study in Anti-Gnostic Polemics: Irenaeus, Hippolytus, and Epiphanius*, vol. 1, Studies in Christianity and Judaism (Ontario: Wilfrid Laurier University Press, 1981), 7.

the other, but not in the form of "anti-pope" and "schism" that we have come to know. The reason for the dispute was the alleged theological errors of Callistus.

The authority conflict between Hippolytus and Callistus might be understood by recognizing that probably only a generation earlier had the church established a single *episkopos* over the elders of the churches. The letters of Clement of Rome and of Ignatius suggested that the change came with tension. Alastair Campbell evidences how elders may have lost some liturgical and political power but retained social influence.[96] If Hippolytus indeed was able to lead congregations from unity with other congregations faithful to what was perceived as a false bishop, then he might be viewed a typical case of the slow transition from local congregations to a united catholic church.

There are two main areas of objection to Callistus' theology and praxis by Hippolytus: the Trinity and the lapsed.[97] Concerning the Trinity, Hippolytus accuses him of Sabellianism: "He maintains that the Father is not one person and the Son another, but that they are one and the same; and that all things are full of the Divine Spirit, both those above."[98] The latter of these two theological violations has a greater bearing on this book because it reveals Hippolytus' insistence on facing one's persecution and passion for suffering for Christ. At the time of the writing of the *Commentary on Daniel*, Callistus' lenient policy of forgiving those who denied Christ under persecution may have, for Hippolytus, temporarily eclipsed his Trinitarian deficiency. Callistus seems to have maintained only moderate discipline of those who escaped martyrdom or persecution by denying the Christian faith. Schaff summarizes that for Hippolytus, Callistus "obtained the object of his ambition, the papal chair,

---

[96] Campbell, *The Elders*, 210-35.

[97] Scholars have analyzed other areas that he opposed that are of secondary importance. Related to our interests of martyrdom, *Philosophoumena* IX.12 describes how Callistus tried to secure martyrdom by standing outside a synagogue on the Sabbath and deriding the Jews. Not only does Hippolytus criticize him for this, he accuses him of not dying for Christ but trying to escape his creditors! With Workman, one can realize that this episode may have been an exception in Callistus' life or a misrepresentation. Herbert Workman, *Persecution in the Early Church: A Chapter in the History of Renunciation* (London: Charles H. Kelly, 1906), 119, n.1. For a complete analysis of Callistus' theology, see Ronald E. Heine, "Christology of Callistus," *Journal of Theological Studies* 49 (1998): 56-91.

[98] *Philosophoumena*, IX.7 His developmental narrative from Noetus to Callistus is seen in IX.2-3, 5-7; X.23. Modern scholars assess Hippolytus' effort to avoid Sabellianism to result in what appears to be a "tritheist" position at times. For example, Hamell mentions that Callistus accuses Hippolytus of holding to two gods, "Ditheismus." He also suggests that Hippolytus "unconsciously defended a form of Subordinationism." Hamell, 81. From a post-Nicene view, however, Hippolytus can be seen as acknowledging an orthodox Christology: "The Logos is God, being the substance of God." *Philosophoumena*, X.29. Hamell calls him "sincerely orthodox at heart."

taught heresy and ruined the discipline by extreme leniency to offenders."[99]

This was only one violation of administrative and moral laxity that Hippolytus charged to the bishop. He accused Callistus of carelessly relaxing policy on marriage for clergy and on second baptism, as well as showing excessive favor to the lapsed. Although Roman law forbade marriage between certain social classes, he supposedly allowed women of high rank to live *in contubernium* with slaves or free men.[100] Against traditional trends, Callistus supposedly allowed twice-married bishops, priest and deacons to continue in clerical office. He provided forgiveness to clergy who had committed adultery or homicide. Adultery and homicide were two of the three "sins of death."[101] Apostasy or denial of the faith was the third, and this sin became an obsession for protest for Hippolytus—a final straw toward disqualification from the faith. In a way, the subject of this monograph reflects this same passion of Hippolytus in his *Commentary on Daniel* not to deny the faith under persecution but to suffer for it even unto martyrdom.

The issue of the lapsed greatly challenged the church in the early third century. Bishop Callistus' reputed decision to favor the forgiveness of sins even to those who denied their faith during persecution seems to have infuriated Hippolytus. *The Refutation of All Heresies* reports:

> The impostor Callistus, having ventured on such opinions, established a school of theology in antagonism to the Church, adopting the foregoing system of instruction. And he first invented the device of conniving with men in regard of their indulgence in *sensual* pleasures, saying that all had their sins forgiven by himself.[102]

When Callistus relaxed the treatment of the penitent who had been guilty of this mortal sin, Hippolytus accused him of having divorced himself from the tradition of the Church through his leniency. Although God could forgive such sins, the church ought not to pardon mortal sin after baptism.[103] Funk says,

---

[99] Schaff, *History of the Christian Church*, 765.

[100] *Philosophoumena*, IX.7. Workman believes these accusations to be preposterous. He remarks, "The highly coloured additions may be discounted as due to Hippolytus' hatred of Callistus or a transference of what Tertullian says about the Gentiles." Workman, *A Chapter in the History of Renunciation*, 148, n.1. There is a recurring error in the scholarship of referencing IX.12 for these misdeeds of Callistus, while another version of *Philosophoumena* does not seem to be evident. Workman, *A Chapter in the History of Renunciation*, 148, n.1; W. H. C. Frend, *Early Church* (Philadelphia: Fortress Press, 1982), 78, n.17.

[101] Three sins of *impudicitia* (shamelessness), murder, and idolatry were unpardonable. Hamell, 83.

[102] Hippolytus, *The Refutation of All Heresies*, IX.7.

[103] C. Bernard Ruffin, *The Days of the Martyrs* (Huntington, IN: Our Sunday Visitor,

"Hippolytus can be quoted to prove that the Roman Church, prior to Callistus, held that [certain sins] were absolutely unpardonable both in theory and in practice."[104] Hippolytus strongly accused the bishop when he claimed that Callistus "connived at the sensual pleasures of men by saying that sins were forgiven to everyone by himself."[105] A consenting voice with Hippolytus' claim is Tertullian of Carthage, who also blasted a bishop, presumably Callistus, in his work *On Purity*:

> I hear too that an edict has been published—and one of the fullest authority at that—i.e., the High Priest... bishop of bishops has decreed: I remit the sins of adultery and fornication to those who have done penance. What an edict! No good will be ascribed to it.[106]

Both of these pioneers of Western Christianity agree on the violations of purity that comes from the moral laxity of the Roman bishop Callistus. Frend condenses the issue and the conflict in this statement:

> Was the church to remain a company of the elect on earth, hedged around with the taboos of purity derived from Leviticus, or was it to be a school for sinners bound together by a sacramental life administered by an ordered hierarchy? Callistus favored the second view, Hippolytus, championing apostolic tradition, the first.[107]

Likewise, Sadowski has noted, "Hippolytus is an example of how the Irenaean tradition could be developed in an unhealthy direction, toward a blanket hatred of pagan thought and toward a 'Puritan' church of the elect."[108] Siding with Callistus, Frend seems to think that the elected bishop had a clearer picture of the needs of the church at that time when he declares, "Christianity was rapidly expanding. Standards required in apostolic times were no longer

---

1985), 120.

[104] Hamell, *Handbook of Patrology*, 83.

[105] *Philosophoumena*, IX.7; Frend, *Early Church*, 78, n.17.

[106] Tertullian, *On Purity* I, vol. 394, Sources Chrétiennes, trans. Claudio Micaelli (Paris: Éditions du Cerf, 1993). "Audio etiam edictum esse propositum, et quidem peremptorium, Pontifex scilicet maximus... episcopus episocoporum, edicit. Ego et moechiae et fornicationis delicta poenitentia funcis dimitto. O edictum cui adscribi non poterit bonum factum." Frend notes that with Tertullian's accusations against Callistus, "The first round of a century-long duel between Rome and Carthage had begun." *The Early Church*, 79. For an argument against Origen's allusion specifically being about Callistus when discussing the priestly forgiveness of sins, see Henri Crouzel, *Origen*, trans. A. S. Worrell (San Francisco: Harper & Row, 1989), 230.

[107] Frend, *Early Church*, 78.

[108] Sadowski, *The Church Fathers on the Bible*, 255.

possible to maintain."[109] Indeed, such standards become the basis of Hippolytus' exhortations to martyrdom in his *Commentary on Daniel*; the same principles of suffering seen in the schismatic activities become the goal of Hippolytus' appeal to martyrdom. He claims that Callistus justified his policies biblically by appealing to the apostle Paul, "Who art thou that judgest another man's servant?" and to Jesus himself, "'Let the tares grow among the wheat' or, in other words, let those who in the church are guilty of sin remain in it."[110]

Apparently, Hippolytus was so outraged that he became a competing bishop of a schismatic community in Rome. So adamant was he in his doctrinal beliefs and his passion for suffering martyrdom for the faith that when Callistus was elected pope in 217, Hippolytus evidently opposed his election and a dissenting community followed him. For this reason, he is often noted as the first "anti-pope," although the term should not be meant to necessitate a monarchial bishop seen later in Rome nor acknowledge any Hippolytan claim to the see for himself. Allen Brent builds a foundation for demonstrating the gravity in Hippolytus' creation of a schismatic Roman community. He notes the curiosity that only one person should be singled out for mention in the controversy when Hippolytus is simply one confessor or presbyter amongst a community full of opposition to Callistus.[111] Hippolytus' opposition to Callistus is clear in his objection: "The imposter Callistus.... established a school of theology in antagonism to the church" with a particular policy "saying that all had their sins forgiven by himself."[112] Instead, he insisted on a pure church and took a rigorist position against forgiving serious sins after baptism. For Hippolytus, Callistus epitomized leniency and moral laxity that ought not to characterize the Christian life. In a way, this anti-heretical work, written about 210, is preemptive of the Novatian controversy in the mid-third century.

From the picture of his conflict with Callistus and his willingness to separate, we see Hippolytus' unwavering passion for the theological issues that were confronting the church. The character and passion of Hippolytus can help to substantiate a schism and fuel a zeal to affirm the faith under persecution. Hippolytus did not favor automatic grace to those who had denied Christ and eluded suffering. Instead, the point highlighted in his *Commentary on Daniel*

---

[109] Frend, *Early Church*, 78.

[110] *Philosopoumena*, IX.7. Romans 14:4 states, "Who are you to pass judgment on the servant of another? It is before his own master that he stands or falls. And he will be upheld, for the Master is able to make him stand." In Matthew 13:29-30, Jesus stated, "No; lest in gathering the weeds you root up the wheat along with them. Let both grow together until the harvest; and at harvest time I will tell the reapers, Gather the weeds first and bind them in bundles to be burned, but gather the wheat into my barn.'"

[111] Brent, *Hippolytus and the Roman Church*, 379. Although Brent is establishing a case for multiple authors in the Hippolytan corpus, his case suggests that a whole community of followers opposed the bishop of Rome and not merely one presbyter.

[112] *Philosopoumena*, IX.7.

and brought out in this book is the very opposite: the Christian ought to be willing to suffer even martyrdom for their faith. Again, this passion and purity for the Christian faith in the face of Callistus' laxity is the same spirit of martyrdom witnessed in his *Commentary on Daniel*. For example, the preeminence of the Christian faith required in Hippolytus' mind an *ultimate* sacrifice from Christians, so he exhorted his audience to preparedness: "Be firm and steadfast, O man, not stammering in matters of faith, and when you receive a call to become a martyr promptly obey so that your faith will shine forth."[113] Godspeed suggests that Hippolytus writing in Greek rather than Latin might even reflect how he had been out of harmony with the dominant element in the Roman church most of his later life.[114]

It is difficult to speculate about the exact association between this schismatic controversy and the writing of the commentary. To compare the sentiment expressed in the commentary with the criticism of laxity assumes two things. First, because the commentary writing precedes Callistus by several years, one should beware reading the schism into the commentary, yet recognizing the same vigor and zeal inherent in the author of both the commentary and the schism. Hippolytus does not respond directly to the laxity of Callistus in the *Commentary on Daniel* because the authorship of the work probably preceded the bishop's new policies. Additionally, the commentary focuses primarily on the text and its application. So, the enemy in the Danielic text is not a substandard ecclesiastical leadership but a foreign, religiously pagan oppressor and the corresponding empire.

Second, any view that recognizes similarities between works and assumes identical authorship must face scholars who are beginning to reject one Hippolytus on source critical grounds. Yet such a study might help to establish one "Hippolytus" between the works. Without overstating the case, we ought at least to consider the shared principles of suffering persecution appearing in both works.

On the other hand, an anti-heretical work in the Hippolytan corpus serves its author as a better place to respond to the bishop. The relationship between these two church leaders is intriguing, but the insights from the schism offer only a secondary impetus for weaving a martyrdom motif into the commentary. It is better to link the works here by their zealous flavor for martyrdom. The passionate presbyter that challenges Callistus' avoidance of persecution matches the same passionate encourager to suffer under persecution through his reading of the Danielic text. The *logos agonistikos* quality parallels perfectly.

---

[113] ἑδραῖος οὖν γενοῦ, ὦ ἄνθρωπε, μήποτε τῇ πίστει βαμβαίνων, ὅτ' ἄν κληθῇς εἰς μαρτύριον προθύμως ἐπάκουσον, ἵνα ἡ πίστις σου φανῇ. *Commentary on Daniel*, II.37.5.

[114] Edgar J. Goodspeed, *A History of Early Christian Literature*, revised and enlarged by Robert M. Grant (Chicago: University of Chicago Press, 1966), 144.

What we can do is link the passion for suffering for Christ exhorted and revisited in the commentary with the willing passion to suffer seen in the conflict with Callistus.

Still, some details of Hippolytus' life remain uncertain as scholars continue to settle on his corpus of works, his ecclesiastical office, and his geographical location. For the purposes of this book, Hippolytus' understanding and use of the scriptural text as our subject ultimately evades the scholarly debates about the provenance of the work. The thesis about the role of martyrdom in this commentary succeeds regardless of our ability to identify the provenance, as long as the location allows for a milieu of persecution. However, because the external factors bear significantly upon the writer and his work, some functional conclusions will be made about the commentary's origins. This study will tentatively function under the traditional provenance of the *Commentary on Daniel* as a work crafted by a presbyter in a Roman milieu who later came to stand in opposition to the bishop of Rome. The application of the martyrdom motif in antiquity could apply to Christian congregations under persecution throughout the empire. Andrew Gregory's study of the apostolic fathers concludes the suitability of such a functional basis for other patristic sources: "Such social and theological situations as can be discerned behind such texts need not be distinctive to their geographic settings, even if they are grounded in them: similar situations might equally be found elsewhere under similar circumstances."[115]

Unveiling a Martyrdom Motif

Hippolytus' use of exegesis to further the cause of martyrdom materializes in this book by first examining the historical and theological context that surrounded the writing of the commentary in the upcoming chapter 2. The increased persecution against Christians during the rule of Septimius Severus led to new religious and social concerns within the church. This chapter examines the options confronting a persecuted church, as well as the specific third century setting in which he crafted his *Commentary on Daniel*. Discerning this milieu will suggest the content and strategy of the commentary.

Chapter 3 will bring out the martyrological motif from the pages of the commentary. The martyrological passages display themes such as faithfulness, heroism, suffering, endurance, persecution, sovereignty, and death that collectively establish an overall martyrdom motif. This highlighted motif in the commentary then becomes clearer in chapter 4 by examining Hippolytus' exegetical method of scripture that sanctioned the motif. This section considers

---

[115] Andrew Gregory, "Disturbing Trajectories: *1 Clement*, the *Shepherd of Hermas* and the Development of Early Roman Christianity," in *Rome in the Bible and the Early Church*, ed. Peter Oakes (Grand Rapids: Baker Academic, 2002), 163.

the systems of Christian and Jewish exegesis that he inherited, mainly the methods of Old Testament writers, the rabbis of the post-exilic period, and the early Christian writers. In some ways, this study answers Frances Young's call to recognize more literary segments in patristic works that function as interpretive genres, "segments interlinked by connecting threads, issues which keep recurring, and which defy simple organization."[116]

In addition to unlocking Hippolytus' exegetical methodology, this work recognizes that his interpretation of scripture only succeeds by his insistence on the divine authority of scripture. Additionally, the eschatological components of his theology must be considered, as they construct his understanding of the text of Daniel. The apocalyptic overtones of the text complement the martyrdom motif with their otherworldly solutions to Christian suffering.

This book will culminate by refining our comprehension of this intentional martyrdom motif by Hippolytus in chapter 5. It will review how Hippolytus exhorted his Christian congregation suffering Roman persecution. His method will be related, as he offered theological explanation of the disasters, contextualizing the events into a larger paradigm of world history in which God is in control. He intended to encourage Christians to remain faithful despite the suffering and persecution that they would experience. By endowing his exegetical activities with a positive interpretation of martyrdom, Hippolytus of Rome offered hope and definition to an oppressed and beleaguered church.

---

[116] Frances M. Young, *Biblical Exegesis and the Formation of Christian Culture* (Cambridge University Press, 1997), 1. In chapter 4 below I will, however, not wholeheartedly accept her assessment of the "inadequate" traditional categories of exegesis.

CHAPTER 2

Provenance and Overview of the *Commentary*

The first chapter viewed and analyzed Hippolytus' life and some of his works attributed to him. It concluded that he was most likely a presbyter around Rome, author of numerous works, opponent of lax ecclesial policy, schismatic leader of a Roman community, and eventual martyr, based on much of patristic tradition and modern scholarship. It also laid the groundwork for examining Hippolytus' *Commentary on Daniel* by revealing a personality so passionate about the Christian faith and earnestly opposing ecclesial leniency for the lapsed that he would be moved to analyze scripture in a way that exhorted those who are suffering persecution in the face of martyrdom. Conflict is a regular part of this historic character's life. Narrowing in on his important *Commentary on Daniel*, this chapter examines the exact political and theological ambiance that gave rise to this work and this call to martyrdom. Historically, this chapter examines how one hundred and fifty years of persecution shaped the church's self-identity and expectations of suffering. It also considers the immediate effect of Emperor Serverus' persecution, showing how past and present cause both an enduring but wearing effect on the church during this time. Theologically, this chapter explores the complex and powerful tradition of martyrdom theology inherited from Jewish ideology, lived and taught by Christ, and developed by the apostles and the fathers that the church integrated into their teaching on suffering. The historical and theological explain how Daniel functioned in a third section that gives reason for Hippolytus to utilize a motif of martyrdom in this writing. This provenance study precedes an overview of the commentary, including manuscripts, editions, style, structure, and content, bringing us to the position of accurately understanding the martyrdom motif in the commentary.

Defining the Historical Milieu

The historical milieu in which Hippolytus wrote his *Commentary on Daniel* was one of apprehension and confusion within the church, as it felt the social and political pressures of the Roman Empire that both instituted unfriendly policies and ignored mob violence against Christians. The early third century church's view of their own persecution was founded on a strong tradition of martyrdom and persecution, a tradition based on an interpretation of the suffering of God's people recorded in scripture from the time of the Jews into the church era. This legacy of persecution prompted the church to construct a theology of martyrdom based on their understanding of the maltreatment of Christians. An examination of the history of persecution and the theology that accompanied it will supply the necessary backdrop to discern how Hippolytus would wed martyrdom and exegesis in his commentary.

Christian Persecution in Prior Eras

The church had been persecuted for one and a half centuries before Hippolytus, so his Christianity in the early third century was no stranger to maltreatment. At times the persecution was sporadic and only local, but the Roman state and local governments never offered permanent security to the church nor guaranteed freedom from future persecution.[1] These centuries of persecution negatively impacted the church by prompting fear of capture, hardships of living and worshipping in secrecy, and the embarrassment of apostasy, in addition to questions about God's providence and the divine purposes of their suffering. These issues shaped Hippolytus' own expectation of suffering and being a Christian in the Roman Empire. An historical survey of Christian persecution will demonstrate three important factors shaping Hippolytus' understanding of martyrdom and persecution: (1) the extensive history and nature of persecution that intimidated the early third century Christian century around Rome, (2) the options for avoiding death that would confront any persecuted believer, and (3) the theologically-based optimism available to any candidate for martyrdom who was willing to persevere. The following pages will examine each factor in detail.

(1) Extent of Persecution. Scholars often classify the empire's historical animosity against Christians in three chronological groups: persecution first by the hands of the Jews, then by society, and finally the government. As early as the Book of Acts, there is record of organized and spontaneous opposition to the growth of Christianity by the Jewish leadership and people (Acts 4:17-18, 8:1, 12:1-5, 17:13). It seems that a pattern developed in which local Jews either pressured Roman authorities for arrests or personally drove out Christians themselves. By Hippolytus' own day, there remained a remnant of Jewish persecutors even in Rome, who "do not cease to think of persecution and tribulations against the church."[2] However, persecution by the Jews receives

---

[1] In fact, Roman policy still operated under the guidelines of Trajan: it was illegal to be a Christian but not worth the state's efforts to take the initiative to capture them. See the letter to Trajan treated on p. 35 below.

[2] διωγμοὺς καὶ θλίψεις ἐγείρειν κατὰ τῆς ἐκκλησίας. *Commentary on Daniel*, I.14; cf. Gal. 2:4. Lists of Hippolytus' works include a treatise *Against the Jews*, while *Philosophoumena*, IX.13-25 and X.26-27 contain attacks against Jewish philosophy,

only a little attention in Hippolytus' writings and the commentary primarily has Roman persecution in view.

The greatest nemesis of the early church in the first three centuries was the Roman imperial policy and the crowds of Roman citizens that took liberty to unite in action against Christians. An examination of the nature of persecution against the church in these eras will begin to inform us of the nightmare in which Hippolytus found himself, and a brief tracing of imperial policy regarding Christians from Nero to Severus divulges good reason for the church in Hippolytus' day to take seriously the reality of martyrdom and persecution.[3] From Tacitus the historian we know that the imperial court was already despising Christians by the summer of 64, even before Nero blamed them for the crime of burning Rome. Nero implemented a policy that was personal and only against Christians in Rome, engaging in several types of persecutions, including theatrical torturous martyrdoms in the palace yards.

Historians consider sporadic and local persecution to be normative for the Roman Empire even until the persecutions of Decius (r. 249-251). This includes episodes of persecution under the reign of Domitian (r. 81-96) as a champion of state religion, and the notorious policy of Trajan (r. 98-117) preserved in his letter to Pliny. This invaluable historical letter shows the attitude of Rome toward Christians that remained typical of policy to follow: to be a Christian was illegal and was worthy of a trial, but it was not worth a special hunt to go and find them within the empire. Any such trial ought to provide an opportunity to recant, Trajan said, that would allow their release if they denied being a Christian. In this regard, the Roman authorities tried to preserve citizens professing Christianity more often than trying to eliminate them. Scholars speculate that they had a genuine preference to spare the lives of its citizens while also recognizing the growing success of the martyrs. This manipulation to recant yielded the greatest practical quandary for the early church and a major grief in the Hippolytus schism: what to do with the lapsed upon their return to the church.

That Christians would be mocked in their persecution was not uncommon, as under Nero, and particularly under Marcus Aurelius (r. 160-180). In the 170's, a series of empire debacles such as famines and the German and Parthian uprisings resulted in anti-Christian sentiment within Roman society. In the decree *Senatus consultum de pretiis gladiatorum minuendis*, the emperor announced that Christians could be used as prisoners in the gladiatorial games, while continuing Trajan's policy of executing those coming through the courts. He ignored the mob actions taken against the Christians in various parts of the

Jewish religious sects, and Jewish chronologies that he claims are seeds for Christian heresy.

[3] This summary of the history of imperial persecution against the church is readily available (see p.19 n.68 above), but I am directly indebted to Frend, *Martyrdom and Persecution*.

empire that resulted in mass tortures and brutal executions such as in Lyons and Philadelphia. Society successfully engendered its own persecution in various parts of the empire with evidence of high levels of anti-Christian sentiment.[4]

This is the era into which Hippolytus was born, about 170 CE. Oddly, Aurelius' son Commodus (r. 180-192) did not inherit this passion against the Christians and his father's Stoic disdain for their religion, nor his political acumen.[5] A period of common peace between the empire and the Christians extended from 192 unto 204, when Emperor Severus (r. 193-211) made a proclamation that shook the Christian world and prompted the writing of Hippolytus' *Commentary on Daniel*. Someone like Hippolytus, reared in the late second century, would know the legends and witness the residual fear among Christians that remained throughout the empire from an era of persecution gone by. This time of peace under Commodus would only serve as a stark contrast to the dark profile of imperial policy under Severus.

(2) *Options for Avoiding Death.* During these times of trial in imperial courts, Christians were usually given opportunity to recant their Christian faith and escape with their lives. This was the policy that Trajan had instructed to Pliny in 117 that remained a sort of index for emperors and local administrators to follow. Thereafter, those that obeyed usually had to offer a sacrifice to the gods or to the emperor as a demonstration of his or her faith and were called "lapsed Christians," or "apostates," by others within the church. In the eyes of the church, there were three types of persecuted apostates: (1) the *sacrificati* who had fully sacrificed to the gods, (2) the *thurificati* who had only offered a few grains of incense in order to honor the emperor, and (3) the *libellatici* who had not offered a sacrifice but had obtained a certificate called a *libellus* protecting them from further persecution.[6] In an effort to persuade and to prevent martyrs, the Roman governors allowed them to offer a simple pinch of incense or simply swear a little oath.[7] The simplicity of the act diluted the sense of full sacrifice to pagan gods while allowing the Christian to escape with their lives. This system produced a large number of "denials" by lapsed Christians.

Scholars suggest that there may have even been three categories of betrayal: those rushing to offer sacrifice to avoid any tribulation, those who yielded after arrest and short imprisonment, and those that eventually compromised only

---

[4] Marcus Aurelius' reign was marked by a series of horrific persecutions by local government, such as those in Lyons and Philadelphia. His successor Commodus was friendlier toward Christians; his reign was not without Christian persecution, however. For example, Tertullian notes that a group of "fanatical Christians" were killed in Phrygia. For patristic sources on the persecutions immediately preceding and contemporary to Hippolytus, see the brief but detailed entry by Williams, "Persecution," 712-717, or the very detailed analysis in Frend, *Martyrdom and Persecution*, 197-239.

[5] Williams, "Persecution," 714.

[6] Lesbaupin, *Blessed Are the Persecuted*, 40.

[7] Lane Fox, *Pagans and Christians*, 421.

after being tortured. Perhaps the worst form of betrayal was by those who surrendered sacred books or provided names and addresses of other Christians.[8] The details are less important for Hippolytus and his congregations than the overall effect of persecution. Christian churches fell under pressure to release material or names, and individual Christians were confronted with cooperation, punishment, or death. The temptation of this "escape" option becomes an important concern that Hippolytus addresses in his *Commentary on Daniel.*

(3) *Perseverance.* Meanwhile, numerous Christians did not deny their faith, but remained faithful to Christ and suffered harm. There developed a category of those who confessed Christ before threatening authorities and were eventually released: they were called "confessors." The *Apostolic Tradition* distinguishes further between those confessors who were physically harmed or formally charged and those who were only casually or informally tried.[9] The former, "a confessor in chains," who is presented for the office of diaconate or presbyter does not need hands laid on him, as he receives the office by his confession. For the latter, "A confessor who was not brought before a public authority nor punished with chains nor condemned to any penalty but was only by chance derided for the name, though he confessed," then hands were still to be laid on him for any formal order. This distinction found in Hippolytus' own writing reveals the high respect the church gave to any confessor, to the Christian who suffered for Christ's sake. There was greater glory given to those who confessed Christ and died who were hailed "martyrs."[10]

For Christians after Severus' reign, the recorded testimony of Perpetua and Felicitas provided models of confessors who persevered even unto death. This account of the martyrdom of some Carthaginian Christians comes as unique documentation about the way Christians understood perseverance under suffering and consequential martyrdom.[11] Events and legends of the martyrs such as this one led to a complex theology of martyrdom in the mind of Christians that will be described below when the theological milieu is defined. For now, the persevering example of Christians suffering served as a heroic inspiration for other believers. Christians facing execution had likely seen other Christians die in the arena. They had seen or heard of various ways that believers were executed. The testimony and faithfulness of recent martyrs surely strengthened their resolve. Tertullian's work *To the Martyrs* circulated to inspire the persecuted church to martyrdom; surely the spirit of this work if not the work itself was well-known during the Septimian persecutions. Tertullian

---

[8] Lesbaupin, *Blessed are the Persecuted*, 40. The record of voluntary martyrdom and the contemporary scholarship on it is interesting but does not bear on our commentary analysis.

[9] Hippolytus, *Apostolic Tradition*, X.

[10] Eusebius also tells us of the high reverence given to those who surrendered their life for the faith in *Ecclesiastical History*, V.1 and V.2.

[11] For an analysis of this legend, see Smith, *Fools, Martyrs, Traitors*, 89-116.

had argued that if pagans showed little fear of death, then Christians ought not to fear it. Earlier Christian martyrs provided stories of bravery that circulated throughout the empire, such as the twelve Scillitan martyrs at Carthage and the slaughter of some of the church at Lyons. The legend of Perpetua and Felicitas preceded the probable writing of Hippolytus' Daniel commentary, so that even this recent event could have inspired and shaped this presbyter as he sought to articulate the expectations of Christians that might confront martyrdom.

Persecution under Septimius Severus

Imperial Rome ruled the world into which Hippolytus was born and continued through his lifetime. The reigns of Marcus Aurelius and Commodus governed his youth; perhaps he witnessed some of the legislation or the social assaults rendered against the church himself. The reign under Septimius Severus began peaceful in 193 CE, and his sudden policy against Christians follows along these lines. In the early third century, Severus ended a series of civil wars in the Empire. Facing remaining dissident groups and the possibility of rebellious legions, the emperor prompted policy to promote religious harmony. All subjects were to come together under the worship of the *Sol Invictus*—the Unconquered Sun—and all religions and philosophies were be syncretized under it. As expected, Jews and Christians refused to yield to any such syncretism. The tenth year of Septimius Severus witnessed renewed persecution on the church as well as on Judaism. In 202, the emperor issued an edict that outlawed all new conversions to Christianity. This policy complimented the *Leitmotiv* of Trajan's policy that seemed to have been prevalent since the early second century, mainly that Christians were not be sought out for trial but, upon arrival in court, had to be tried under good witness to either recant their faith or face execution. Now, however, a new policy was initiated that would be maintained by a number of emperors to come in which the state and public authority began to assume the initiative for persecutions. This marks the close of Trajan's rule to not to 'go looking for Christians' and the beginning of the era of persecution by edict had begun.[12]

Scholars have scrutinized the conflict between the church and the empire in a way that explains the logic of Roman persecution and the decree that were typical for Hippolytus' milieu. The intent was to prevent conversions to Christianity and not primarily to exterminate the Christians. Workman remarks, "Severus, alarmed by the rapid rate of the new religion, and the increasing menace of its tone, possibly resenting also certain indiscretions in the army,

---

[12] Lesbaupin, *Blessed are the Persecuted*, 8. The intentional effort by the Roman state to take new lengths to suppress Christianity is monumental. Shelley comments, "Thus the importance of Severus' action rests less in the application of the edict than in the fact of it." Bruce L. Shelley, *The Cross and the Flame: Chapters in the History of Martyrdom* (Grand Rapids: Eerdmans, 1967), 36.

found it necessary to take active measures against Christianity."[13] Bowersock identifies the nature of this hostile era "when Rome still had its empire and empowered its far-flung bureaucracy to process recalcitrant Christians within the legal system of the age."[14]

However, T. D. Barnes has argued that the decree by Severus is not historical and had no direct relationship to the martyrs. He accuses the historical record of inventing the edict of Severus, claiming that the emperor mentioned in Hippolytus' *Commentary on Daniel* could not be definitely identified.[15] The historical basis for the decree is the *Commentary on Daniel*, where Hippolytus writes:

> They watch for the favorable day when all [Christians] are praying and singing hymns to God, they enter into the house of the Lord, drag them out, and speak violently through blackmail, threatening to testify against them. When they do not consent, they testify against them before the tribunal, accuse them of acting contrary to the decree of Caesar and condemn them to death.[16]

This clear reference to some policy of the state is either the ongoing policy of Trajan or more likely a new edict by Severus. In the face of the numerous martyrs during the reign of Severus, Barnes' denial of a decree becomes difficult to maintain when one considers the suddenness and the severity of the persecutions, both from imperial interests and local actions. During this year of Severus' reign, Eusebius claims that there was a great increase in local persecutions reminiscent of those of the second century.[17] With prior imperial

---

[13] Herbert Workman, *Persecution in the Early Church* (Oxford: Oxford University Press, 1980), 95. Unfortunately, there is not any evidence that might reveal any evidence of "indiscretion," and any "increasing menace of its tone" is uncertain. Shelley adds, "The vigorous witness was the key to the influx of believers into high places. This was the government's way of bolting the door before it swung wide open." Shelley, *Cross and Flame*, 36.

[14] Glenn W. Bowersock, *Martyrdom and Rome* (Cambridge: Cambridge University Press, 1995), 25.

[15] Barnes, "Legislation Against the Christians," *Journal of Roman Studies* 58 (1968): 41-43. Barnes points out that besides leaving the Caesar unnamed, the rhetorical nature of the statement is casual (comparing this speech to that of Tertullian) and implies the commonly used phrase "the decree of Caesar" (as in Acts 17:7 describing Roman accusations against the apostles' behavior).

[16] παρατηροῦνται ἡμέραν εὐθῆ καὶ ἐπεισελθόντες εἰς τὸν οἶκον τοῦ Θεοῦ προσευχομένων ἐκεῖ πάντων καὶ τὸν Θεὸν ὑμούντων, ἐπιλαβόμενοι ἕλκουσί τινας καὶ κρατοῦσι λέγοντες δεῦτε, συγκατάθεσθε ἡμῖν καὶ τοὺς Θεοὺς θρησκεύσατε, εἰ δὲ μὴ, καταμαρτυρήσομεν καθ᾽ ὑμων. τούτων δὲ μὴ βουλομένων προσάγουσιν αὐτοὺς πρὸς τὸ βῆμα καὶ κατηγοροῦσιν ὡς ἐναντία τοῦ δόγματος Καίσαρος πράσσοντας καὶ θανάτῳ κατακρίνοται. *Commentary on Daniel*, 1.20.3.

[17] "When Severus began to persecute the churches, glorious testimonies were given everywhere by the athletes of religion." He notes that North Africa experienced the

decrees (viz., Marcus Aurelius), the mobs may have found approval in their actions even if the event were separated from the decree by a couple of years. Society's violence sometimes operated outside imperial policy, yet the proximity of the decree to the rise in local persecutions seems conclusively related to Roman imperial initiative. Furthermore, one would be hard pressed to dismiss the remark by Hippolytus as referencing an edict under any other emperors in his lifetime. For such reasons, most scholars hold to a decree by Serverus.[18] Even if Barnes is correct, we can clearly see that Christians in Hippolytus' locale suffered formal persecution by Roman courts.

During this period, the major centers of Carthage, Alexandria, Rome, Corinth, and Antioch all hosted burnings, beatings, and beheadings of Christians.[19] The severity of persecution at Carthage is preserved in the *Acts of Perpetua and Felicitas*, where we see several elements that typified Roman persecution: amphitheater entertainment, rejection by families, hostile mobs, severe punishment, and feeding to wild beasts. Clement of Alexandria notes that "roastings, impalings, and beheading" were common experiences during this time.[20] Tradition notes that Irenaeus of Lyons, mentor and friend of Hippolytus, even suffered martyrdom during this time.[21]

The effect on the church was dramatic. Frend estimates the impact of this era:

> The Severan persecution was the first coordinated worldwide move against the Christians. While it affected only the relatively small class of Christian converts and was confined to the major centers, it provided a precedent for later official actions. Perhaps because of the relatively high social standing of some of the victims, it produced a profound impression on the Christians themselves.[22]

---

greatest attention, and included in his record of martyrs is Leonides, the father of Origen. Eusebius, *Ecclesiastical History*, VI.1; cf. VI.7. For an additional, interesting, yet technical analysis of the persecutions under Severus, see the eighteenth century work by Thieleman J. Van Braght, *The Bloody Theater or Martyrs Mirror of the Defenseless Christians*, trans. Joseph F. Sohm, 11th ed. (Scottdale, PA: Herald Press, 1977), 126.

[18] Lesbaupin, *Blessed are the Persecuted*, 9; Frend, *Martyrdom and Persecution*, 240, 321, 482, n.70; Smith, *Fools, Martyrs, Traitors*, 101, 386, n.53.

[19] Frend remarks, "Perhaps what repelled the Christians more than anything, the judicial consignment of high-born women converts to the *lupanaria*." Frend, *Martyrdom and Persecution*, 240, 482, n.71.

[20] Frend, *Martyrdom and Persecution*, 240.

[21] Quasten, *Patrology*, vol. I, 288. He reports that the first historical reference to Irenaeus' martyrdom is by Gregory of Tours, *Historia Francorum*, I.27.

[22] Frend, *Martyrdom and Persecution*, 240. Frend analyzes the events that lead to the edict as well as numerous reports of persecutions. "Apart from the years 202-203, and the situation which had developed between the Christians and pagans in Carthage, the reigns of Septimius Severus and his son Caracalla (211-217) were tolerant." Frend, *Martyrdom and Persecution*, 242.

Eusebius says about these years, "So mightily did the agitation of persecution, then prevailing, shake the minds of many."[23] Beginning in this period, Hippolytus started producing a large collection of exegetical and dogmatic treatises for the church that were highly apocalyptic in nature. In particular, he wrote his *Commentary on Daniel* that it might offer hope to this era of persecuted Christians. Frend comments how this biblical commentary was drafted "in the midst of the persecution, or when its memory was still vivid."[24] The consequence of one hundred and fifty years of imperial executions and the vigilante mob acts was a special veneration of martyrs who gave their lives in witness of their belief in Christ. For example, such events led to the martyrdom of Ignatius, Polycarp, and (later) to Irenaeus in a way that produced a powerful theological milieu of martyrdom, and popular legends such as *Martyrdom of Polycarp* and *Perpetua and Felicitas* elevated the martyrs as heroes and heroines. This tradition of martyrdom eventually claimed Hippolytus himself, but not until he captured the spirit of sacrifice through martyrological ideologies, apocalyptic expectations, and pastoral exhortations founded on a biblical exegesis of the Book of Daniel. This historical legacy of suffering becomes the foundation for a strong martyrdom theology within the church that the next section will consider.

Defining the Theological Milieu

The generations that suffered persecution before Hippolytus laid a commanding foundation for a martyrdom theology that could lead him to interpret the Book of Daniel with the suffering church in mind. The genealogy of theological concepts about martyrdom proceeding the early third century is well-known in scholarship,[25] but it deserves attention here insomuch as they construct a larger theological framework that influences Hippolytus. Although this chapter at times seems detailed and encumbersome, each quote by Jesus, each concept of Old Testament persecution, each early church martyr could have been a gigantic factor in shaping the theological milieu that constructed the *Zeitgeist* of early church's view of martyrdom.

The early church perceived the conflict with the "world" to be a clash between what was good and true by God against what was evil and false; the persecution they experienced was of the latter category and even viewed as

---

[23] Eusebius, *Ecclesiastical History*, VI.7.

[24] Frend, *Martyrdom and Persecution*, 343, n.167.

[25] For example, Everett Ferguson summarizes them in, "Martyr," in *Encyclopedia of Early Christianity*. The classic treatment of the foundation and episodes of early Christian persecution is Frend, *Martyrdom and Persecution in the Early Church*. See also Daniel Boyarin, *Dying for God: Martyrdom and the Making of Christianity and Judaism* (Stanford: Stanford University Press, 1999).

Satanic in origin. This somewhat dualistic framework is seen best in the Johannine works of the New Testament, but notions of it can be witnessed in the Synoptic, Pauline, and general epistles as well.[26] The death of the saints at the hands of these worldly powers epitomized this conflict, preparing them to meet Christ whom they imitate in his passion and death. The martyrs became heroes for the people, and Christians idealized those experiencing this noble death. We will see that this ideology was basically apocalyptic in origin, providing a philosophy from which a Christian theology of martyrdom was built. Frend remarks: "Behind their actions lies the whole theology of martyrdom in the early Church. They were seeking by their death to attain to the closest possible imitation of Christ's passion and death. This was the heart of their attitude."[27] This did not mean that Christians were to seek out martyrdom, but like Jesus in the Garden of Gethsemane, if this suffering was a "cup passed to them," they should resolve to accept it. They were willing to suffer martyrdom as an obligation of their faith, as Christ had surrendered his life for their redemption.

We have already seen the beginning of a theology of martyrdom that he inherited from generations of elevating martyrs into heroes such as Ignatius, Polycarp, the apostles, and particularly Christ. Of particular interest to Hippolytus would have been the oral theological tradition of martyrdom that was handed down face-to-face from mentor to pupil from the Apostle John to Ignatius of Antioch to Polycarp of Smyrna to Hippolytus' own teacher Irenaeus of Lyons—a tradition from the East to the West.[28] We will now augment our study of this martyrdom theology with (1) notions of martyrdom inherited from Jewish and Christian writings, especially those centered on Christ and the Maccabees, (2) notions of apocalyptic in Jewish literature and in Revelation, and (3) the function of Daniel among the communities of God's people, and sequentially consider how these factors lent themselves to the tragedies of persecution in the Christian communities in Hippolytus' lifetime.

The second century closed some formative years of the Christian church in establishing doctrine, liturgy, theology, and organizational developments. Because the third and fourth centuries would prove so abundant in Trinitarian and Christological definitions in the ecumenical councils, Hultgren has

---

[26] For a discussion on the uniformity between the Synoptics and John against those who would call Johannine theology one, dualistic strain of early Christianity, see D.A. Carson, "Understanding Misunderstandings in the Fourth Gospel," *Tyndale Bulletin* 33 (1982): 59-91.

[27] Frend, *Martyrdom and Persecution*, 15.

[28] There is a need for a conclusive study demonstrating an inherited ideology of martyrdom from the East to the West, or from the earliest fathers to the later church; it is lacking in scholarship while certainly seeming to be logical from Patristic studies and a powerful theological force from the apostles through the fathers. For a survey of a similar phenomenon—the related apocalyptic tradition among the fathers of these eras— see Tsiripanlis, "The Antichrist and the End of the World," 5-17.

suggested that figures such as Hippolytus lived during a time of transition from "more urgent and fundamental tasks of defining the scope and limits of what Christianity itself was to become."[29] Although driven into questions of the Trinity and the similarity of "substance" between the Father and Son, Hippolytus remains trapped in a life-threatening time of testing from external forces, forces that churches in both East and West survived, partially due to a foundational theology of martyrdom and persecution.

Our study of the theological milieu of this frightful era begins below with an investigation of the general concept of martyrdom before proceeding to Christ's teaching on martyrdom and Old Testament and Apocryphal notions inherited by church that were basic to their outlook. This achronological approach helps to capture Hippolytus' perspective better, as Christ's teaching and example of martyrdom was the greatest influence on the early church martyrs. This tradition becomes the lens through which this early church presbyter interprets the book of Daniel in his commentary.

The Concept of Martyrdom

Martyrdom is universally recognized as dying for a cause. Nicole Loraux distinguishes between tragedies in which deaths are reported and martyrs in which deaths are also seen. Martyrdom is thus murder in public spaces due to a particular cause; they are *thanatoi en toi phanaroi*, "deaths that are seen."[30] Joyce Salisbury simplifies early Christian martyrdom as a clash of cultures in a way that recognizes the threat that Christianity posed to established culture and religion: "Things are never simple when paradigms shift and ideologies conflict. Martyrdom represents perhaps the most vivid moment in such a clash of cultures. During the early centuries of Christianity, individuals were willing to die, and die horribly, to bear witness to a new idea that was displacing an old one."[31]

When the early Christians came into the public square in the presence of spectators, they brought their own series of expectations. For them, their reason for being there was clear: they were about to be tested for their faith, and their resolve to stand firm was everything. Joyce Salisbury describes their expectations as almost programmatic by the time of Perpetua and Felicitas faced martyrdom.[32] The heroic examples of earlier martyrs described above, as well as visions, miracles, obedience, and sacrifice seen in a larger supernatural arena constructed the willingness of Christians to die for their faith. The

---

[29] Hultgren, *The Earliest Christian Heretics*, 2.

[30] Nicole Loraux, *Tragic Ways of Killing a Woman*, trans. Anthony Forster (Cambridge, MA: Harvard University Press, 1987), vii.

[31] Joyce E. Salisbury, *Perpetua's Passion: The Death and Memory of a Young Roman Woman* (New York: Routledge, 1997), 4.

[32] Salisbury, *Perpetua's Passion*, 135.

primary inspiration for them, however, probably came from the teaching and example of their Lord for whom they died.

Martyrdom in the Teaching and Rejection of Christ

The early church looked to the gospels for Jesus' warnings that his own persecution would foreshadow their own (Matt. 10:16-42, John 15:18-35).[33] The teachings of Christ include descriptions of a suffering servant reminiscent of the figure of Isaiah 53 (Matt. 20:17-28), as well as encouragement and promise of reward to his followers who suffered for his sake.[34] As we saw how the Roman persecutions came with opportunity for disavowal, so the New Testament spoke predicatively that some would deny Christ, and there was preliminary judgment against such people (Matt. 10:33, Rev. 3:5).[35] The one who overcomes persecution inherits God's reward, while those who are "cowardly" are ranked among the unbelievers, abominable, and murderers (Rev. 21:6-8). Willingness for self-sacrifice is obvious in some sayings of Christ such as Matthew 10:38, "He who does not take his cross and follow me is not worthy of me," and Luke 14:33, "Whoever of you does not renounce all that he has cannot be my disciple." Readiness and enthusiasm toward sacrifice are indicative of a spirit of one of Christ's own. The Apostle Paul knew this readiness for martyrdom in Romans 8:36: "For thy sake we are being killed all the day long; we are regarded as sheep to be slaughtered." Paul speaks of a redemptive kind of suffering in which a Christian willingly experiences hardship such as persecution and martyrdom, hoping "that I may know him and the power of his resurrection, and may share his sufferings, becoming like him in his death" (Phil. 3:10).[36] This teaching becomes foundational to the spirit of rigor and suffering in the name of Christ that characterizes the pleas and exhortations of Hippolytus in the commentary. Droge sums up the model of

---

[33] Matthew 10:24-26 declares, "If they have called the master of the house Beelzebul, how much more will they malign those of his household." John 15:20 typifies this passage, "If they persecuted me, they will persecute me."

[34] Matthew 5:10-12 states, "Blessed are those who are persecuted for righteousness' sake, for theirs is the kingdom of heaven. Blessed are you when men revile you and persecute you and utter all kinds of evil against you falsely on my account. Rejoice and be glad, for your reward is great in heaven, for so men persecuted the prophets who were before you."

[35] Matthew 10:33 depicts Jesus saying, "But whoever shall deny me before men, I will also deny before my Father who is in heaven." Revelation 3:5 predicts, "'He who conquers shall be clad thus in white garments, and I will not blot his name out of the book of life; I will confess his name before my Father and before his angels.'"

[36] Additional allusions in the Pauline Epistles to willful suffering for Christ's sake or in love of other believers include Romans 8:17-18, Ephesians 3:13, 5:1-2, Philippians 1:29, Colossians 1:24, 1 Thessalonians 3:4, 2 Thessalonians 1:5, 2 Timothy 1:8.

Christ, "Behind every description of martyrdom lay the example of Jesus."[37]

Martyrdom in the Maccabean Literature

Less directly influential but quite foundational to the shaping of Christian martyrology was the view of self-sacrifice in the Maccabean literature. The Jewish piety in the literature from the critical years of the revolt against the Hellenistic king Antiochus IV (173-164 BCE) shaped an ideal of Jewish martyrdom.[38] Frend comments: "Without Maccabees and without Daniel a Christian theology of martyrdom would scarcely have been thinkable."[39] Likewise, Augustine used the suffering of the Maccabees under Antiochus as an example for God's people to follow: "May men learn from them to die for the truth."[40] The early second century shared this same sentiment and found inspiration to suffer under persecution because of the legends of the Maccabees. The events of the revolt are recorded in 1 Maccabees, 2 Maccabees, and again in 4 Maccabees. However, 2 Maccabees 6:18-7:41 is perhaps the most important summary for our purposes. The next section will examine the development of national prophetic eschatologies, Jewish historical perspectives on Antiochus, and the understanding of atonement through suffering.

NATIONAL AND PROPHETIC ESCHATOLOGIES

A substantial change occurs in the *Weltanschuung* of Judaism after the return of the Jews from the exile with respect to how that God was leading his people. Prior to their exile, Jews gloried in the "golden age" under Solomon, their national and religious identity came with the Temple, and their ongoing reverence for the divinely provided Mosaic Law guided them. But even in this post-exile era, they were servants of generations of established foreign command (Persians, Greeks, Ptolemaics, and Seleucids) with a need for a reestablishment of a national identity, as they possessed some religious freedom but only as a people still under foreign occupation. This pressure and

---

[37] Arthur J. Droge and James D. Tabor, *A Noble Death: Suicide and Martyrdom among Christians and Jews in Antiquity* (San Francisco: HarperSanFrancisco, 1992), 156.

[38] Scholarly work on this topic is immense, but two helpful analyses are Smith, *Fools, Martyrs, Traitors*, 41-62, and Frend, *Martyrdom and Persecution*, 22-57 and 133-154. For an analysis of the literature in the Hellenistic period related to theology of martyrdom, see Droge and Tabor, *A Noble Death*, 72-76.

[39] Frend, *Martyrdom and Persecution*, 54. So powerful is the Jewish martyrdom tradition upon Christian thought, that Frend further remarks, "It has sometimes been said that Judaism was itself a religion of martyrdom." Frend, *Martyrdom and Persecution*, 22.

[40] Elias Bickerman, *The God of the Maccabees: Studies on the Meaning and Origin of the Maccabean Revolt*, vol. 32, Studies in Judaism in Late Antiquity, ed. Jacob Neuser, trans. Horst R Moehring (Leiden: E.J. Brill, 1979), 92.

restlessness led to a period of substantial theological change that deserves more attention.

At this historical point, Paul Hanson and Otto Plöger suggest that two different eschatological worldviews began to develop: a national eschatology and a prophetic eschatology.[41] The national eschatology expected God to deliver his people from this oppressive rule by military means. Just as God led the Israelites victorious in battle into the Promised Land, so he would again deliver these current kingdoms into the hands of the Jews, throwing off the yoke of the Gentiles and allowing them to have self-rule and entire freedom to worship as God's people. However, many Jews still held to a prophetic worldview in which God would speak through his prophets who would announce his upcoming judgments on these nations. God himself would divinely intervene and Israel would be fully restored. John J. Collins likes to coin the two groups "revolutionaries" and "visionaries."[42] The former would give rise to the Maccabees and the second century BCE armed revolt, while the latter group did not take up arms but awaited God to miraculously deliver them. This latter group give rise to the Pharisees, scholars believe, as well as developing the use of apocalyptic as a justification for their times of suffering. They can be recognized as the *maskilim* "wise ones" who are called by God to receive a divine message for the people, which in turn will be a source of encouragement and hope in times of loneliness, alienation, oppression, and persecution.[43] Sections of Daniel are highly apocalyptic in this fashion and their degree of historical detail has prompted some scholars to date it in the early second century BCE.[44]

---

[41] Paul D. Hanson, *The Dawn of Apocalyptic: The Historical and Sociological Roots of Jewish Apocalyptic Eschatology* (Philadelphia: Fortress Press, 1979); Otto Plöger, *Theology and Eschatology*, trans. S. Rudman (Richmond: John Knox Press, 1978).

[42] John J. Collins, *Apocalyptic Imagination: An Introduction to Jewish Apocalyptic Literature*, 2nd ed. (Grand Rapids: Eerdmans Publishing, 1998).

[43] For an analysis of the identity and goals of the *maskilim*, see Steven Thompson, "Those Who Are Wise: the *Maskilim* in Daniel and the New Testament," in *To Understand the Scriptures: Essays in Honor of William H. Shea*, ed. David Merling (Berrien Springs, MI: Institute of Archeology of Andrews University, 1997), 215-220.

[44] The accuracy and nature of the book's prophetic claims about Antiochus in chapter 11 has especially contributed to this later dating. There are some conservative scholars who maintain a sixth century BCE dating of the book based on literary and historical data, but the mainstream of scholarship sees such efforts as hard-pressed. For a commentary generally representing of this earlier dating, see Joyce G. Baldwin, *Daniel: An Introduction and Commentary*, Tyndale Old Testament Commentaries, ed. D.J. Wiseman (Downers Grove, IL: InterVarsity Press, 1978). For good arguments justifying an earlier date, see Gleason L. Archer, *A Survey of Old Testament Introduction* (Chicago: Moody Press, 1994), 421-447. For a more critical analysis, see Arthur Ferch, "Authorship, Theology, and Purpose of Daniel," in *Symposium on Daniel*, ed. Frank B. Holbrook, vol. 2, Daniel and Revelation Committee Series (Washington, D.C.: Biblical

Hippolytus found himself in a socio-political situation very similar to the Maccabees, while his interpretation of Daniel falls along the prophetic, "visionary" line of response. As presbyter, he had a duty to guide his congregations as they faced foreign oppression to look to God for deliverance or patiently wait to die for him. Like the *maskilim*, these Christians did not look for military victory but thought their piety might glorify their Lord who will either rescue them or accept the sacrifice of their lives. The hope of a "national" Christian vision is out of view for his era of the church. Hippolytus draws from the prophetical material of Daniel 11 as a model for the suffering which Christians confronted in the early third century CE, tying together the events of Antiochus and a future, final Antichrist.[45] Likewise, Cyprian would later view Antiochus as that final figure: "In Antiochus Antichrist was set forth..."[46]

Through the force of the *maskilim* movement, the Maccabean events enforced within Judaism a resolve of death; those defending their faith should expect to die instead of hoping for deliverance through divine intervention. The Maccabean revolt of 167 BCE established a paradigm of suffering for Judaism; now the death of God's people accomplishes a greater achievement than being rescued—they demonstrate God's bridled judgment while foreshadowing his imminent advent. In the Jewish mind, formerly God received glory by delivering Daniel, Shadrach, Meschach, Abednigo, and Susanna, but now the divine sovereign volition prefers that the post-exilic, Maccabean era Jews offer a sacrifice of death. This was a time of theological transition in which the death of the godly became a sacrifice to God that saved them, and some began to look beyond immediate deliverance from earthly harm for eternal rewards in heaven. Williams notes how "the suffering in persecution was the willing sacrifice made by the righteous for the unrighteous."[47] However, not all the Maccabean tradition emphasizes these sacrificial notions that enhance a later Christian theology of martyrdom, and examination of the literary accounts deserves individual attention.

HISTORICAL PERSPECTIVES ON ANTIOCHUS

In *The God of the Maccabees*, Elias Bickerman suggests that Daniel, 1 Maccabees, and 2 Maccabees offer different historical perspectives on the

---

Research Institute, 1986), and also see Collins, *Apocalyptic Imagination* as well as his *Daniel: With an Introduction to Apocalyptic Literature* (Grand Rapids: Eerdmans, 1984). For a less well-known survey focusing on how Daniel was written with a specific apocalyptic purpose in a Seleucid milieu, see Alexander Di Lella, *Daniel: A Book for Troubling Times* (Hyde Park, NY: New City Press, 1997).

[45] His understanding of current persecution and a future Antichrist are examined below as commentary data in "The Prophecy of the Great Tribulation," pp. 99-110, and in analysis in "History and Eschatology," pp. 137-139.

[46] Cyprian, *Exhortation to Martyrdom, Addressed to Fortunatus*, Treatise XI.11.

[47] Robert Lee Williams, "Persecution," 712.

situation of Antiochene persecution.[48] This critical scholar describes the three
Jewish sources in a way that could potentially influence an early church writer
differently, and it is not difficult to see how the text of 2 Maccabees might
speak to Hippolytus the most. Contrasting these three individual sources will
help to demonstrate this influence. The major contributions of each are
considered below in chronological order of their writing: Daniel, 1 Maccabees,
and 2 Maccabees. Although the traditional dating for Daniel is the sixth century
BCE, critical scholars date Daniel in 165-64 BCE. All scholars date 1
Maccabees in the broad 135-04 BCE and 2 Maccabees just before the end of
the second century BCE.

The book of Daniel sets the anticipated military and religious action in the
context of future prophecy. Elias Bickerman pits the Greek practical, civilized,
propaganda account of Epiphanes against the Jewish prophetic, theological
account. The biblical understanding of history, as it was conceived by the great
prophets, can discover meaning in any event only in connection with God's
activity on behalf of his people. So, when the "nations" rise up against Israel,
this catastrophe can be understood only as a punishment decreed by God.[49] In
the early fifth century, Jerome would identify this in his *Commentary on
Daniel*: "It is by the will of God that they [kings and empires] are governed,
altered, and terminated. And the cases of individuals are well known to Him
who founded all things."[50] Thus, prophecy functions to explain the reasons and
duration for the oppression of an alien ruler. Daniel's account takes special
effort to display the arrogance of the Gentiles and the divine intentions behind
their actions. This sets the stage for divine justice, which usually follows a
period of tribulation of God's people.

However, the book of 1 Maccabees is characteristically different than
Daniel, as it continues the line of biblical judges and kings in Israel during the
time of Seleucids and the Maccabean rebellion. Bickerman points out that the
story's sense and significance would be missing except for the contrast between
Israel and the nations. In this Hasomaean account, the Maccabees naturally
become a point of reference for righteousness, and their deeds are often
justified and defended. In this book, the blame for unrighteousness does not lie
with these rulers but the godless Jews who "hated their nation" (1 Macc. 11:21)
and made "a covenant with the Gentiles" (1 Macc. 1:11), in addition to the
sinful, arrogant "Gentiles" that persecuted them. Unlike Daniel, this book does
not find God's wrath calmed through repentance and prayer. Unlike 2
Maccabees, this book does not propitiate God's wrath through the blood of the
martyrs.[51]

The account of 2 Maccabees offers the most theological interpretation of the

---

[48] Bickerman, *The God of the Maccabees*, 14-23.

[49] Bickerman, *The God of the Maccabees*, 15.

[50] Jerome, *Commentary on Daniel*, II.21.

[51] Bickerman, *The God of the Maccabees*, 17-21.

persecution events.[52] The temple and the holiness of the Lord are the focal points in which both Jews and Gentiles have disobeyed the Lord. Antiochus IV was an instrument of heavenly justice against a disobedient people, while he is also guilty of a crime of ungodliness himself. Bickerman identifies a formula for changes in the history of the temple: sin + repentance by Israel; arrogance + punishment of the Gentiles. There is divine grace for God's people and divine retribution for those who not belong to him. "He never withdraws his mercy from us. Though he disciplines us with calamities, he does not forsake his own people" (2 Macc. 6:16).

ATONEMENT THROUGH SUFFERING

The greatest martyrological ideal developed in this book is that the blood of the martyrs in these events becomes the reason for God's satisfaction for Jewish disobedience. With the Maccabees, especially this account, scholars see a paradigm shift in martyrdom in which the suffering experience begins to provide atonement for sin and vindication through forgiveness. In 2 Maccabees, there is a sense in which the participants were purged of their sins and that their reward was immediate and eternal upon their death. Essentially, their suffering accomplished their salvation. As God's people, the Jews saw themselves as "having an active role as God's advocates in the midst of an evil and unsympathetic world" on both an individual and national level.[53] Oppressed and afflicted, the suffering of these people came to be regarded as atoning for Israel's collective sins. Eleazar suffered for the sake of the faith "to die a good death willingly and nobly for the revered and holy laws" (2 Macc. 6:28). He died as "a vicarious sacrifice on behalf of his people (2 Macc. 7:37), to stay the wrath the Almighty (2 Macc. 7:38)."[54] From the Maccabean era into early Christianity, suffering began to function as something atoning for the righteous ones among God's people, and this is evidenced in the later Christian *Acts of the Martyrs*.

Accompanying this remuneration was the expectation of divine deliverance of the nation of Israel through a reprisal for her enemies. The martyr became the instrument for testifying about the imminent judgment of Yahweh; his children's suffering served to prelude a divine judgment and retribution that was to come. 1 Maccabees 2:37 states, "Let us die in all innocence: heaven and earth shall testify for us that you put us to death wrongfully." Likewise, Judas cries out to God to honor their sacrifice of life: "They besought the Lord to look upon the people who were oppressed by all...to hearken to the blood that cried out to him" (2 Macc. 8:2-3). So also the suffering of the young man in 2

---

[52] Despite this supernatural explanation, there is also a natural one that explains the actions of the Greek: Antiochus Epiphanes "left Egypt and took the city by storm" (2 Macc. 5:11). Bickerman, *The God of the Maccabees*, 22-23.

[53] Frend, *Martyrdom and Persecution*, 23-24.

[54] Frend, *Martyrdom and Persecution*, 35.

Maccabees 7:37-38 had an important function, as he defended their suffering by "appealing to God to show mercy soon to our nation and by afflictions and plagues to make you confess that he alone is God, and through me and my brothers to bring to an end the wrath of the Almighty which has justly fallen on our whole nation." John J. Collins remarks that the martyrdoms in 2 Maccabees add human a dimension of sacrifice that complement the 1 Maccabean account of human military action. The martyr deaths are "not the only factor which arouses the vengeance of God, but it is at least clear that the zealot warriors are not the only ones who contribute to the victory. They also serve who only stand and suffer."[55]

Even a critical dating of Daniel allows the book to inspire the Maccabees through ideas of hope for those suffering for the Lord's sake with its themes of sovereignty, deliverance, resurrection, judgment, and eternal rewards.[56] Before being thrown into the furnace, the three youths found consolation in possible death. Addressing Nebuchadnezzar they declared:

> If it be so, our God whom we serve is able to deliver us from the burning fiery furnace; and he will deliver us out of your hand, O king. But if not, be it known to you, O king, that we will not serve your gods or worship the golden image which you have set up. (Dan. 3:17-18)

Daniel 12:2 predicts that in the end personal resurrection to eternal life awaits those who have died for the faith, while the enemies of God go on to eternal disgrace and contempt. Likewise, Daniel's deliverance from the lions' den, the youths' deliverance from the dietary penalties, and the hopes of the destruction of the kingdoms of the world also provided either hope of rescue or reassurance that their sacrifice was not in vain. These themes are shared with the Maccabean literature and foundational to the early church's rising martyrdom theology.

The following passage from 2 Maccabees typifies this important understanding of their obedience, suffering, and sacrifice:

> But you, unholy wretch, you most defiled of all men, do not be elated in vain and puffed up by uncertain hopes, when you raise your hand against the children of heaven. You have not yet escaped the judgment of the almighty, all-seeing God. For our brothers after enduring a brief suffering have drunk of everflowing life under God's covenant; but you, by the judgment of God, will receive just punishment for your arrogance. I, like my brothers, give up body and life for the

---

[55] John J. Collins, *The Apocalyptic Vision of the Book of Daniel*, Harvard Semitic Monographs, ed. Frank Moore Cross (Missoula, Montana: Scholars Press, 1977), 198.

[56] Smith, *Fools, Martyrs, Traitors*. For a essay identifying the use of Daniel in Maccabean ideology, see C. Thomas McCollough, "Daniel," in *Encyclopedia of Early Christianity*. There is no thorough work devoted exclusively to Daniel's contribution to a Christian theology of martyrdom and persecution.

laws of our fathers, appealing to God to show mercy soon to our nation and by afflictions and plagues to make you confess that he alone is God, and through me and my brothers to bring to an end the wrath of the Almighty which has justly fallen on our whole nation. (2 Macc. 7:34-38)

Thus, Bickerman finds that 2 Maccabees' "idealizing representation" is the strongest among the sources that helped the Jewish people understand the oppression after the event.[57] 2 Maccabees displays many particular parallels with the situation of Hippolytus that surely influenced this early church presbyter, beginning with the parallel between the King of the North in Daniel 11 and the historical record of Antiochus in 2 Maccabees 6-8. It centers on a royal decree by Antiochus that required Jews to "forsake the laws of their fathers and cease to live by the laws of God" (2 Macc. 6:1; cf. Dan. 11:31). Such were the notions of martyrdom from tannaitic Judaism.

Before moving to the Christian enhancements of martyrdom, a glance at Boyarin's arguments for Jewish martyrdom from the Maccabean period is worth noting. He challenges Frend's claim that "Judaism was itself a religion of martyrdom" because it "completely obscures and indeed annihilates the historical specificity of the new formations that developed both with the Rabbinic community and among the Christians of late antiquity."[58] His assessment seems a worthy one, as it softens the martyrdom force that Frend flushes out of his study of Jewish and Christian ideology. Martyrdom and persecution combined for only one strain of shared thought from the tannaic to the Christian periods, and even then it was not so neat and clean. For our purposes, Boyarin's call to epistemological changes is significant: "No practice or discourse arises entirely *de novo*, but we must be prepared to mark epistemic shifts."[59] Patristic writers had a way of picking and choosing Jewish concepts that complimented their own faith understanding. In Hippolytus' case, his willingness to use heterodox sources as scripture offers him more credibility; besides his use of the Apocrypha's Maccabean accounts, he embraces the episodes of Daniel in Theodotian's version of the Septuagint that are not found in the Masoritic texts.[60] However, I would suggest that for Hippolytus, as for other patristic writers on martyrdom, the text and ideas of the Maccabees were not the primary driving force for their theology of suffering, but the New Testament holds that place of privilege.

Christian Enhancements to Martyrdom

Christians understood the notions of martyrdom inherited from Judaism to be

---

[57] Bickerman, *The God of the Maccabees*, 21-22.
[58] Boyarin, *Dying for God*, 127.
[59] Boyarin, *Dying for God*, 127.
[60] See "Authority of Scripture," pp. 124-128 below.

exemplified and taught further by Christ. Ferguson writes, "The significance of martyrdom in the early church is shown by the important theological premises that were used to interpret the event."[61] By the third century CE and the administration of Hippolytus, Christians had just such theological premises adopted from their Jewish ancestors to fit into a Christian theological and apologetic framework. It is necessary to explore the Christian development in ways important to Hippolytus and his congregations around Rome at the dawn of Severus' persecution.

This section examines how many influential martyrological events following the Maccabees through the reign of Marcus Aurelius preceded and shaped appreciably the composition of this particular Daniel commentary. First, it examines how the church used Maccabean literature to develop its own Christian martyrological ideology. Then, it considers other Christological developments that reinforced the theological justification for the church's suffering. Finally, it reports how the possibility of suffering persecution and martyrdom became a stand Christian expectation for Hippolytus and other Christian writers. For example, the legends of the martyrs popularized and actualized the reality and possibility of the persecution for Christians everywhere.

TRANSITION FROM JEWISH TO CHRISTIAN IDEOLOGIES

The Jewish Maccabean period preceding the early church produced and nourished works that provided Christianity with a theology of persecution. These works were generally accepted by the early church as scripture. Bickerman describes how "the church incorporated the books of the Maccabees in her canon as testimonies of steadfastness during persecution, and she recognized the blood witnesses of the imperiled faith under Epiphanes...as the forerunners of her own martyrs."[62] Origen calls the Maccabean perseverance "a magnificent example of courageous martyrdom."[63] Bickerman lists other Christian figures on whom this traditional interpretation of heroic martyrdom by the people of God and Antiochus as a precursor to Nero, Decius and Diocletian. Maccabean influence can be seen in Gregory of Nazianzius, Leo, Prudentius, and Victorinus, as well as some German monks, many Byzantine theologians, and modern Catholic thought.[64]

Just as the Jews gained inspiration from the legends of the Maccabees preserved in their literature, so the early Christians shared these events and

---

[61] Ferguson, "Martyr," 577.

[62] Bickerman, The God of the Maccabees, 24.

[63] Origen, Exhortation to Martyrdom 23, in Alexandrian Christianity: Selected Translations of Clement and Origen with Introductions and Notes, trans. John Ernest Leonard Oulton and Henry Chadwick, ed. Henry Chadwick (Philadelphia: Westminster Press, 1954).

[64] Bickerman, The God of the Maccabees, 24.

began preserving also preserved their own legends who had given their life for Christ, gaining new hope from their faithful acts. The Greek words *martureo* μαρτυρῶ "to give testimony" and *martus* μάρτυς "witness" were used to describe the testimony offered by the faithful, at first as eyewitnesses to the events of Christ's life, as well as for any later attestation of the faith such as submitting to hostile punishment. Revelation 2:13 speaks of Antipas as a sort of blood witness, and by the end of the second century it had become a technical term for those who die for the faith.[65] The church distinguished between those persecuted that confessed Christ before authorities and lived, whom they called "confessors," and those not surviving called "martyrs." Here, the special denotation of "blood witness" took on its full meaning, and martyrdom became a heroic ideal of ultimate testimony to the faith. The sacrifice of some martyrs in the church led some to become Christians, such as Justin Martyr and Tertullian.[66] The social impact of the Christian martyrs is measured in the many references among pagans and Christian writing that witnessed it. Tertullian's quotation is commonly used to describe the church's effect on many pagans: "The blood of the martyrs is the seed of the faith."[67] With different rhetoric, Hippolytus writes: "All, at the sight of this marvel, are full of surprise ... and a great number, drawn to the faith by the martyrs, also become God's martyrs."[68]

Despite the ancestral connection of early Christianity with the Maccabean period, Talmudic scholar Daniel Boyarin wants to abandon the kinship metaphors that scholars use to describe the relationship between Judaism and Christianity. Ideas such as the mother-daughter affiliation or the sisterhood of Talmudic Judaism and early Christianity can minimize their ideological relationship. He prefers Wittgenstein's idea of "family resemblance as a semantic, logical category." Here, all forms of Judaism and all forms of Christianity are not merely parallel but "crisscrossing lines of history and religious development."[69] Such developmental models are interesting, but we need only acknowledge a transference of core values from the Maccabean period, as this work seeks relationship and influence rather than development and formation. Our study seeks to identify principles of martyrdom and redemption from this seminal Maccabean period, with an eye for cross-pollination of continuing traditions into the third century that almost certainly influenced Hippolytus' theological worldview.

---

[65] Ferguson, "Martyr," 575. This is evidenced in *Martyrdom of Polycarp*, 2; Irenaeus, *Against Heresies*, 5.9.2; and Clement of Alexandria, *Stromata*, 4.4-5, 21.

[66] Justin, *2 Apology*, 12; Tertullian, *Apology*, 50. For a detailed survey of the witness of the Christian martyrs in the pagan world, see Willy Rordorf, "Martyr, Martyrdom," in *Encyclopedia of the Early Church*, ed. Angelo Di Berardino, trans. Adrian Wolford (New York: Oxford University Press, 1992).

[67] Tertullian, *Apology*, 50.13.

[68] *Commentary on Daniel*, II.38.

[69] Boyarin, *Dying for God*, 8.

Unlike their Jewish predecessors, Christian martyrs possessed in Jesus' death and resurrection absolute confidence that martyrdom was worthwhile. The Jews at the time of the Maccabees believed passionately that their theories of suffering and martyrdom were legitimate, yet they lacked positive empirical evidence that Christians possessed in Christ's resurrection and the consequential hope of their own future resurrection. The real harbinger to their faith was the belief in the resurrection of Jesus. Therein lay the "proof" that God was on their side, rewarding their martyrs with eternal life. The Apostle Paul could guarantee the necessity of it, "But if there is no resurrection of the dead, then Christ has not been raised; if Christ has not been raised, then our preaching is in vain and your faith is in vain" (1 Cor. 15:13-14).

The power and hope of the resurrection invigorate Hippolytus' exhortations for Christians to stand firm under persecution. The writers of the biblical text, such as Daniel, served to bolster both Jewish and Christian faiths, even though God delivered those in the Daniel stories but did not rescue those in the second century. Christians possessed a richer theology of martyrdom, knowing that their reward included personal future victory over the death they were about to meet, or over the cruel deaths their loved ones had suffered for Christ's sake. So, Christians joined the ranks of those godly Old Testament believers who had also suffered for the Lord. Surely Hippolytus understood this concept, as Frend notes: "The martyrs represented a continuance in the church of the righteous examples of the Old Testament."[70]

Like 2 Maccabees, early Christian theology reveals that the church sometimes saw their sacrifice as purgative of sin. *Shepherd of Hermas* records the notions that the elect would be tried by fire, "chosen by God for eternal life" as they passed through it, with mention of blood and fire together being purifying.[71] The sacrifice has a positive effect that results in union with God, not of a negative purgative notion. The work announces a place for those who have "suffered for the sake of the Name,"[72] and elsewhere, "The sins of these have been taken away because they have suffered for the name of the Son of God."[73] Ignatius of Antioch particularly took up the theme of sacrifice through martyrdom, using the rare term ἀντίψυξον "ransom," speaking how his spirit can serve as a redemptive substitution for his followers' lives.[74] This same tradition is displayed in Tertullian who presents martyrdom as the supreme

---

[70] Frend, *Martyrdom and Persecution*, 118.

[71] *The Shepherd of Hermas* 24, in *The Apostolic Fathers: Greek Texts and English Translations*, ed. Michael W. Holmes (Grand Rapids: Baker, 1999). See p. 333 in this volume for comparisons and conversion of difference references systems for the *Shepherd*.

[72] *Shepherd of Hermas*, 9; cf. 10.

[73] *Shepherd of Hermas*, 105.

[74] Frend, *Martyrdom and Persecution*, 152-53.

atonement for sin.[75] According to the legend of Polycarp, to be a martyr for the faith was to be counted worthy of God.[76] Additionally, confessors originally were believed to be able to forgive sins, restoring contrite believers to the church.[77]

FURTHER CHRISTOLOGICAL DEVELOPMENTS OF MARTYRDOM

The early church held a high ideal that a Christian who suffered for Christ was sharing in the same act of Christ's passion. This was a change from Jewish theology, as the New Testament ideas of suffering become even more positive when one personally witnessed to the truth and imitation of Christ's suffering.[78] Martyrdom came to represent a reenactment of his death, and would-be martyrs naturally anticipated a corresponding resurrection to immortality. The Apostle Paul wrote of "sharing in [Christ's] sufferings" (Phil. 3:10), while Ignatius pushed for the need to imitate and share Christ's passion: "Suffer me to follow the example of the Passion of my God."[79] Polycarp believed that a consequence of being a Christian involved death at the hand of the authorities like his master had done had done.[80] Tertullian insists that Christians confronting martyrdom should view their suffering as an event preceding full salvation.[81] A belief in a heavenly reward as a consolation to their persecution characterized the apocalyptic worldview of Christians in this era, one of several concepts to be spelled out below. Christians saw their death as a means of *autoapotheosis*, "a shortcut to immortality."[82] Origen declared his passionate willingness to suffer

---

[75] Tertullian, *Against Marcion*, IV.39.4.

[76] *Martyrdom of Polycarp*, 14: "I give Thee thanks that Thou hast counted me, worthy of this day and this hour, that I should have a part in the number of Thy martyrs, in the cup of thy Christ, to the resurrection of eternal life, both of soul and body, through the incorruption [imparted] by the Holy Ghost. Among whom may I be accepted this day before Thee as a fat and acceptable sacrifice, according as Thou, the ever-truthful God, hast foreordained, hast revealed beforehand to me, and now hast fulfilled." Cf. Ferguson, "Martyr," 577.

[77] Eusebius, *Ecclesiastical History*, 5.2.5; Tertullian, *On Purity*, 22; see Ferguson, "Martyr," 578, for additional patristic sources. Ferguson says that the basis of this belief was Luke 12:11ff, where the Holy Spirit is promised to believers when they are drug before the courts on account of their faith. This led to so many problems that eventually Cyprian insisted on bishops as determining the efficacy of ecclesiastical reconciliation.

[78] Frend, *Martyrdom and Persecution*, 150, Ferguson, "Martyr," 575; *Martyrdom of Polycarp*, 1, 6ff.; see Ferguson, "Martyr," 577 for additional patristic evidence. Droge remarks, "For some Christians, 'following' meant a vicarious reenactment of Jesus' death and resurrection thought the ritual of baptism." Droge and Tabor, *A Noble Death*, 126.

[79] Ignatius, *Epistle to the Romans*, 6.3.

[80] Ignatius, *Epistle to the Philippians*, 8.2.

[81] Tertullian, *Against Marcion*, IV.39.4.

[82] Droge, 129. The expectation of eternal reward for suffering for the faith can exist in early Christians' experiences without Droge's insistence that it requires voluntary death.

with immortal expectations:

> Bring wild beasts, bring crosses, bring tortures. I know that as soon as I die, I
> come forth from the body, I rest with Christ. Therefore let us struggle, therefore
> let us wrestle, let us groan being in the body, not as if we shall again be in the
> tombs in the body, because we shall be set free from it, and shall change our body
> to one which is more spiritual. Destined as we are to be with Christ, how we groan
> while we are in the body.[83]

Origen also declared that sins committed after the baptism of water can only be
forgiven by a baptism of blood.[84] This was a grace that God only gave to some,
and it seems that the church thought one was chosen especially by God to
experience it.[85]

Early Christians also believed their struggle was a personal encounter with
Satan. Like Christ whom God delivered in infancy from the hand of Herod,
who battled Satan in the temptation in the wilderness, and who permitted
himself to mockery and death, Christians engaged in their own temptation to
surrender to the buffeting of Satan. The *Epistle of Barnabas* presents the state
as an instrument of Satan: "The worker of evil himself was in power."[86] The
experience of death did not defeat their spiritual enemy, and the agonies of
persecution did not redirect the evils of the world or God's inevitable judgment
on them. It was victorious, nonetheless, as Smith notes: "Death and dying
became for the Christian a triple-sign: the reenactment of the folly of Calvary, a
bloody but potent proof of the power of faith, and a warranty to share with
Christ in his glory within the tabernacle of the Lord."[87] The pain of martyrdom
may be agonizing but eternal life was the reward; it had been written, "Every
one who acknowledges me before men, I also will acknowledge before my
Father who is in heaven" (Matt. 10:32). Christians' adversary the devil was
their only remaining obstacle to paradise, and martyrdom overcame that hurdle.

The martyrs came to play a central role in the self-identity of the church.
The public display of torture and the witnessing of the death of others helped
Christianity bring into focus what Judith Perkins calls a "new subjectivity" with
the self as sufferer.[88] In the early Roman Empire "the suffering body became a
focus of significant cultural concern," and Christianity developed its own
particular view of self that provided "a new basis of power and enabled the
formation of new [Christian] institutions incorporating this power."[89] Such

---

[83] Origen, *Dialogue with Heraclides*; so noted in Droge, 164, n.100.

[84] Origen, *Exhortation to Martyrdom*, 30.

[85] *Commentary on Daniel*, III.26. For additional patristic evidence, see Ferguson,
"Martyr," 577.

[86] *Epistle of Barnabas*, II.1; cf. IV.36.

[87] Smith, *Fools, Martyrs, Traitors*, 92.

[88] Judith Perkins, *The Suffering Servant* (London: Routledge, 1995), 7.

[89] Perkins, *The Suffering Servant*, 12.

principles were crucial development for the martyrdom theology of the early church. The ultimate result is that for Hippolytus martyrdom has more of a Christological basis rather than a Maccabean one.

EXPECTATION OF CHRISTIAN SUFFERING

These inherited notions of martyrdom developed into a complicated Christologically-minded experience that was the exact chord to which Hippolytus appealed. His life was one of conflict: challenge to a substandard bishop, confronted with persecution with inherited legends of church leaders' martyrdoms, and scripture instructing followers of Christ to expect conflict with the world. So, Hippolytus encouraged his congregation to be ready for martyrdom as if it were a duty or an obligation that one owed their savior who was martyred for them. If faith is a free, total surrender of self to God, then it entails a readiness and willingness to die for Christ. His own record demonstrates this principle when he was so rigorous in his devotion for the Lord. Hippolytus would scrupulously oppose even a bishop if he seemed to be lax on those who deliberately eluded suffering for the Christian faith.

The legends of the early Christian martyrs themselves became part of a larger impetus for believers to be willing to suffer for Christ. The heroic acts of Christians, the miracles that surrounded some of the legends, the bravery of standing naked in the public square—such stories of courage came to function as a motivation in itself that complemented the Christological, Maccabean, and prophetic dimensions to the church's theology of martyrdom. Several of them deserve mention here because they offered weight and credibility to Hippolytus' interpretation of the book of Daniel in his commentary, and offered a primary rationale for this first commentary on an Old Testament book: its potential for modeling suffering for God. This section examines a few remaining historical events and writers that also shaped Hippolytus' theory of suffering Christian martyrdom.

Tertullian crafted his work *To the Martyrs* in 197 CE to explain and encourage the persecuted church as "athletes" who struggle against Roman persecution.[90] He wrote to those in prison in order to firm their resolve in the tempting face of lapsing. As he considered the nature and rewards of martyrdom, he suggested that a cleaning of sin came through martyrdom. Tertullian had argued that if pagans showed little fear of death, then Christians ought not to fear it.[91]

In July 180, a proconsul of Africa ordered the execution of twelve Scillitans at Carthage for refusal to sacrifice to the Roman gods. The legend of their fortitude in the face of danger became well-known, and these martyrs would

---

[90] Salisbury reveals in detail how Perpetua's suffering is a metaphor for a Roman athletic contest in a work usually attributed to Tertullian. Salisbury, *Perpetua's Passion*, 109-112.

[91] Tertullian, *To the Martyrs*, *passim.*

inspire a rallying cry for African Christians under imperial persecution for two centuries: *Hodie martyrs in caelis sumus*, "Today the martyrs are in heaven!"[92]

If one accepts the evidence that Hippolytus was a direct disciple of Irenaeus, then the devastating persecution that left the episcopate of Lyons void leading to Irenaeus' appointment unquestionably influenced Hippolytus' sober reality of persecution. Those who refused to deny the faith were found guilty of criminal offense and either thrown to the beasts or beheaded. The individual legends of many of the forty-eight are preserved in Eusebius, who reports how their bodies were exposed for six days, burned, and cast into the Rhone because their persecutors wanted to frustrate their hope of any resurrection. He reports that such sufferers were "so zealous in their imitation of Christ...they cheerfully yielded the title of martyr to Christ, the true and faithful martyr (witness), the first begotten from the dead, the prince of divine life."[93] Frend remarks how "conditions in the second century had provided a test of survival which the Christians had surmounted."[94] On the other hand, Eusebius reports that in 177, ten Christians renounced Christ under pains of death. Their denial of the faith causing sorrow and fear among those not yet arrested. Salisbury describes the effect well: "Just as the constancy of some martyrs spurred others on to bravery, the weakness of others spawned timidity."[95]

The legend of Perpetua and Felicitas preceded the probable writing of Hippolytus' Daniel commentary, so that even this recent event could have inspired a presbyter who sought to articulate the expectations of Christians that might confront martyrdom. Visions, miracles, and obedience in a larger supernatural arena reinforced the willingness of Christians to die for their faith. Surely the spirit of this work—if not the work itself—was well-known during the Septimian persecutions.

Thus, earlier Christian martyrs provided stories of bravery that circulated throughout the empire. Many Christians in the early third century had likely seen other Christians die in the arena. They had seen or heard of various ways that believers were tortured or executed. The testimony and faithfulness of recent martyrs surely strengthened the resolve of many. The possibility of such persecution became so real and very likely that we see Tertullian emphasize a willingness to be martyred as an imperative for every Christian. "Thus ought every servant of God to feel and act, even one in an inferior place, that he may come to have a more important one, if he has made some upward step by his endurance of persecution."[96]

The ideal of martyrdom in the early church was so attractive that some

---

[92] Frend, *Martyrdom and Persecution*, 233.

[93] Eusebius, *Ecclesiastical History*, V.1.62. The accounts of the Lyon martyrs fill *Ecclesiastical History*, V.1.1-63.

[94] W.H.C. Frend, *The Rise of Christianity* (Philadelphia: Fortress Press, 1984), 184.

[95] Salisbury, *Perpetua's Passion*, 135.

[96] Tertullian, *On Flight and Persecution*, 11.

Christians began to voluntarily seek their own death at the hand of Roman oppressors.[97] They willingly surrendered themselves and hoped to gain the high honor that was due any martyr of the Lord. The church did not look honorably upon these, however, believing that one should be faithful on trial but should not seek this suffering out.[98] Although the suffering was voluntary, the trial and punishment were not to be self-initiated. Bowersock in *Martyrdom and Rome* justifies their efforts when he states, "Suffering and death at the hands of persecuting magistrates so elevated the status and presumably future prospects of martyrs that, by the late second century, there were many Christians who actively courted their own deaths as martyrs." [99] Smith describes, "The Christian theory of martyrdom transformed suffering into a matter of free will and fashioned foolhardy disobedience and obduracy into divine necessity."[100] Their willingness reflects the elevated and attractive status of the martyrs that the church had placed on them. The martyrdom ideal in the early church justifies the martyrdom motif in ancient works like Tertullian and Cyprian, and likewise in this commentary by Hippolytus.

Christian Enhancements to Apocalyptic Literature

In this unfavorable political situation of persecution and martyrdom, Hippolytus also inherited a tradition of apocalyptic writings. From the pre-Maccabean and Maccabean periods,[101] a corpus of Jewish apocalypses were composed that would influence New Testament and post-New Testament writings, contributing to the Christians notions of martyrdom through its eschatological framework. Christian eschatological interest was common from subapostolic times through the third century. Martin Werner has suggested that this was a time of somber reinterpretation of Christian revelation due to the

---

[97] Droge and Tabor reduce virtually all the martyrs as voluntary, but most scholars more accurately hold to social and state persecution and the church's consequential theology of martyrdom as leading only a minority to volunteer for martyrdom.

[98] Ferguson, "Martyr," 576. *Martyrdom of Polycarp*, 4 states that Christians were not to seek out martyrdom because it is not instructed in scripture. After a Phyrgian named Quintius forced his way forward for martyrdom, he saw the beasts and was afraid. The text reads, "Wherefore, brethren, we do not commend those who give themselves up [to suffering], seeing the Gospel does not teach so to do."

[99] Bowersock, *Martyrdom and Rome*, 2. He adds that it is impossible to postulate the exact number of the martyrs during this era.

[100] Smith, *Fools, Martyrs, Traitors*, 89-91.

[101] Most scholars insist that Jewish apocalyptic owes some proto-apocalyptic influence to a Babylonian matrix. Collins maintains that the writing of the earliest apocalypses in eastern Diaspora "cannot be decisively verified at present," although most scholars remain convinced of the majority of apocalyptic provenances. Collins, *Apocalyptic Imagination*, 21-22.

non-fulfillment of the parousia.[102] Jaroslav Pelikan disagrees, describing Werner's point as a "gross exaggeration of the evidence" of the early church's understanding of the biblical teaching.[103] Regardless of the historical reasons for apocalyptic issues, Dunbar rightly asserts, "It is clear that the unexpected extension of history was the cause of speculation, disagreement, and doctrinal and institutional development among the early Christians."[104]

TRANSITION FROM JEWISH APOCALYPTIC WRITINGS

Apocalyptic literature functions to offer hope and comfort to the oppressed in times of suffering, to encourage and edify believers in their resistance to what they see as forces of evil. Certain features characterize this genre: (1) A dualism between the kingdoms of this world, led ultimately by Satan himself, and the kingdom of God which ultimately will prevail. (2) A postponing of the judgment and justice that is due to each member of these kingdoms until a time imminent or in the next life. (3) A transcendence of God's people above the events of this world by the promise of resurrection and eternal life, with death becoming a passageway into the next life. (4) The use of catastrophic language and imagery to describe the events of the end of the world. (5) A conclusion that events are divinely approved; that God is in control, still sovereign, and had even foreordained many events. All of these characteristics functioned to offer hope to God's people in the absence of theological explanation of chaotic and harmful events. Simply put, Collins has remarked: "Apocalypses are usually regarded as crisis literature."[105] The result is that apocalyptic literature provides theological credibility to the suffering of God's people. This section considers how Jewish apocalyptic writings helped God's people to explain the persecution and injustices against them. This also gives rise to the apocalyptic Daniel and Revelation considered in the next section.

Hippolytus inherited a four hundred year old tradition from Judaism and early Christianity in this literary genre that was augmented by several factors: constant foreign rule with intermittent oppression, increased Jewish expectation of the Messiah, and Christian anticipation of Christ's return. This unfavorable contemporary situation explains what prompted Hippolytus' analysis of an apocalyptic section of scripture to explain the crises and martyrs. Although their crises were varied in kind and intensity, apocalyptic literature consistently contained a confrontation with death and a search for salvation beyond this world.[106] Jewish apocalyptic literature provided an impetus for resurrection

---

[102] Dunbar, "The Eschatology of Hippolytus," 322.

[103] Jaroslav Pelikan, *The Christian Tradition: A History of the Development of Doctrine,* vol. I, *The Emergence of the Catholic Tradition (100-600)* (Chicago: University of Chicago Press, 1971), 23-24.

[104] Dunbar, "The Eschatology of Hippolytus," 322.

[105] John J. Collins, "Apocalyptic Literature," in *Encyclopedia of Early Christianity,* 58.

[106] Collins, "Apocalyptic Literature," 56-59.

beliefs, empowering the notion of the afterlife. Notions of resurrection from the dead arose in popularity in Jewish circles from the Hellenistic period until the second Jewish revolt (132-35 CE). This, in turn, bore on the church's understanding of her own suffering. The power of God's people to transcend death by dying and entering into immortality offered a next-life solution to this world's suffering. Martyrdom became a means of achieving this goal and a solution for the experience of agonizing persecution. Caroline Walker Bynum confirms this, showing that by the end of the third century, the belief in the resurrection of the soul and the body was common.[107] Besides the corpus of Jewish apocalyptic composed in the late third century BCE onward and the compositions of Qumran, early Christian works that were Jewish in nature contributed to the tradition of apocalyptic tradition inherited by the early church.[108]

How did the early church employ this apocalyptic genre from the Daniel text? Hippolytus' martyrological interpretation of scripture is the topic of chapter 3 below, but the precedent was established prior to him and followed along these lines. Under the stress of Roman rule, apocalyptic Christianity found a definite hearing. Martyrdom was an apocalyptic mechanism serving as a prelude to the final coming of Christ, when Michael and Satan would engage in a cosmic battle of good and evil (Dan. 12:1). For now, the army of the Christian elect was becoming staffed, and already beginning to battle the servants of the Antichrist. This apocalyptic vision gave a place to martyrdom in the larger operation of God's kingdom, thus encouraging those who may face it.

Unlike the Jewish model of martyrdom seen in the Maccabean account, most Christians did not find strength in corporate, shared martyrdom. Instead, they stood alone before a hostile mob, naked in a public square. Unlike the Jewish prototype of martyrdom in the Maccabean and some of the Daniel narratives, the Christian martyrs did not see themselves as part of a national destiny. They were not at war with their foreign occupant, Rome, as were the Maccabees; their gain was not earthly-minded like former Jewish martyrdom models. In fact, many Christians saw themselves as loyal citizens of the Roman Empire. They were not defending the institutional church, as the hierarchical institution was not yet fully shaped. Furthermore, they believed that their very souls were

---

[107] Caroline Walker Bynum, *The Resurrection of the Body in Western Christianity, 200-1336* (New York: Columbia University Press, 1995), 21-43.

[108] Parts of Ezekiel, Isaiah 24-27, 40-66, Zechariah 9-14, and Joel are considered proto-apocalyptic. Only Daniel 2:29-45 and 7-12 are truly considered Old Testament apocalyptic literature. Synoptic parallels of Mark 13:1-37, Matthew 24:1-44, Luke 21:5-36, and Revelation are notably apocalyptic. Whereas the *Shepherd of Hermas* was probably Roman in origin, its motifs of tribulation, visions, and supernatural intervention probably carried certain influence.

being challenged by the incarnate power of Satan, an ordeal of both body and spirit. This encounter with Satan was profoundly personal and individualistic, rather than organizational or national.[109]

Instead, a new, greater, and more demanding martyrology was at work. Just as God delivered Daniel and three youths from various trials such as a fiery furnace, lion's den, dietary demands, and imprisonment, so he could also deliver believers in each era that followed. Rewards were in the next life, and their suffering functioned to validate an imminent judge. Smith describes, "The martyrs were men and women filled with the Holy Spirit who did immediate and violent battle with Satan and reaped the rewards of their victory."[110]

To a great extent, millenarianism and apocalyptic has been an essential component of Christian thought and piety. Apocalyptic literature interprets real events through a spiritual or divine perspective, causing unfavorable events to take on a new meaning as favorable events. When the audience, such as persecuted Christians, sees the events as larger than their own suffering, it results in encouragement and purpose to them. Such hope is extremely evident in the Book of Revelation.

MARTYRDOM IN THE BOOK OF REVELATION

The Book of Revelation's themes made it an important work for many Christians, especially those with a strong Jewish theological heritage such as Papias, Justin, and Irenaeus.[111] It deserves attention here because it shares apocalyptic ideas with the book of Daniel. Of particular theological importance, both Daniel and Revelation seem to anticipate a persecution of God's people by a godless figure whose actions are a blasphemy to the Lord. The difficult acceptance of Revelation by some in the early church is well known, but for Hippolytus this writing is viewed as scripture. In general, the book of Revelation fared better in the West.[112] This position is evidenced by his citations to the work and overall eschatology seen in *On Christ and the Antichrist* and even in his Daniel commentary, and probably by his willingness to write his commentary on Revelation now non-extant. Recognizing Irenaean influence on Hippolytus the commentary writer, especially in a Roman milieu, it comes as no surprise that Irenaeus accepts Revelation as end of the first

---

[109] See pp. 101-112, 139-142 below to see how these individualistic notions in Maccabean thought came to bear on the development of Christian apocalyptic theology.

[110] Smith, *Fools, Martyrs, Traitors*, 94.

[111] David E. Aune, "The Book of Revelation," in *Encyclopedia of Early Christianity*, 782. For a survey of apocalyptic tradition in these patristic figures in particular, see Tsiripanlis, 5-17.

[112] See the historical discussion surrounding Hippolytus' acceptance of Revelation as Scripture below in "The Complementary Role of the Book of Revelation," pp. 69-71.

century and Johannine.[113]

A main theme of the work is God's faithfulness to those who remain faithful to him under persecution, seen in numerous verses where those persevering will receive rewards of eternal life, the right to eat of the Tree of Life, authority over the nations, white garments, right to reign, and the inheritance of heaven.[114] Of particular interest are the passages of Revelation 6:9-10 and 7:9-17, where those killed for the sake of Christ are personally around the throne of God and rewarded for their sacrifice—a special honor only for the martyrs. On the other hand, those who are not faithful, those who do not persevere to the end, those that deny Christ and lapse in their faith will suffer eternal punishment, according to Revelation 3:16, 21:8. In apocalyptic literature, this rewards/punishment theme finds an important function in offering comfort and encouragement to those who are experiencing the trials and being persecuted for their faith. There is eternal blessedness awaiting those who remain faithful under these trials, especially the martyrs. According to Revelation, they are even given a place of special honor in heaven around the throne of God and in a state of happiness (7:9-17).

In the midst of this time of tribulation against God's people, the book gives surety that God has power over all these events, that Jesus is "Lord of lords and King of kings" (Rev. 17:14). The enemy of God in all its form of powers will be destroyed (Rev. 17-19), while the faithful of God will inherit heavenly Jerusalem (Rev. 21-22). Final punishment of this enemy includes vengeance for those whom the Antichrist figure harmed during this time of great tribulation (Rev. 6:9-10).

In particular, the early church could now view the text of Daniel through a lens of Revelation, with the events of Daniel 10-12 being seen as types of the future. The tyranny of the King of the North is, in Antiochus, a type of the Antichrist and the final tribulation, to be followed by a resurrection of believers that is already essential to New Testament eschatology. Cyprian would later view Antiochus as spiritually alien to God, "In Antiochus Antichrist was set forth-sought to pollute the mouths of martyrs, glorious and unconquered in the spirit of confession."[115] This phenomenon was part of the larger use of Daniel in the Christian community to which we now turn. This deserves closer attention because of its immediate influence on the biblical exegesis of Hippolytus. Early Christian apocalyptic works came to Hippolytus as models for Christian interpretation of apocalyptic literature in a way that inspired him in his exegesis of Daniel.

---

[113] Irenaeus, *Against Heresies*, 5.30.3. See also Eusebius, *Ecclesiastical History*, 3.18.2-3 and 5.8.6, and Francis X. Gumerlock, "The Date of Revelation in the Early Church," in *The Early Church and the End of the World*" by Gary Demar and Francis X. Gumerlock (Powder Springs, GA: American Vision, 2006).

[114] Revelation 2:7, 2:11, 2:13, 2:17, 2:26, 3:5, 3:12, 3:21, 6:9-10, 7:14, 21:6-8.

[115] Cyprian, *Exhortation to Martyrdom, Addressed to Fortunatus*, Treatise XI.11.

Function of Daniel in the Christian Community

Initially, it may be hard to find the logic for an early church father to choose a text like Daniel to create a commentary on scripture when such literature hardly existed within the church. When we consider how this father was living in a milieu of martyrdom and persecution, with his churches engaged in a greater apocalyptic conflict, it explains more clearly Hippolytus' choice of this book to project a martyrdom motif through its literary examples, prophetic allusions, and practical exhortation. The early church used the text directly, as well as its themes and rhetoric, to develop an understanding to its own relationship with a caustic Roman society and culture.

Traditional Lines of Interpretation

Even before Hippolytus employed the Book of Daniel for his commentary, the main lines of interpretation had been established.[116] From the time of its writing, God's people have employed the Book of Daniel to encourage and revitalize them. The early church was no exception, using the book as an inspiration for persecuted, suffering Christians. Scholars have always agreed that martyrdom profoundly shaped the character of early Christianity and aided its triumph over the empire. As we have surveyed in this chapter, the early church fathers developed this theme of martyrdom into a prominent theology for understanding the world in which they lived. Lacey Baldwin Smith notes, "Quite consciously the early Christian fathers were articulating a psychology of martyrdom [in their writings]. That suited the troubled souls and anxious minds of late antiquity."[117] The way that the church used Daniel prior to Hippolytus will clarify his exegesis.

Thomas McCollough groups the types of Christian interpretation along three main lines that best represent the way that Daniel functioned in the church: eschatological, messianic or Christological, and moral.[118] First, they developed an eschatological reading of the dreams and visions found in chapters 2, 7, and 11. Christians treated the imagery contained there as prophetic of the end of the world. Wilken remarks, "The Book of Daniel was seen as a fertile source of prophecies about the coming of Christ and the destruction of the Temple in Jerusalem, a topic which assumed a major role in the early Christian view of history."[119] Secondly, they developed a messianic reading of the return of Christ

---

[116] For a unique article surveying the use of Daniel throughout church history, see Gammie, "A Journey Through Danielic Spaces," 144-56. He gives an adequate review of Hippolytus while recognizing his contribution to the history of interpretation of Daniel in the church unto today.

[117] Lacey Baldwin Smith, *Fools, Martyrs, Traitors*, 95.

[118] McCollough, "Daniel," 254-55.

[119] Robert L. Wilken, *The Christians as the Romans Saw Them* (New Haven, CT: Yale University Press, 1984), 139.

centering on the 70 weeks of Daniel 9:24-27. This passage about seventy weeks was seen as eschatological, as the seventieth week represented the beginning of the end, the time of chaos just before Christ return. But the church also saw this prophecy as predictive of the first advent of Christ. In the first three years of the third century, one named Judas calculated the seventieth week to occur in the tenth year of the reign of Severus (202 CE) and that the Antichrist was at hand.[120] Thirdly, they practiced a reading of the stories of trials and persecution against God's people Daniel 1-6 for moral exhortation. For example, the Jewish youths in Babylon who demonstrated faithfulness to the Lord were models for Christians. Two of these lines of interpretation—paraenetic and eschatological—will be considered. In particular, an eschatological hope developed amidst earthly persecution and a paraenetic reading of the text encouraged those fearful of suffering or those mourning loss of fellow believers.

Probably the most popular use of Daniel in Christian writings during the first two centuries was concentrated on the eschatological visions of the stone in Daniel 2 and the glorious one in Daniel 7 that judged the kingdoms of the world and redeemed his people who were persecuted by them.[121] With respect to these apocalyptic beliefs, Thomas McCollough can establish three chronological traditions of interpretation. First, Christian writings at the time of Irenaeus and Tertullian tended to be chiliastic, with the saints reigning with Christ for a literal thousand years.[122] The subsequent era favored only a heavenly fulfillment of the reigning saints while portraying "the Roman Empire as the predicted scene of the conflict between the Antichrist and the faithful" as seen in Eusebius, Jerome, and Theodoret. Third, the Syriac writers Ephraem the Syrian, Aphraates, and Polychronius saw the prophetic visions fulfilled with the Seleucid king Antiochus. However, all three traditions of interpretation deem that the text referred to "in an indirect or secondary sense to the events related to the advent of Jesus."[123]

The book of Daniel witnessed the destruction of the Temple in Jerusalem (Dan. 11) and helped to identify Christ as the expected Messiah (Dan. 2 and 7). Josephus says that Daniel was the quintessential prophet because "he not only prophesied of future events but also determined the time of their fulfillment."[124]

---

[120] Eusebius, *Ecclesiastical History*, VI.7. Cf. p. 89.

[121] Reinhard Bodenmann reports how the most extensive citations in the second century CE are found in Justin's *Dialogue with Trypho*, where Daniel 2:34 and 7:9-28 are interpreted as prophecies of Christ. Bodenmann, *Naissance d'une exégèse*.

[122] McCollough presumes without analysis that Hippolytus preferred a literal thousand-year earthly reign; chapter 4 below will suggest that this father was not so noticeably conforming to this trend.

[123] McCollough, "Daniel," 255.

[124] Josephus, *Jewish Antiquities*, 10.267. For a complete discussion on how Daniel's prophecy has been used for as a prediction for Christ's exact arrival, see Allan A.

For such a reason, it was useful for early Christianity's appeal to prophesy in order to legitimate Christian claims about Jesus to the Jews and to authenticate Christianity to the pagans.[125]

Contemporary with Hippolytus were two millenarians who use the text of Daniel and other eschatological sources to foster apocalyptic expectations among the people of God. The first is the mysterious Judas reported by Eusebius who crafted an exegetical project on Daniel.[126] Noted as the first chronographer, Judas fit a record of historical events within the framework of Daniel's prophecy of 70 weeks.[127] He proposed this prophetic time range to end in 202, the tenth year of Severus, which became a year of persecution and speculation about the Antichrist. With Judas, we witness how historiography can be seen as an extension of apocalyptic writing—an effort that Hippolytus would repeat in chronological treatises.[128] Secondly, Sextus Julius Africanus wrote a chronology similar to Hippolytus, both teaching from scripture that Christ had been born in the year 5550 after creation. With this teaching, Bonwetsch remarks that Hippolytus "cut the nerve of expectation of the end in that the Second Coming would come only in the distant future."[129] This explanation will set him apart from the millenarian eschatology tradition that we see in Irenaeus so as to postpone an immanent apocalypse and millennium.

The use of Daniel after Hippolytus' death further demonstrates its importance to the Christian community. Jerome's *Commentary on Daniel* is the second in breadth only to that of Hippolytus. Besides employing Daniel's eschatological material, Jerome used the book for additional purposes such as preserving Jewish interpretation, furthering the cause of eunuchs, and apologetics against the pagan critic Porphyry.[130] In the *City of God*, Augustine

---

MacRae, *The Prophecies of Daniel* (Singapore: Christian Life Publishers, 1991), 193-202.

[125] This is particularly true of the vision of the statue of four elements (Dan.2) and the four beasts (Dan.7) as representing the rise and fall of the Babylonian, Median, Persian, Greek empires. Justin Martyr provides an sample of its apologetic service, writing: "But lest someone argue against us, 'What excludes the supposition that this person whom you call Christ was a man, of human origin, and did these miracles you speak of by magic arts, and so appeared to be God's son?' We will bring forward our demonstration. We....are forced to believe those who prophesied before [the events] happened, because we actually see things that have happened and are happening as was predicted." Justin, *Apology* 1.30.

[126] Eusebius, *Ecclesiastical* History, VI.7.

[127] Daniel 9:20-27.

[128] Hippolytus, *The Chronicle* and *The Determination of the Date of Easter*, per Quasten, 176-178; Frend, *Rise of Christianity*, 417.

[129] G. Nathanael Bonwetsch, *Studien zu den Kommentaren Hippolyts zum Buche Daniel und Hohen Liede* (Leipzig: J. C. Hinrichs, 1897), 53; Gammie, "A Journey Through Danielic Spaces," 148, n.11.

[130] Gammie, "A Journey Through Danielic Spaces," 150.

contrasted the church and the Roman Empire, evidencing that Christians were still optimistic about relief from the state through the coming of Christ's reign. Referring to Daniel 7:15-28, he remarked, "He who reads this passage, even half asleep, cannot fail to see that the kingdom of Antichrist shall fiercely, though for a short time, assail the church before the last judgment of God shall introduce the eternal reign of the saints."[131]

Despite Daniel's eschatological visions of heavenly victory, the book also affirms the present realization of worldly opposition. Christians drew strength and hope from the tales of exemplary acts of faith in the book. For them, the Daniel text reported his deliverance from those who oppress God's people, such as preserving them while not eating unlawful food (Dan. 1:15), safety in a den of lions (Dan. 6:22), and relief from a blasphemous dictator and oppressor (Dan. 12:1). With respect to deliverance, the church believed Christ himself to be present in the fiery furnace with his suffering faithful (Dan. 3:25). The Book of Daniel also provided predictions of Jesus' defeat of worldly empires (Dan. 2:34), the establishment of his eternal rule (Dan. 2:35-36), the crucifixion of Jesus (Dan. 9:26), and his final return and distribution of just rewards (Dan. 12:1-3).[132] Such stories and believed predictions with their apocalyptic flare provided encouragement and meaningfulness to the suffering church, thus causing unfavorable events to take on a new meaning as favorable events.

So, in writing his *Commentary on Daniel*, Hippolytus admirably reinforced the popular, victorious theology of martyrdom by employing the Daniel text along the first line of interpretation that later parallels Tertullian and Cyprian. As a study of his historical milieu showed, persecution and martyrdom were almost expected for Christians living in a non-Christian world under pagan rulers. The readers of the *Commentary on Daniel* would see their circumstances modeled by God's people in Babylon, and they would understand themselves to be God's new people in a new Babylon.[133] The Book of Daniel was a popular resource in the first two centuries, enabling the church to justify their hardships. There is no effort to reform society collectively and public life is shunned, but the concern is primarily with avoiding sin and cleansing oneself through suffering. Instead, earthly hope is redirected to heavenly hope and reward, first accomplished through an anticipation of upcoming eschatological events that

---

[131] Augustine, *City of God*, 20.23.

[132] For additional details in the use of certain parts of the Book of Daniel, see McCollough, "A Journey Through Danielic Spaces," 254-55, and Vanyó, "Daniel," 219-220.

[133] This notion is already seen in 1 Peter 5:13, where Christians recognize Rome as a "Babylon," and Revelation, where the theme of "Babylon" as the national enemy of God's people almost certainly represents the Roman Empire (14:8, 17:5, 18; 18:2). It is present in extra-biblical Jewish writings and in Old Testament imagery as a place of exile, or a wicked or arrogant city. For an analysis of Babylon in early church imagery, see Peter H. Davids, *First Epistle of Peter*, New International Commentary on the New Testament, ed. F. F. Bruce (Grand Rapids: Eerdmans Publishing, 1990), 201-203.

include tribulation. Thus, the church's suffering in this life can be inexorably linked to greater eschatological events.

Given this great tradition of reading the book of Daniel, John Gammie laments the limited effort among modern scholars to recognize its use in the early church, reminding us of its importance throughout the history of Christian thought and piety. Scholars who "stress the original matrix of the scripture have, as a rule, played down the way in which the New Testament itself and centuries of Christian theology have seen in the prophet Daniel a number of wondrous predictions of the first and second coming of Jesus the Christ."[134] In conclusion, we see that Hippolytus does not stand alone in his use of Daniel while standing as a pioneer to its capabilities. He addresses the same problems facing Christians throughout the empire in a new and unique way—by finding the justification for the events in the scriptures and uncovering hidden hope for their troubles. Therefore, it becomes less surprising that the earliest known Christian commentary on scripture was Hippolytus' *Commentary on Daniel.*

Hippolytus' Choice of Daniel as a Text

With such lines of interpretation shaping the church's use of scripture, it becomes easier to hypothesize why Hippolytus would respond to persecution by writing a commentary on Daniel. He surely saw how this Old Testament book provided important principles for Christians living in a context of persecution. This presbyter was moved to interpret the biblical text to encourage a harassed and beleaguered church, and to do so in a way that justified their suffering.

In the process of unpacking the commentary evidence of this theory, however, a reader would rightly imagine that there is more to the commentary than a martyrdom motif. Our project at hand in no way intends to reduce the commentary to a single martyrdom theme supported by additional textual commentary. First and foremost, Hippolytus wrote a commentary for Christians to understand the scriptures, probably primarily for his own congregations to read and analyze for themselves. The commentary explores many types of issues relevant to an early church community besides suffering. For example, the faithfulness and obedience of the Daniel characters are natural examples for Hippolytus to inspire his audience in their own faith in less dramatic ways than persecution. Like so many other patristic authors, for Hippolytus the scripture is worthy of study simply because it is God's Word. From neophyte to bishop

---

[134] Gammie, "A Journey Through Danielic Spaces," 156. He goes on to emphasis a preservation of criticism of the text while also recovering a Christological benefit in our understanding of Daniel: "If in comparison to previous centuries the Book of Daniel today seems more peripheral, less central to the faith, one of the obvious reasons for this decline in mainline Christian circles is the retreat of Christological interpretations." Certainly, the early church fathers including Hippolytus support such an interpretation.

throughout antiquity, Kannegiesser remarks that "Scripture never failed to satisfy the needs and to respond to the expectation of early Christians."[135]

Given the milieu in which he served the church by writing, Hippolytus could not ignore the impending pressure of martyrdom and persecution that bore on his audience. If the author were a presbyter around Rome, he would be writing this work in a sort of cultural and political headquarters of his persecutors. Even if he were in the East, there is no guarantee that the local and sporadic patterns of Roman persecution would not have been any less intense. One particularly pressing matter is certain to the provenance of this writing: persecution keeps the commentary author returning to encourage his audience to stand fast under impending social and religious maltreatment. Thus, this becomes a commentary with a special purpose. We expect biblical commentaries to elucidate texts both on the literary level, but Hippolytus interprets on the historical and theological levels to bolster the faith of Christians surrounded by persecution that may soon come face to face with the reality of potential martyrdom.

Complementary Role of the Book of Revelation

A final note on the importance of the book of Revelation in understanding Daniel deserves attention here. The apocalyptic nature of this book was often interpreted by the early church as a more detailed prophecy of a final era of persecution against the people of God, with a final Antichrist figure publically blaspheming God while pursuing the church in persecution. Hippolytus views the book of Revelation as scripture and he explicitly lists it alongside the prophets, the apostles, and the teaching of the Lord as he calls them all scripture.[136] His allusions to Revelation seem to be along the lines of interpretation seen in Irenaeus; their very comparable eschatological outlooks parallel their common anti-heretical spirit and similar methods of exegesis throughout their works.[137] Although Hippolytus is at times more tentative in his eschatology, both provide detailed comments about the events that will construct history's end.[138]

Although its acceptance in the developmental process was precarious in parts of the empire, in the second and third centuries, the book of Revelation

---

[135] Kannengiesser, *Handbook of Patristic Exegesis*, 13.

[136] *Commentary on Daniel*, IV.49.2. Περὶ τούτου πᾶσα γραφὴ οὐκ ἐσιώπησεν, καὶ προφῆται ... καὶ ὁ κύριους... καὶ ἀπόστολοι ... καὶ τὸ τούτου ὄνομα δι ἀριθμοῦ μυστικῶς Ἰωάννης ἐν τῇ Ἀποκαλύψει ἀφανέρωσεν.

[137] A summary of their eschatological views can be found in Daley, 28-32 (Irenaeus) and 38-41 (Hippolytus). See also Tsirplanis, 5-17.

[138] Considering how Irenaeus and Hippolytus crafted anti-heretical works, perhaps Gnosticism's denial of the importance of this world's action on the future, as well as its alteration of the hope of resurrection of the body among Christians, prompted similar thought between these two church fathers.

was more widely accepted in the Western churches.[139] The Ligorian statue includes a work by Hippolytus *On the Gospel of John and the Apocalypse* in which he defended a Johannine authorship of Revelation against Gaius, presbyter at Rome, who denied it. The supposed reasons for rejecting it, Bruce Metzger says, relate to "its garnish imagery and millenarianism." Meanwhile, "The differences between the Synoptic Gospels and John's Gospel were taken to prove that the latter is wrong and so ought not to be included among books recognized by the Church."[140] Addressing also the error of the Alogi, the works shows the author defending a Logos doctrine as well as the authenticity of Revelation.[141] Such a defense of John's Apocalypse as scripture fits nicely into a Western milieu where the book was more generally widely accepted. In fact, perhaps the Western trend to accept the apocalyptic principles seen in Daniel 7-12 and the book of Revelation allowed a more favorable use of this material by Hippolytus as he wrote to his congregations.

Meanwhile, the apocalyptic eccentricities of certain early church trends such as the Montanist movement had a way of aggravating the overall church. Robert Lee Williams suggests that Montanism could have been seen as a prophetic authority that competed with apostolic succession, oracles "theologizing" from Scripture rather than exegeting passages in worship, and generally upsetting the growing legitimacy of the church in Roman society.[142] About its apocalyptic effects, Bruce Metzger remarks: "Not only did such a feeling tend to discredit several apocalypses that may have been, in various parts of the church, on their way to establishing themselves, but...even the Apocalypse of John was sometimes brought under a cloud of suspicion because

---

[139] For a discussion on reasons and patristic positions on Revelation, see von Campenhausen, *The Formation of the Christian Bible*, 215-18, 235-42.

[140] Bruce M. Metzger, *The Canon of the New Testament: Its Origin, Development, and Significance* (Oxford: Claredon Press, 1987), 105. Some Syriac fragments of Ebedjesu (c. 1300) report that this work defended the theological debate to us, while Dionysius bar Salibi (d. 1171) calls Gaius a heretic for rejecting the Apocalypse and the Fourth Gospel. F. F. Bruce, *The Canon of Scripture* (Downers Grove, Ill.: InterVarsity Press, 1988), 178.

[141] Metzger, *The Canon of the New Testament*, 149-151. For an older analysis of the technicalities of the work, see John Gwynn, "Hippolytus and His 'Heads Against Gaius'" in *Hermathena* 6 (1888): 397-418.

[142] Robert Lee Williams, "'Hippolytan' Reactions to Montanism: Tensions in the Churches of Rome in the Early Third Century," in *Studia Patristica* 39 (2006): 131-138. Cf. Hippolytus, *The Refutation of All Heresies*, 8. For additional discussion on the reception of Montanism at Rome in the late second century, see Alistair Stewart-Sykes, "Papyrus Oxyrhynchus 5: A Prophetic Protest from Second Century Rome," in *Studia Patristica* 31 (1997): 196-205.

of its usefulness in supporting the 'new prophecy.'"[143] This event leads F. F. Bruce to think that "this work of Hippolytus might have played an important part in the history of the New Testament canon."[144] Thus, the apocalyptic contents of Revelation are not out of Hippolytus' view. It is a book of scripture whose own martyrdom motif and apocalyptic imagery will, at times, escort his interpretation of Daniel. Likewise, other associations with the New Prophecy might have influenced this presbyter.

Commentary Overview

Now we will consider an overview of the commentary as a final preparation to examine the theology contained in the text. The commentary's style, structure, and divisions familiarize the reader with the work as a final step toward recognizing the underlying martyrdom motif to be elucidated fully in the next chapter.

Manuscripts and Textual Versions

The *Commentary on Daniel* may have enjoyed a wide spread circulation in antiquity, as it was copied early into Paleo-Slavonic, Armenian, and Syriac.[145] Despite its apparent popularity, this commentary was rarely copied in its entirety, and we possess these texts mostly in many loose fragments. Marcel Richard reports how the entire text is fully preserved in its original Greek, the result of further manuscript scrutiny since the edition of the French translation.[146] The *Ante-Nicene Fathers Series* contains the most extensive English collection in the form of assorted fragments of the *Commentary on Daniel*, although it is far from complete.[147] However, this early translation does not consider the significant manuscript discoveries by Diobonoutis in 1911 in

---

[143] Metzger, *The Canon of the New Testament*, 104; see also von Campenhausen, *The Formation of the Christian Bible*, 214-239 for a discussion on the effect of Montanism on canonicity.

[144] Bruce, *The Canon of Scripture*, 178.

[145] For a complete list of the manuscripts, see the *Clavis Patrum Graecorum*, vol. 1, ed. Mauritius Geerard (Turnhout: Brepols, 1947-1987), 259-260, 1873-74.

[146] At the time of his writing of Bardy's introduction to the Sources Chrétiennes version, Richard still denied the availability of the entire text in Greek, so earlier patrologies such as Quasten concur. Bardy, "Introduction," 65, 67; Quasten, *Patrology*, 171. With the deciphering of the Meteor manuscript, there is a working Greek text with some lacunae. Marcel Richard, "Einleitung," in *Kommentar zu Daniel*, trans. Georg Nathanael Bonwetsch (Berlin: Akadamie Verlag, 2000), xxxvii-xli.

[147] Hippolytus, *Commentary on Daniel*, vol. V, Ante-Nicene Fathers, (Edinburgh: T & T Clark, reprinted 1990), 177-94.

the Meteor convent.[148] The *Sources Chrétiennes* version of the commentary has the Greek text juxtaposed to a French rendition. This translation follows the Greek "every time that it is able to do so," with the advantage of also using the Meteor manuscript.[149] Michel Richard has recovered more of the text using ultraviolet light and has rendered a more precise reading of the manuscript.[150] In 2000, the Akadamie Verlag published a revised edition of their classic 1897 *Kommentar zu Daniel* in a German translation by Georg Nathanael Bonswetch. This work renders the Old Church Slavonic (Paleo-Slavonic) into a German version and contains the complete Greek text.[151]

Style and Approach

A reading of Hippolytus' exegetical treatise on Daniel reveals a sense of urgency on the part of the author, provoking one to question the reason for his concern in such writing. The historical and theological milieu that we have just imparted helps to explain its exigency, as he interprets the book for a persecuted community of Christians. His commentary on Daniel is a sober one, confronting the concerns on hand for a contemporary early third century church.

Based on the style of the works in the Hippolytan corpus, scholars as recently as Cerrato entertain the possibility that there is more than one author named "Hippolytus." From Hippolytus' style, however, scholars should entertain the possibility that he was not a native Roman but a transplant to the West. In this way, Hippolytus may even be called a "scion" to the West per Cerrato's theory.[152] He has a vast familiarity with Greek philosophy and pagan religions; and his use of the doctrine of the Logos suggests a Hellenistic training. There is not agreement about his exact Eastern stylistic accent, but

---

[148] For a summary of this manuscript evidence, see the "Einleitung" by Richard with its critical manuscript analysis in *Kommentar zu Daniel*, ix-xlii.

[149] "La présente traduction suit de préférence le grec, toutes les fois qu'elle peut le faire." Bardy, "Introduction," 65. Hippolytus, *Commentaire sur Daniel*, vol. 14, Sources Chrétiennes, trans. Maurice Lefèvre, introduction by Gustave Bardy (Paris: Éditions du Cerf, 1947). For an entire analysis of the translation, see Bardy, 65-67.

[150] Marcel Richard, "Les difficultés d'une édition du commentaire de saint Hippolyte sur Daniel," *Revue d'histoire des textes, tome 2* (Paris: Centre National de la Recherche Scientifique, 1972), 1-10, and "Pour une nouvelle édition du commentaire de saint Hippolyte sur Daniel," in *Kyriakon: Festschrift Johannes Quasten*, ed. Patrick Granfield and Josef A. Jungmann (Munseter Westfalen: Verlag Aschendorff, 1970).

[151] Hippolytus, *Kommentar zu Daniel*, trans. Georg Nathanael Bonwetsch (Berlin: Akadamie Verlag, 2000). Still, this is not a critical edition of the Old Church Slavonic.

[152] W. Brian Shelton, review of Cerrato, *Hippolytus between East and West*, 362; cf. Cerrato, 253-258.

Hanson insists there is no trace of Alexandrian influence in this commentary.[153] His literary expression and thought is Greek, and he is the last of the western church fathers to write in Greek—a fascinating phenomenon when the rest of Christian Rome and North Africa is already writing in Latin. Suchla has suggested that the popularity of his works in the East stems from their being written in Greek,[154] while Goodspeed suggests that his Greek preference may be the mark of someone out of harmony with the dominant element in the Roman church most of his later life.[155] Scholars recognize that the Latinizing process occurred later in Christian communities than the rest of culture, especially because their scriptures were in Greek and their social kinship tended to remain consolidated.[156] Summarizing Hippolytus' style, Quasten remarks: "His entire mentality, in short, indicates that he came from the East."[157]

His commentary is filled with lengthy quotations of the biblical text with comments in between. Methodologically, Hippolytus comments on passages of the Book of Daniel, sometimes briefly but sometimes elaborately. Often the exchange is only a phrase or two long, but his regular deliberations make for a thoroughly interactive commentary.[158] Hippolytus offers a sort of running commentary on the entire twelve chapters of Daniel, including *Susanna* and the *Hymn of the Three Youths* found in Theodotian's Greek translation of the Old Testament. He does not comment on every verse, but his commentary is novel because it treats the book in an entire sense and does not omit the largest of its components. His rhetorical style is loaded with scriptural quotations that accompany his comments on the text, demonstrating how scripture is authoritative for Hippolytus, as well as being a medium for basing pastoral exhortations toward holy living.

---

[153] Hanson, *Allegory and Event*, 114. Quasten alone believes Hippolytus was connected with Alexandria, while Daniélou and Simonetti prefer a Palestinian or Syrian influence. Quasten, *Patrology*, 163; Daniélou, *Gospel Message*, 260; Simonetti, *Biblical Interpretation*, 27.

[154] Suchla, "Hippolytus," 288.

[155] Goodspeed, *A History of Early Christian Literature*, 144. No one has suggested that his schismatic tendencies caused a lack of popularity in the West, and the lack of any Latin translation is puzzling.

[156] Christine Mohrmann, *Liturgical Latin: Its Origins and Characteristics* (Washington, D.C.: Catholic University Press, 1957), 30-35.

[157] Quasten, *Patrology*, 163. Quasten's basis for his stylistic analysis is the entire collection of works attributed to Hippolytus, especially his knowledge displayed in the *Philosophoumena*.

[158] Trakatellis took a number of pages at random and determined the distribution of biblical texts cited *verbatim* to Hippolytus' comment was 3:2. Trakatellis, ΛΟΓΟΣ ΑΓΩΝΙΣΤΙΚΟΣ, 529, n.5.

Structure and Content

The Greek manuscripts have a four-fold division of the commentary that is preserved in the translations by both Bonswetsch and Lefèvre. The four books, entitled λόγοι, analyze larger sections of the Book of Daniel. Table 1 below displays their titles. Besides the four book titles, the Bardy/Lefèvre edition adds some section headings within chapters that highlight the main issues that Hippolytus discusses. However, the Paleo-Slavonic manuscripts do not use these divisions, preferring to break the commentary into a number of visions. Bardy believes that the Greek text appears to be the primitive one because it refers the preceding book in a way not observed in the Slavonic.[159]

Table 1: Book Titles in the Greek Manuscripts

Book No.	*Book Title*
Book I	Concerning Susanna and the Dragon
Book II	Concerning the Statue which Nebuchadnezzar The King Made
Book III	Concerning Nebuchadnezzar and Concerning Daniel When He Was Thrown to the Lions
Book IV	Concerning the Vision of the Prophet Daniel

Table 2 below displays the divisions in the Slavonic manuscripts as they correspond to the four books in the Greek manuscripts. The original division headings reveal the sections of Daniel that are most important to the *Commentary*'s author. In Book 1, Hippolytus analyzes the story of Susanna to demonstrate how God's servants can remain faithful despite even an organized attack against their personal character. Hippolytus mostly uses allegory to present his model confessor here: Susanna, falsely accused before an ungodly court, parallels the persecuted church in excessive detail. Book 2 presents the stories surrounding Shadrach, Meschach, Abednego, and Daniel as they receive pressure to compromise their religious convictions for Babylonian religious policy, mainly the statue that Nebuchadnezzar made to be worshipped. Hippolytus hails them also as models of perseverance, not through allegory but as historical figures that are heroic models. Book 3 considers the unwillingness of Daniel to cease his daily prayers to the Lord and redirect them to King Darius. When he is thrown into the lion's den, Hippolytus parallels his suffering to that of his fellow believers persecuted by the Jews and the Romans

---

[159] "Hippolyte renvoie au moins une fois le lecteur à ce qui a été dit dans le livre precedent, ἐν τῇ πρὸ ταύτης βίβλῳ (IV.2), et cette reference est exacte. La version slave n'observe pas cette division." Bardy, "Introduction," 65.

before his time and at the time of the writing. Book 4 offers a distinct interpretation of the vision of the nations with their armies that surround Jerusalem recorded in Daniel 10-12. Hippolytus offers an interpretation to the events that would instruct his congregations and generations of the Christians afterward as they looked to eschatology to explain contemporary and future events.

Table 2: Book Divisions in the Slavonic versus Greek Manuscripts

Slavonic Manuscript Heading	*Corresponding Greek Division*
First Vision	I.1-11
Concerning Susanna and two old men; Second Vision	I.12-33
The account of the third vision	II.1-13
Fourth Vision of the prophet Daniel; On the statue and on the three young men	II.14-38
Fifth Vision; On the dream related to the tree and how Nebuchadnezzar was exiled	III.1-12
Sixth Vision; On the fingers of the hand	III.13-18
Seventh Vision; Daniel thrown in the pit of lions	III.19-31
Vision of four beasts	IV.1-25
Ninth Vision; On the goat and the ram	IV.25-28
Tenth Vision; On nine weeks and sixty-two weeks	IV.28-36
Eleventh Vision and on the kings of the South & North	IV.36-41
Twelfth Vision; The treatise of the three kings	IV.41-60

There are other themes in the commentary, even though the thesis of this book is Hippolytus' emphasis on suffering persecution and the willingness for martyrdom in the Christian life. For example, Trakatellis has explored the exegetical style of "agonistic speech" in Hippolytus' use of scripture against the enemies of Christianity, and in matters of eschatology, martyrology, and Christology. Additionally, Dunbar has systematized the eschatology of Hippolytus from his works, of which the *Commentary on Daniel* provided unique insights toward this end, as it began to lay out Hippolytus' entire system of eschatology. This book about how this church father endowed his exegesis with martyrdom adds to this collection.

CHAPTER 3

Analysis of the Martyrological Passages

The last chapter considered how the historical and social setting of Roman persecution against Christians prompted Hippolytus to write his *Commentary on Daniel*. It demonstrated how generations of persecution against God's people resulted in a complex theology of martyrdom and persecution that Hippolytus inherited. This chapter will observe how he employed the Book of Daniel as a source of encouragement to the threatened congregations in his presbytery based on this theology of martyrdom. When Hippolytus comments on the persecution stories contained in the Book of Daniel, the force of his commentary is paraenetic and pedagogical. The commentary readers should apply the principles seen in Daniel to the current persecutions experienced in their own world. This application is most clearly evidenced by his occasional shift from the Babylonian king and his evil advisors to "the tribunal,"[1] transferring attention across eight hundred years from Babylon to Rome. This application finds support through an interpretation of the Danielic characters and events as types and parallels. The persecution of the Roman Empire, a dramatization of the events of scripture to serve as heroic examples, and a positing of the sovereignty of God as overarching all of history, adds to the many clear proposals to be willing to suffer martyrdom for Christ. By all these forms of application, Hippolytus explains biblically the state of his fellow suffering Christians and prepares them for possible martyrdom.

My organizing principle for analyzing the martyrdom motif in the commentary will be Hippolytus' own grouping of Daniel into four books, with martyrological material arranged thematically within each. I will combine the data from book 2 on the three youth and book 3 on Daniel in the lions' den because of the similar way that he draws typological-based exhortations from narrative material. When analyzing the martyrological passages, I will postpone technical issues of exegetical method until chapter 4 in order to reveal all of the commentary data on martyrdom and persecution first. This way, we can best evidence the martyrological purpose of Hippolytus' exegesis of Daniel.

It is noteworthy how a martyrdom motif becomes evident to the reader in the opening lines of the commentary. Hippolytus states the importance of discovering the mysteries of the Book of Daniel "which has produced 'martyrs

---

[1] *Commentary on Daniel*, I.20, II.37. Additional shifts from historical, scriptural analysis to contemporary events can be seen in I.14 and III.30.2.

full of faith' in the world.″[2] The same preamble claims that Daniel's impressive witness inspired these martyrs. His "witness" is particularly noteworthy because Hippolytus uses the Greek cognate μαρτυρῶ: "When he [Daniel] witnessed in holiness and righteousness to men, he became a prophet and witness of Christ."[3] Hippolytus credits to Daniel's witness the written preservation of the accounts of the would-be martyrs among the Jews in Babylon. The prominence of this theme in the opening of the work constructs a martyrological framework and sets a mood of the preeminence of martyrdom that will go on to reveal how some of God's people were persecuted yet were steadfast in their faith.

Allegory and Exhortation in the Susanna Story

In book 1 of his *Commentary on Daniel*, Hippolytus displays Susanna as a heroine in the face of persecution. In this story, Susanna is a Jewish woman during the Babylonian exile who was beautiful and who feared the Lord. She was the wife of one Joakim, a wealthy judge that other elders and judges would visit for matters of lawsuits. One afternoon, two such elders trapped her alone in the garden and threatened to accuse her falsely of a marital affair if she did not lay with them. When she refused, they took her to court where she was found guilty and condemned to death until Daniel interceded for her. The story relates how he sagaciously separated the elders and revealed the contradictions of their claims, acquitting Susanna and prompting the people to praise God for giving Daniel to them as a judge. The intention of the story is to show that although Susanna is harassed and wrongly accused by authorities, she remains faithful to God in purity and faith and he delivers her.

Arguing that the text belongs among the scriptures,[4] Hippolytus declares that her loyalty to God amidst persecution is a model for suffering third century Christians. He uses several features to accomplish this principle, and in the story of Susanna his use of allegory stands prominent. He identifies the members and components in the story as representing people and forces in church history involved in the persecution of God's people. He directs his interpretation to his own congregations currently undergoing persecution by using explicit comparison and exhortation to suffer martyrdom, thus accomplishing his task of a pastorally minded exegesis.

---

[2] μάρτας πιστοὺς ἐν κόσμῳ προήγαγεν. *Commentary on Daniel*, I.1.

[3] καὶ αὐτὸς μαρτυρήσων ὁσίῳ καὶ δικαίῳ ἀνδρὶ προφήτῃ καὶ μάρτυρι Χριστοῦ γεγενημένῳ. *Commentary on Daniel*, I.1.

[4] The episode of Susanna was not retained in the Hebrew scriptures but is included in the LXX. Hippolytus accuses them of scorning the story because it presents two Jewish elders in a dubious fashion. "The Jewish leaders wanted to abridge Susanna from the scripture, pretending that it is not a real product from Babylon, because they are ashamed of what the elders have done in this era." *Commentary on Daniel*, I.14.

Two Elders: Symbols of Christian Persecution

Hippolytus offers a comprehensive allegorical interpretation through several characters in the story. The two old men who try to seduce Susanna are seen as *typoi* for those who want to damage God's people.[5] Each of them represents a group of persecutors against Christians: "The Church is in fact harassed and brought into agony not only by the Jews, but also by the Gentiles and by those who pretend to be Christians but are not. Seeing her wisdom and stability they exert themselves to destroy her."[6] While the Susanna text calls them "chief of the people" and "judges," Hippolytus comments that they signify those "with power and law who render unjust judgments against the just."[7] The way that the two men "observed" Susanna in the garden "represents how the church is the object of wicked espionage and surveillance" by those who persecute her.[8]

As a type of those who harass God's people, the two elders for Hippolytus point to the Roman state that presently persecutes the church. He shifts his focus from the narrative of Susanna to explicitly portray the persecutions of his own day. He writes how the persecutors of Christians "agree to seduce the saints, they watch for the favorable day and break into the house of the Lord when everyone is praying and singing hymns to God," an obvious illustration of the persecutions against the church.[9] When Christians do not consent, they lead them "before the tribunal and accuse them of acting contrary to the decree of Caesar" and condemn them to death.[10] This is a clear reference to the policy and actions of the Roman state in the early third century. He claims that wicked

---

[5] οἱ δὲ δύο πρεσβύτεροι εἰς τύπον δείκνυνται τῶν δύο λαῶν τῶν ἐπιβουλευόντων τῇ ἐκκλεσίᾳ, εἰς μὲν ὁ ἐκ περιτομῆς καὶ εἰς ὁ ἐξ ἐθνῶν. *Commentary on Daniel*, I.14. Although Hippolytus uses the term "type," he often parallels the Daniel characters, events, and places to contemporary events in an allegorical fashion much removed from the literal meaning of the text. A discussion of his use of typology and allegory are below, pp. 128-134.

[6] ἡ γὰρ ἐκκλησία οὐ μόνον ὑπὸ Ἰουδαίων θλίβεται καὶ στενοξωρεῖται ἀλλὰ καὶ ὑπὸ ἐθνῶν καὶ ὑπὸ τῶν λεγομένων μέν, οὐκ ὄντων δὲ χριστιανῶν, οἱονεὶ τὸ σῶφρον καὶ εὐσταθὲς ταύτης ἐνορῶντες φθείρειν ταύτην βιάζονται. *Commentary on Daniel*, I.21.2; cf. I.29.

[7] ὅτι ἐν τῷ αἰῶνι τούτῳ ἐξουσιάζουσι καὶ ἄρχουσι, κρίνοντες ἀδίκως τοὺς δικαίους. *Commentary on Daniel*, I.14.

[8] τοῦτο σημαίνει ὅτι ἕως νῦν παρατηροῦνται καὶ περιεργάζονται τὰ ἐν τῇ ἐκκλησίᾳ. *Commentary on Daniel*, I.15.

[9] ἡνίκα γὰρ οἱ δύο λαοὶ συμφωνήσουσι διαφθεῖραί τινας τῶν ἁγίων, παρατηροῦνται ἡμέραν εὐθῆ καὶ ἐπεισελθόντες εἰς τὸν οἶκον τοῦ Θεοῦ προσευχομένων ἐκεῖ πάντων καὶ τὸν Θεὸν ὑμνούντων. *Commentary on Daniel*, I.20.

[10] τούτων δὲ μὴ βουλομένων προσάγουσιν αὐτοὺς πρὸς τὸ βῆμα καὶ κατηγοροῦσιν ὡς ἐναντία τοῦ δόγματος Καίσαρος πράσσοντας καὶ θανάτῳ κατακρίνονται. *Commentary on Daniel*, I.20; cf. II.37.

people do not cease to cry out against them, saying, "Remove them from the earth, the people of this sort—it is not necessary for them to live!"[11]

Susanna is a type of the church who suffered by the hand of the old men, and in Hippolytus' day people also suffered by the "princes of Babylon."[12] Babylon is consistently used in the early church as a symbol to refer to Rome. Rome shared literary allusions to Babylon in a way that reflects the early Christian self-understanding as a people exiled, prisoners in paganism's capitol, and surrounded by hostility against the elect of God. In apocalyptic fashion, Hippolytus also understands these events to be part of a greater, cosmic battle between God and Satan. He writes of these symbols of Roman persecution: "These words are easy to understand: the two people are incited by Satan who operates through them, not ceasing to plan persecution and tribulation against the church. They search how to destroy, but they work in vain."[13]

Susanna as an Allegorical Heroine

Susanna symbolizes the church and the bath into which she descends represents Christian baptism.[14] Her bathing represents how the church, the bride of Christ, ought to "consider herself before God as a young and pure spouse."[15] Hippolytus identifies her husband Joachim as a type of Christ, probably due to the marital imagery between the church and Christ in scripture. Possibly Hippolytus also saw Joachim as a righteous judge, or as an Adam figure who is the custodian of the garden (cf. Gen. 2:15).

Allegorically, the garden represents the Garden of Eden through a figure and a model of a heavenly paradise. The description of a pure woman in a garden about to be lured into sin is an obvious image of Eve in Eden. Hippolytus wants this paradise image to become the focus of the persecuted Christian, rather than their experience of pain and potential loss of this life. Hippolytus indicates, "From this earthly garden we must lift our eyes upon the heavenly garden, leaving the symbolic to understand the spiritual...setting our hopes on eternity."[16] The church itself is not a place, but a community, a "spiritual garden

---

[11] Αἶρε ἐκ τῆς γῆς τοὺς τοιούτους, οὐ γὰρ καθῆκον αὐτοὺς γῆν. *Commentary on Daniel*, I.23.

[12] ταῦτα καὶ νῦν ὁμοίως ὑπὸ τῶν ἀρχόντων τῶν ἐν τῇ νῦν Βαβυλῶνι ἐπιτελεῖται. *Commentary on Daniel*, I.14.

[13] καὶ γὰρ ἐστιν ἀληθῶς καταλαβέσθαι τὸ εἰρημένον, ὅτι πάντοτε οἱ δύο λαοὶ κατανυσσόμενοι ὑπὸ τοῦ ἐν αὐτοῖς ἐνεργοῦντος σατανᾶ βουλεύονται διωγμοὺς καὶ θλίψεις ἐγείρειν κατὰ τῆς ἐκκλησίας, ζηλοῦντες ὅπως διαφθείρωσιν αὐτήν, αὐτοὶ ἑαυτοῖς μὴ συμφωνοῦντες. *Commentary on Daniel*, I.15.

[14] *Commentary on Daniel*, I.16.

[15] ἡ ἐκκλεσία ὡς Σωσάννα ἀπολουομενη καθαρὰ νύμφη θεῷ παρίσταται. *Commentary on Daniel*, I.16.

[16] ἐκ γὰρ τῶν ἐπιγείων δεῖ τὰ ἐπουπάνια ἐνοπτρίζεσθαι καὶ ἐκ τῶν τυπικῶν τὰ πνευματικὰ ἐπιγινώσκειν καὶ ἐκ τῶν προσκαίρων τὰ αἰώνια προσδοκᾶν. *Commentary on Daniel*, I.17.1. For quotations of I.17, I follow the Greek text as deciphered by

of God, planted by Christ."[17] The trees planted in the garden represent several things: the early patriarchs, the works of the prophets accomplished after the law, the chorus of the Apostles who had knowledge of the Word, the virgins sanctified by water, the chorus of the doctors, the church fathers, bishops, and Levites. However, one in particular concerns us: "the chorus of martyrs saved by the blood of Christ."[18] The mention of them among the spiritual giants in the history of God's people reveals an elevated view of the martyrs and an established theology of martyrdom. Hippolytus says that there are two trees today in the garden of the spiritual church: the Law that gives knowledge of sins and the Word that gives life and forgiveness of sins.[19] Whereas the garden represents the community of saints, Babylon represents the world at large—the typological background for the suffering church.[20] The two female servants who attend to her in the garden represent "faith and charity which also accompany the church."[21]

Hippolytus asserts that Susanna instructs Christians when she figures in herself, in all points, the mysteries of the church in which faith, piety, and wisdom within the body are demonstrated even up to his own day.[22] Her beauty is of faith, of wisdom, and of holiness.[23] She had been instructed from infancy in the law of God and had become pure and wise to render the old men's testimony—the claims of the inimical world—as unbelievable. Hippolytus is implicitly presenting the church's desirable qualities through her type in Susanna. There is a clear contrast between exhortations to these qualities and the deliberate persecution and martyrdom against the church.

Susanna calls to the heavenly Avenger, crying out how God knows the lies brought against her and the impending reality of her death. The text reports that God heard her prayer, allowing Hippolytus to tell his own persecuted congregations, "All who call God from a pure heart, he hears them."[24] The

---

Marcel Richard since the publishing of the Sources Chrétiennes version. Richard, "Les difficultés d'une édition," 1-10.

[17] γίνεται ἐκκλησία οἶκος Θεοῦ πνευματικός. The text here uses the word οἶκος "house" instead of "garden" here, but Bonwetsch notes that it must refer to the garden. *Commentary on Daniel*, I.17.6, Lefèvre, 103, n.b.

[18] μαρτύρων τε πάντων δι᾽αἵματος Χριστοῦ σεσωσμένων. *Commentary on Daniel*, I.17.

[19] *Commentary on Daniel*, I.17.

[20] *Commentary on Daniel*, I.14.

[21] καὶ ὡς αἱ δύο παιδίσκαι αἱ αὐτῇ παρακολουθοῦσαι πίστις καὶ ἀγάτη. *Commentary on Daniel*, I.16.

[22] *Commentary on Daniel*, I.22.

[23] *Commentary on Daniel*, I.25.

[24] ὅσοι γὰρ ἐπικαλοῦνται αὐτὸν ἐκ καθαρᾶς καρδίας τούτων ὁ Θεὸς ὑπακούει. *Commentary on Daniel*, I.26. Cf. II.35, where God rescued Daniel because of his "simplicity of heart." Susanna makes an interesting allusion to the blood associated with martyrdom, crying, "I'm clean of the blood!" She seems to be claiming no responsibility for her own death, reminiscent of the martyr of an innocent Christ when Pilate washed his hands (cf. Matt. 27:24).

moment that she prayed to God and was heard, at this instance an angel was
sent to help her, a rescue that Hippolytus compares to the events of Tobit and
Sarah, as well as an assertion of the prophet Amos, all of which describe God's
assistance.[25] In this collection of allegorical symbolism, Susanna becomes the
prominent figure; Hippolytus implies and explicitly exhorts that she is the
example that suffering Christians ought to model.

Analysis of the Exhortations

Amidst his exegetical activities, Hippolytus directly encourages his
congregations to stand strong in the face of organized persecution. Susanna had
lamented to the elders, "I am hemmed in on every side. For if I do this thing
[adultery], it is death for me; and if I do not, I shall not escape your hands"
(Sus. 1:22). Hippolytus remarks that it is better to fall into the hands of accusers
than to sin before God and so escape physical harm. The Christian reflecting on
the martyrs and apostates of his own day ought to see the wisdom in Susanna's
lament and be inspired to faithfulness in the face of suffering.

For his readers who are mentally weighing the suffering they see against
Hippolytus' theological explanations, this presbyter enhances the contrast by
revealing the ultimate destiny of the martyrs and the apostates.[26] Those who no
longer listen to God but listen to men essentially desire death and eternal
punishment; those who stumble due to the name of Christ are dead to God and
live for the world. However, if they obey God, they will not escape the hands of
the judges and will probably die. Which is better, according to Hippolytus? "It
is preferable to die because of unjust men, to live close to God, rather than to
have dealings with them, to be delivered by them yet to fall into the hands of
God."[27] He tells them, "Prefer the death that does not endure but for an instant,
in order to escape the torment of fire."[28] He urges his readers, "If we are eager
to imitate the just ones we will be saved as they were," while those doing
otherwise God will condemn.[29] He calls Christ the one who reigns over the
living and the dead due to his own suffering death and resurrection.[30] As a
result of mentally weighing the options, the distressed readers gain a clear sense
that they ought to suffer for the faith.

---

[25] Tobit 3:16-17; Amos 3:7. The reference to Sarah is unclear; perhaps he means the
angelic appearance to Hagar during the Sarah incidence.
[26] *Commentary on Daniel*, I.21.
[27] τοῦτο γὰρ διαφορώτερον ἀποθανεῖν ὑπὸ ἀνθρώπων ἀιδίκων, ἵνα παρὰ Θεῷ ζήσωσιν
ἢ συνθεμένους αὐτοῖς καὶ ἀπολυθέντας ὑπ' αὐτῶν ἐμπεσεῖν εἰς τὰς χείρας τοῦ θεοῦ.
Commentary on Daniel, I.21.
[28] τὸν πρόσκαιρον θάνατον αἱρησαμένη, ἵνα τὸν δεύτερον τοῦ πυρὸς θάνατον ἐκφύγῃ.
Commentary on Daniel, I.22. Cf. Matt. 10:28, Luke 12:5.
[29] *Commentary on Daniel*, I.14. Cf. I.24, in which a reward is reserved for those after
death, but a double penalty for those claiming to believe but acting like unbelievers.
[30] *Commentary on Daniel*, I.22.

There arises a predictable anxiety for any Christian facing possible martyrdom: whether God will miraculously rescue them or allow them to die. Hippolytus points out that it is the Lord who saves and the same sovereign God who gives them confidence in the face of danger can also resolve to rescue them or not to rescue them: "When he wants one of his servants to be protected, he can protect and save whomever he wants and as he wants."[31] Hippolytus develops this possibility of death by explaining the greater purpose that God has to perfect the character of his children. "When he wants something to prove perfect, he waits with patience, to be able afterwards to glorify him by crowning him as a good athlete. When Susanna had prayed and had been hearken to, the angel of the Lord was sent, he who avenges and rescues in order to ruin the enemies of Susanna."[32] Their suffering is part of the plan of God to sanctify them and bring glory to himself.

In exhorting his congregations, Hippolytus uses Pauline rhetoric to compare the desires of the flesh and the temptation to succumb to apostasy. "Thus watch, all you saints; I will pray for you. Love truth and think on the purity of Susanna, so as not to become a slave to the pleasures of the flesh. Do not listen to old men but guard in your heart the fear of the Savior, and prefer the death that doesn't endure but for an instant, in order to escape the torment of fire."[33] He quotes the Apostle Paul in application to his congregations, "But I am afraid, lest as the serpent deceived Eve by his craftiness, your minds should be led astray from the simplicity and purity *of devotion* to Christ."[34] He asks all that read these pages of scripture—women and virgins, small and large—to beware the deception of their own day:

> Imitate Susanna so that you do not discard the glory of God, and the Word that lived in Daniel, and that you can be saved from the second death. You men, imitate the purity of Joseph. You, women, imitate the purity and the faith of Susanna, and do not permit any reproach to be uttered against you nor prove the word of the old men to be in you. For a number of lying seducers have come in our day who deceive the souls of the saints. They seduce some by their vain

---

[31] πῶς οὖν; ὅτε θέλει τινὰ τῶν δούλων αὐτοῦ ῥύσασθαι, δύναται ῥύσασθαι αὐτὸν καὶ σῶσαι, ἡνίκα ἂν θελῃ καὶ ὡς ἂν θέλῃ. *Commentary on Daniel*, I.27.3.

[32] τῆς γὰρ Σουσάννης προσευξαμένης καὶ εἰσακουσθείσης, ἐξαπεστάλη ἄγγελος κυρίου ἔκδικος αὐτῆς καὶ βοηθὸς γενάμενος, ἵνα τοὺς κατ' αὐτῆς ἐπιβούλους διολέσῃ. *Commentary on Daniel*, I.27.4.

[33] ἀνανήψατε πάντες οἱ ἅγιοι, παρακαλῶ. τὴν ἀλήθειαν ἀγαπήσατε καὶ τὸ καθαρὸν τῆς Σουσάννης ἐπιγνῶτε, ἥτις οὐ σαρκί, ἐπιθυμίᾳ ἡδονῆς, ἐδουλώθη, οὐδὲ προσώποις πρεσβυτέρων συνηρπάγη, ἀλλὰ τὸ Θεὸν ἐκ ὅλης καρδίας ἐφοβήθη, τὸν πρόσκαιρον θάνατον αἱρησαμένη, ἵνα τὸν δεύτερον τοῦ πυρὸς θάνατον ἐκφύγῃ. *Commentary on Daniel*, I.22.

[34] 2 Cor. 11:3; *Commentary on Daniel*, I.22.

words; they pervert others by their heretical precepts, in this fashion desiring to satisfy their passion.[35]

Besides the person of Susanna herself, Hippolytus employs certain items in the story to exhort believers to remain faithful, to stand firm under persecution, and to taste the things of heaven:

> We must take care in everything ...imitate Susanna, and enjoy your delicacies in the garden. Wash yourself in the inexhaustible water, wiping away all your stains, and sanctify yourself in the heavenly oil, in order to present yourself to God with a pure body. Light your lamps and await your husband, so that, as soon as he knocks, you receive him, you sings hymns to God by Christ, to whom be the glory forever. A-men.[36]

Given the large amount of martyrological passages preceding this exhortation, we can recognize how Hippolytus urges believers to complete devotion in a context of persecution.

Throughout the Susanna story, Hippolytus can find textual material to connect with the issues of persecution and martyrdom surrounding the church of his time. He does not reduce the text to merely martyrological media, but is able to employ the text for commentary on plenty other issues, including prophecy, the character of scripture, God's working in history, and personal holiness. However, he has a clear objective in allegorizing the Susanna story to present a heroine in the face of martyrdom to be a model for all of God's people confronting decisions of suffering.

Daniel and the Three Youths: Models for Suffering

In the first thirteen chapters of book II, "On the Statue that was made to Exalt King Nebuchadnezzar," Hippolytus describes how Daniel came to interpret the king's dream about a great statue as parts representing powerful kingdoms to come. In the final fourteen chapters of the commentary, he scrutinizes Daniel 2-

---

[35] μιμήσασθε ταύτην καὶ ὡς Σουσάννα ὑπὸ Θεοῦ ἐκδικηθῆναι καὶ ὑπὸ τοῦ ἐν τῷ Δανιὴλ πολιτευσαμένου λόγου ἐκ τοῦ δευτέρου θανάτου ῥυσθῆναι δυνήσεσθε. Οἱ μὲν γὰρ ἄνδρες ζητοῦντες τὸ σεμνὸν τοῦ Ἰωσήφ, αἱ δὲ γυναῖκες τὸ ἁγνὸν καὶ πιστὸν τῆς Σουσάννης, μὴ δότε ψόγον βλασφημίας καθ᾽ ὑμῶν, ἵνα μὴ στήσητε τὰ ὑπὸ τῶν πρεσβυτέρων εἰρημένα ὡς ἀληθῆ. παρενέδυσαν γὰρ πολλοὶ ψευδολόγοι καὶ φρενατάται, ἐξαπατοῦντες τὰς τῶν ἁγίων ἀκεραίους ψυξάς, οἱ μὲν τὰς γυναῖκας πιθανοῖς λόγοις διαφθείροντες καὶ πρὸς τὰς ἰδίας ἐπιθυμίας ἐφέλκοντες. *Commentary on Daniel*, I.22.

[36] προσέχειν οὖν ὀφείλομεν ἐν πᾶσιν....τὴν Σουσάνναν μιμήσασθε καὶ τὸν παράδεισον ἐντρυφήσητε καὶ τοῦ ἀεννάου ὕδατος ἀπολαύσατε καὶ πάντα ῥύπον ἀποσμήξασθε καὶ ἐλαίῳ ἐπουρανίῳ ἁγιάσθητε, ἵνα σῶμα καθαρὸν Θεῷ παραστήσητε καὶ τὰς λαμπάδας ἐξάψητε καὶ τὸν νυμφίον προσδοκήσητε, ἵνα κρούσαντα τοῦτον εἰσδέξησθε καὶ Θεὸν διὰ Χριστοῦ ἀνυμνήσητε, ᾧ ἡ δόξα εἰς τοὺς αἰῶνας. Ἀμήν. *Commentary on Daniel*, I.33.

4 for its heroic examples of faithfulness under the reign of Nebuchadnezzar. From these stories about the mistreatment of God's people, Hippolytus can find biblical relevance for his suffering congregations. Besides exhorting them to be like these willing to suffer, Hippolytus constructs a systematic revelation about God's sovereignty over history that functions to offer a theodicy reinforcement to the suffering. Likewise, in book III "On Nebuchadnezzar and On Daniel When He was thrown to the Lions," he further analyzes the text for important themes and examples relevant to the suffering of God's people. The example of Daniel's faith and the divine ordering of these events help establish his case for martyrdom here also.

In both of these books commenting on narrative sections in Daniel, Hippolytus uses the text in several different ways in order to enlighten his readers to the reasons for the sufferings among fellow Christians and to prepare them for their own possibility of martyrdom. Hippolytus commented on these two books of narrative in a similar fashion that I will categorize into three groups: (1) dramatizing the narrative events, (2) presenting the three youth as models of perseverance, and (3) positing God's sovereignty over all the events of their day. He also addressed the theological and logical concerns that surround the drastic difference between the time of Daniel and their own day: why they are not being rescued. This particular theodicy question will stand in a separate section that follows.

Dramatizing Narrative Events

Nebuchadnezzar built a statue and decreed that all were to worship it or be cast into a fiery furnace (Dan. 3:1-30). The obstinacy of Shadrach, Meshach, and Abednego against the command infuriated the king, who ordered them to be executed. To the astonishment of the king, the Book of Daniel tells us, the young men did not burn up or suffer harm, and Nebuchadnezzar even witnessed a fourth person in the furnace looking like a son of the gods. Hippolytus alerts his audience to the threat of the king upon the life of the youth, highlighting how the young men's resolve and tenacity in the face of death is a model for Christians. The climax of the conflict occurs when the youth respond in a way typical of the genre of apocalyptic literature, telling the king: "Our God whom we serve is able to deliver us from the burning fiery furnace; and he will deliver us out of your hand, O king. But if not, be it known to you, O king, that we will not serve your gods or worship the golden image which you have set up" (Dan. 3:17-18). From this biblical story, Hippolytus casts a vision for martyrdom that is conveyed rhetorically in several different images to be examined individually in detail: by athletic competition, by graphic descriptions of suffering, and by venerating the courage of would-be martyrs. He implements these features of struggling as part of a larger model of expectation for present and future Christians in the early third century.

Hippolytus uses an impressive number of words and phrases related to athletic competition to describe martyrological struggles. The three youths are called "athletes full of vitality," "good athletes," "faithful martyrs," "they have remained faithful unto death," "they have defeated the whole power of the Babylonians," "they did not let the mob of the Babylonians defeat their faith," "they have been fighting against the myriads of the unbelievers," "they did not let themselves be enslaved," and "they have shown that faith is something unsurpassed."[37] Thus, "Daniel, admiring them as good athletes of the faith, crowned them as victors."[38] The three youth are described as "ready to receive the crown."[39]

Hippolytus sometimes employs very graphic language to describe the maltreatment of Christians. As Arioch the chief cook and wise men were dispatched to kill Daniel and his friends (Dan. 2:14), Hippolytus writes: "As the butcher kills and butchers all the animals, the same way the rulers of the world kill the human beings butchering them as if they were unreasonable animals."[40] In his interpretation of Nebuchadnezzar's dream in Daniel 4 concerning the magnificent tree, Hippolytus observes that the wild beasts who rest under symbolize the military forces that the king dispatches, "Ready to fight and to destroy, and like the wild beasts ready to tear to pieces the human beings."[41] In the vision of Daniel 7, the four beasts that symbolize the four consecutive kingdoms of the earth lend themselves to further enhancement: "By way of type and image, the beasts show the kingdoms that rose up in this world like wild beasts destroying humanity."[42] The opponents of God's people are not merely people, but are the products of the work of Satan himself. The king is portrayed as a "great devil that exercises tyranny."[43] Also, he attributes the activities of the future Antichrist to the manipulation of Satan.[44] The activities of the current Roman Empire are part of a larger battle that Satan is waging against the Lord, and it is Satan who is inciting the persecution and tribulation against the church.[45]

Finally, Hippolytus uses the story of the three youth by venerating their courage in the face of martyrdom. He compares their sagacity with the wisdom

[37] *Commentary on Daniel*, II.19.4-8; II.24.

[38] θαυμάσας τούτους ὡς καλοὺς ἀθλητὰς τῇ πίστει ἐστεφάωσεν. *Commentary on Daniel*, II.22.5.

[39] ἐνορῶν τρεῖς παῖδας μέλλοντας...στεφανοῦσθαι. *Commentary on Daniel*, II.18.

[40] ὥσπερ γὰρ ὁ μάγειρος πάντα τὰ ζῷα ἀναιρεῖ καὶ μαγειρεύει, τῷ αὐτῷ τρόπῳ καὶ οἱ ἄρχοντες τοῦ κόσμου τούτου ἀναιροῦσι τοὺς ἀνθρώπους ὡς ἄλογα ζῷα μαγειρεύοντες αὐτούς. *Commentary on Daniel*, II.4.2.

[41] ὡς θηρία ὑπάρχοντες ἕτοιμοι εἰς τὸ πολεμεῖν καὶ διαφθείρειν καὶ τοὺς ἀνθρώπους ὥσπερ θηρία διασπαράσσειν. *Commentary on Daniel*, III.8.9.

[42] ἐν τύπῳ καὶ εἰκόνι δείκνυσιν τὰς ἐν τῷ κόσμῳ τούτῳ ἐπαναστάσας βασιλείας, ὥσπερ θηρία διαφθείροντα τὴν ἀνθρωπότητα. *Commentary on Daniel*, IV.2.1.

[43] ὡς μέγας διάβολος τυραννεῖ. *Commentary on Daniel*, II.19.

[44] *Commentary on Daniel*, IV.12, 21.

[45] *Commentary on Daniel*, IV.9.1-3.

attributed to Christ in Matthew 10:28: "Do not fear those who kill the body but cannot kill the soul; rather fear him who can destroy both soul and body in hell."[46] They become an example for all people because they do not fear the crowd; they are not frightened by the threats of the king, not trembling when facing the furnace, despising the world that lacks a fear of God.[47] They demonstrate the degree to which God's people are willing to go for their Savior: "We remain faithful unto death."[48] Likewise, Hippolytus speaks for Christians, "If threatened with the sword, we patiently endure death."[49] They are described as "declaring themselves faithful martyrs, glorified by God, so that Nebuchadnezzar was covered in shame and the idols of the Babylonians were proved to be nothingness."[50]

Besides his extensive presentation of the three youths as exemplary martyrs and athletes, Hippolytus enhances his efforts by employing the example of the heroic seven brothers and their mother from 2 Maccabees 7:1ff.[51] Having presented this second example of martyrdom, Hippolytus turns to his readers and urges them "to study the martyrs" because this is exactly what the spirit of the Father teaches them to do, exhorting them to defy death and to hasten towards the heavenly things. If someone is without the Holy Spirit, "He becomes fearful and ridden by anxiety, he is scared and hides himself, he is afraid of a temporary death, and he crouches in fear of the sword because he is attached to the material and earthly things of this world."[52] It is easy to see that this description points to actual conditions of persecution and to imminent danger based on an examination of the contemporary milieu clearly reflecting such a situation.

Like the Maccabees, the readers of this *Commentary on Daniel* believed their struggle was a personal encounter with Satan, that the adversary was their only remaining obstacle to paradise, and that martyrdom overcame that hurdle. The experience did not defeat their spiritual enemy, and the agonies of persecution did not redirect the evils of the world or God's inevitable judgment on them. It was still victorious for them, as Lacey Baldwin Smith notes, "Death and dying became for the Christian a triple-sign: the reenactment of the folly of Calvary, a bloody but potent proof of the power of faith, and a warranty to

---

[46] *Commentary on Daniel*, II.17.

[47] *Commentary on Daniel*, II.18.

[48] μείνωμεν πιστοὶ ἄχρι θανάτου. *Commentary on Daniel*, II.19.

[49] εἰ μαχαίρᾳ ἀπειλεῖ τὸν θάνατον ὑπομείνωμεν. *Commentary on Daniel*, II.19.7. Bardy renders the declaration in the hortatory, "Supportons la mort."

[50] τρεῖς οὗτοι πιστοὶ μάρτυρες ἐν Βαβυλῶνι εὑρεθέντες, ἵνα δι᾿ αὐτῶν ὁ Θεὸς δοξασθῇ καὶ Ναβουχοδονόσορ καταισχύνθῇ κἀ Βαβυλωνίων τὰ εἴδωλα μηδὲν ὄντα φανῇ. *Commentary on Daniel*, II.18.

[51] *Commentary on Daniel*, II.20.1-4.

[52] ἐὰν γάρ τις χωρὶς ἁγίου πνεύματος ᾖ, οὗτος δειλιῶν ἀγωνιᾷ καὶ φοβούμενος κρύβεται καὶ τὸν πρόσκαιρον θάνατον εὐλαβεῖται καὶ μάχαιραν καταπτήσσει καὶ κόλασιν οὐχ ὑπομένει, τὸν κόσμον τοῦτον πρὸ ὀφθαλμῶν ἔχει, τὰ τοῦ βίου μεριμνᾷ. *Commentary on Daniel*, II.21.2.

share with Christ in his glory within the tabernacle of the Lord."[53] The pain of martyrdom may be agonizing but eternal life was the trade-off; it had been written, "Every one who acknowledges me before men, I also will acknowledge before my Father who is in heaven" (Matt. 10:32). Hippolytus allegorizes the Daniel narrative with his contemporary stage of events. "Today Babylon is the world, the satraps are the power of the world, Darius their emperor, the den is Hades, the lions the angels who administer torment."[54]

There is an instructive and proselytizing purpose for the narrative of the three youths for Hippolytus. The rich use of imagery makes for a more dramatic presentation of the suffering of persecuted Christians. This is part of Hippolytus' effort to elevate the martyrs and ready his own churches to the possibility of martyrdom themselves.

Models of Perseverance

Using the story of the three youths, Hippolytus also intentionally builds a model for persecuted third century Christians who will be persecuted, or who have or will witness martyrdom. He is eager to project through the biblical narrative a powerful theology of martyrdom, and to make it strongly operative in the lives of the faithful. By projecting such a motif, he is promoting a spirit of resoluteness and combativeness among his readers and throughout the Christian community. When facing hostile authorities, the Christian is to remain blameless, not giving any pretext for fault or weakness. Instead, the Christian should be willing to suffer without reproach, "When one suffers for God and one lives here below in purity and in fear, it is not necessary to give the least excuse for accusation to those seeking pretext, for then they are more covered in confusion."[55] Hippolytus suggests that Daniel saw martyrdom as a glorious and commendable experience when he witnessed the three youths' faith. At the time of their execution, Daniel refrained from interfering but instead stood from afar and encouraged them with his smile, "Joyful to be present for their martyrdom."[56]

Hippolytus deliberately redirects from the glorious acts of these youth to challenge his readers about their own priorities in the faith. In one of the most powerful passages in the commentary, IV.37, Hippolytus pleads with his readers to be willing to die for their faith like Shadrach, Meshach, and Abednego had done. He solicits their reflection: "Which interests you, O man?

---

[53] Smith, *Fools, Martyrs, Traitors*, 92.

[54] ἴδε σύ σήμερον Βαβυλών ἐστιν ὁ κόσμος, σατράπαι δὲ τούτου αἱ ἐξουσίαι, Δαρεῖος δὲ ὁ τούτων βασιλεύς, λάκκος, ὁ "Αιδης, λέοντες δὲ οἱ ἄγγελοι κολασταί. *Commentary on Daniel*, III.30.

[55] δεῖ οὖν τοὺς εὖ ἐπιπόνους ἁγνῶς καὶ μετὰ φόβου ἐν τῷ κόσμῳ τούτῳ ζῶντας, μεδεμίαν ἀφορμὴν διδόναι τοῖς ζητοῦσιν ἀφορμήν, ἵνα ἐν τούτῳ αὐτοὶ μᾶλλον καταισχύνωνται. *Commentary on Daniel*, III.24.3.

[56] χαίρων δὲ καὶ αὐτὸς ἐπὶ τῇ τούτων μαρτυρίᾳ. *Commentary on Daniel*, II.18.2.

To suffer martyrdom and to leave this world covered in glory, or to escape, rest here, and continue sinning?"[57] He appeals to his audience's knowledge how some have gone before the tribunal and lost faith, having forfeited their heavenly crown. He exhorts them to stand boldly when faced with a Roman tribunal: "Let him pray, therefore, who is taken before the courts for the name [of Christ]. Let him ask for a martyr's death regardless of the manner... It could be that God wants to prove [your faith] as he proved Abraham of old when he asked him for Isaac."[58] Whether delivered or not, their reward is clear: "When you are before the tribunal, God wants to take you from there, and by this you give glory to God."[59]

Hippolytus specifically states that the three youth are models of perseverance for all people. They did not fear the satraps, they were not threatened by the words of the king, they did not tremble when speaking of the fire of the furnace, but instead they scorned all the people (their enemies) and even the whole world, having only the fear of God before their eyes. They were not seduced by the music, nor subdued by the voluptuous instruments, nor won over by the misleading of the errors of the Babylonians, nor submitted to the edict of the king, nor bowed a knee before a statue made of gold. Hippolytus confidently declares, "These three youth declared themselves faithful martyrs in Babylon, so that God would be glorified, that Nebuchadnezzar would be covered with shame, and that the Babylonian idols would be revealed to be nothingness." They are exemplars of how God's people should embrace the opportunity to testify for the Lord and receive their due inheritance:

> Therefore we who believe in him, let us show ourselves worthy of him by the steadiness of our bodies, of our soul, and of our spirit, in a manner for us to receive the crown of immortality and to sing hymns to God, in the company of the blessed martyrs. To him is the glory forever. Amen.[60]

Those that would be martyrs "receive the martyrs' crown" and "are vanquished of the devil."[61] He exhorts his readers directly by the example of the three youth in the furnace:

---

[57] τί δέ σοι συμφέρει, ὦ ἄνθρωπε, μαρτυρήσαντα ἐν δόξῃ ἐξελθεῖν ἐκ τοῦ κόσμου τούτου, ἢ ῥυσθέντα καὶ ἐνθάδε ἀπομείναντα ἁμαρτάνειν. *Commentary on Daniel*, II.37.1.

[58] ὥστε εὐχέσθω ὁ ἕνεκεν τοῦ ὀνόματος προσφερόμενος οἵῳ δήποτε τρόπῳ μαρτυρήσας ἐξελθεῖν...τυχὸν δὲ ὁ Θεὸς ἐπείρασέν σε ὡς τὸν Ἀβραάμ, ἡνίκα ᾔτησεν τὸν Ἰσαάκ. *Commentary on Daniel*, II.37.4-5.

[59] ἐάν σε προσενεχθέντα θελήσῃ ῥύσασθαι, καὶ ἐν τούτῳ τὸν Θεὸν δόξαζε. *Commentary on Daniel*, II.37.5.

[60] ᾧ πιστεύσαντες καὶ ἡμεῖς ἀξίους ἑαυτοὺς Θεῷ παραστήσωμεν, σωφρονοῦντες σώματι καὶ ψυχῇ καὶ πνεύματι, ἵνα τὸν τῆς ἀφθαρσίας στέφανον καὶ ἡμεῖς λαβόντες ἅμα τοῖς μακαρίοις μάρτυσιν σὺν αὐτοῖς τὸν θεὸν ὑμνήσωμεν αὐτῷ γὰρ ἡ δόξα εἰς τοὺς αἰῶνας τῶν αἰώνων. ἀμήν. *Commentary on Daniel*, II.38.5.

[61] *Commentary on Daniel*, II.18.

Therefore take courage, O man. Let your faith never waiver. And when you are called to be a martyr, answer willingly to the call so that your faith may be evident. God may happen to test you, as he proved of old Abraham by asking Isaac of him. If, when you are before the tribunal, God wants to rescue you from there, in this you give glory to God. Imitate, you also, the three youth and remember their faith. As they answered the king, "God is capable of delivering us, and if he doesn't desire, we are sufficient in him." You respond likewise, "We prefer to die rather than to do what you ask."[62]

Hippolytus reminds his readers of the gravity of the Christian calling by quoting Christ in the gospels: "Therefore, if anyone wants to approach the Word, hear the injunction of the King and Lord of heaven: 'He who does not take his cross and follow after me is not worthy of me' and 'No one of you can be my disciple who does not give up all his own possessions.'"[63]

Hippolytus further understands the Old Testament narrative through an early church Christology. The reason for the three youths' success in the furnace is attributed to the intervening presence of God by his Son. For Hippolytus, that the fourth was "like a Son of God" (Dan. 3:24-5) denotes for him the presence of Christ in the fire with the three youths. By recognizing the pre-existent Christ in the person of the fourth figure, Hippolytus takes an Old Testament passage and transforms it into a Christian story. By giving it a strong Christological interpretation, he directly relates to Old Testament narrative of God's people under oppression to the current Christian situation. This makes the story immediate and actual for his readers. Although the three youths do not actually die, the story is strongly martyrological because it gives an account of a potentially deadly conflict involving faith. The story presents the three youths as superb models of a heroic witness to the true God and obedience to his commandments under conditions of persecution.

Positing God's Sovereignty

Hippolytus opens his treatment of the episode of Daniel in lions' den by recounting Nebuchadnezzar's own prior acknowledgment of God's

---

[62] ἑδραῖος οὖν γενοῦ, ὦ ἄνθρωπε, μήποτε τῇ πίστει βαμβαίνων, καὶ ὅταν κληθῇς εἰς μαρτύπιον προθύμως ἐπάκουσον, ἵνα ἡ πίστις σου φανῇ. τυχὸν δὲ ὁ Θεὸς ἐπείρασέν σε ὡς τὸν Ἀβραάμ, ἡνίκα ᾔτησεν τὸν Ἰσαάκ. ἐάν σε προσενεχθέντα θελήσῃ ῥύσασθαι, καὶ ἐν τούτῳ τὸν Θεὸν δόξαζε. μίμησαι καὶ σὺ τοὺς τρεῖς παῖδας καὶ τὴν τούτων πίστιν κατάοησον εἶπαν γὰρ τῷ βασιλεῖ δυνατὸς ὁ Θεὸς ἐξελέσθαι ἡμᾶς ἐὰν δὲ μὴ θελήσῃ, ἐν ἐξουσίᾳ Θεοῦ ἐσμέν, ἡδέως ἀποθύσκομεν ἢ ποιοῦμεν τὸ ὑπό σου προστεταγμένον. *Commentary on Daniel*, II.37.

[63] Δεῖ οὖν πάντα ἄνθρωπον τῷ λόγῳ προσίοντα ἀκούειν τί προστάσσει ὁ ἐπουράνιος βασιλεὺς καὶ δεσπότης "Ὃς ἄν μὴ ἄρῃ τὸν σταυρὸν αὐτοῦ καὶ ἀκολουθήσῃ ὀπίσω μου, οὐκ ἔστιν μου ἄξιος καὶ ὃς μὴ ἀποτάξηται πᾶσιν τοῖς ὑπάρχουσιν αὐτῷ οὐ δύναται εἶναι μου μαθητής. *Commentary on Daniel*, II.21; Matt. 10:38, Matt. 16:24; Luke 14:33.

sovereignty. This pagan king glorified the Lord after seeing his dreams miraculously interpreted (Dan. 2), after he witnessed the rescue of the youth from the fiery furnace (Dan. 3), and after his humiliation as a beast in the field (Dan. 4). Hippolytus comments how these divine interventions were gracious gifts from heaven, to demonstrate God's glory by the instruction of the Holy Spirit through the prophets. This display of God's sovereignty is furthered when Daniel's words are recalled, "You, O king, the king of kings, to whom the God of heaven has given the kingdom, the power, and the might, and the glory."[64] It is God who reveals mysteries (Dan. 2:47), who rescues his servants (Dan. 3:28), and whose ways are just and who humbles the proud (Dan. 4:37).[65]

These activities group Daniel among the Old Testament prophets, Hippolytus insists, making his visions and writings verifiably prophetic. As a Daniel commentator living three major world kingdoms after Nebuchadnezzar and the giving of Daniel's prophetic visions, Hippolytus can clarify the fulfillment of the vision of the statue and the beasts. He asks his readers: "If we believe he spoke the truth when these things came to pass, why would we not believe also that the future prophecies of the blessed prophets would not also truly come to pass?"[66] This allows Hippolytus to trump the sovereignty of God over all time: "All things will be fulfilled in their own time according to the will of God."[67]

Concerning the martyrs, Hippolytus attributes their success to the power of the Holy Spirit: "The Spirit of the Father inspires the martyrs with eloquence and exhorts them to scorn the death here below, to hurry to reach the good heavenly things."[68] Meanwhile, Hippolytus contrasted in detail the mental anguish that awaits those without the Lord:

But a man deprived of the Holy Spirit is frightened by the struggle, hiding himself in fear, taking precautions against a death which is only passing, terrorized before the sword, falling into panic at the thought of torment, only seeing the world below, only having anxiety toward life.[69]

---

[64] Daniel 2:37; cf. *Commentary on Daniel*, III.2.

[65] *Commentary on Daniel*, III.2.

[66] εἰ γὰρ πιστεύομεν τοῖς ἤδη γεγονόσιν ὡς ἀληθεύει, πῶς οὐχὶ καὶ ἄπαντα τὰ ἐρχόμενα ἔσται ἀληθῆ, ἅτινα οἱ μαρκάριοι προφῆται ἐσόμενα προαπήγγειλαν. *Commentary on Daniel*, III.12.

[67] κατὰ δὲ βουλὴν Θεοῦ ἰδίος καιροῖς προκόπτοντα ἄπαντα πληρωθήσεται. *Commentary on Daniel*, III.12.

[68] ὁρᾷς πῶς τὸ πνεῦμα τοῦ πατρὸς μελετᾶν τοὺς μάρτυρας διδάσκει προτρεπόμενον αὐτοὺς καὶ παραμυθούμενον καταφρονεῖν μὲν τοῦ θανάτου τούτου, σπεύδειν δὲ ἐπὶ τοῦ βελτίονος. *Commentary on Daniel*, II.21.

[69] ἐὰν γὰρ τις χωρὶς ἁγίου πνεύματος ᾖ, οὗτος δειλιῶν ἀγωνιᾷ καὶ φοβούμενος κρύβεται καὶ τὸν πρόσκαιρον θάνατον εὐλαβεῖται καὶ μάχαιραν καταπτήσσει καὶ κόλασιν οὐχ ὑπομένει, τὸν κόσμον τοῦτον πρὸ ὀφθαλμῶν ἔχει, τὰ τοῦ βίου μεριμνᾷ. *Commentary on Daniel*, II.21.2.

By their resistance, Hippolytus claims they showed the king that "the idol he worshipped did not merit the least consideration."[70] Hippolytus stresses how the king ordered the fire to be heated sevenfold before throwing them in an effort to triumph in an earthly fashion, but it was by faith in God that the three young men triumphed.

It is significant that Hippolytus includes a sharp criticism of the Roman state, which he regards as the fourth beast of the vision in Daniel 7:2-12. This is "the kingdom which is now in power," namely "the kingdom of the Romans."[71] He is obviously speaking to persecuted congregations through this martyrdom motif. He develops their faith by explaining how God empowers the martyrs and how death even by Roman antagonists is a passage that ends in heavenly reward.

The youths showed the king their invincible faith in a sovereign God by adding that even if God did not save them, they would remain faithful to their Lord by not worshipping the idol. In an attitude reminiscent of Job, "Though He slay me, yet will I trust in Him" (Job 13:15, KJV), the youth are willing to forfeit their notion of divine rescue for a reward and salvation in the next life— a distinct characteristic of apocalyptic literature. Hippolytus does not view the youth's refusal to bow down and an underlying hope for a reward in the next life as a denial of their ensuing death, as if they are making claims for themselves about imaginary rewards in another world that they can not actually prove. Instead, Hippolytus defines their qualifying statement (Dan. 3:18) as deliberate strategy against any effort of their executors and the devil to brag about their begging for mercy once they are inside of the furnace. "Therefore in order to protect the reputation of the faithful martyrs even after their death, they give themselves all sorts of guarantees, giving the devil no escape."[72] Any martyr who asserts this is wise and certainly not weak. From Hippolytus' claim about their motive, one can see the high view of the martyrs that the early church possessed; the reputation of the martyrs lives on and their achievement is commendable and encouraged.

Moving beyond the actual narrative of the text, Hippolytus reports Daniel's presence at the scene of the fiery furnace and claims that he was "filled with admiration" at the youths' response, that "as good athletes, he might give them the crown of faith."[73] The exhibition of faith in the face of persecution is a heroic model for the church to follow. Reflecting on Daniel's unwillingness to worship King Darius and instead become a martyr for his faith, Hippolytus

---

[70] ἐνδεικνύμενοι, ὅτι μηδὲ λόγου τινὸς ἄξιον εἴη τὸ εἴδωλον τὸ ὑπ᾽ αὐτοῦ προσκυνούμενον. *Commentary on Daniel*, II.24.3.

[71] τὰς βασιλείας τὰς ἔμπροστεν γενομένας; διατί τὴν τῶν᾽ Ῥωμαίων. *Commentary on Daniel*, IV.8.1; 8.2.

[72] ἵνα οὖν καὶ μετὰ θάνατον πιστοὶ μάρτυρες κληθῶσιν, κατὰ πάντα τρόπον ἑαυτοὺς ἠσφαλίσαντο, ὁπωσοῦν τινα παρέχειν ἀφορμὴν τῷ διαβόλῳ μὴ θέλοντες. *Commentary on Daniel*, II.24.7.

[73] προτρεπόμενοι ἀλλήλους ὡς ἔμψυχοι ἀθληταὶ προηγοῦντο. *Commentary on Daniel*, II.19.

remarks, "When one dies for God, one can rejoice at having obtained life eternal."[74] The sacrifice that comes with martyrdom helps accomplish one's salvation, as eternal life is the reward awaiting the martyred believer on the other side of death. This concept is a characteristic of the theology of martyrdom in the early church and in apocalyptic literature: the justice and reward for many events in this life come about in the life to come. Similarly, Tertullian spoke of martyrdom actually accomplishing salvation.[75]

Anticipating his readers' objections, Hippolytus rhetorically asks why the three youths were not also caught in disobedience to the decree alongside Daniel. He assures his readers that their silence does not mean they succumbed to persuasion. Instead, the authorities neglected them because on this occasion "Daniel alone was called to martyrdom" because God had already tested them.[76] The same was true when Daniel chose not to intervene to save the youth doomed for the furnace; God intended another purpose.[77] Hippolytus emphasizes the principle that God calls whomever he wants for martyrdom, thus he points out the importance to his own early third century readers to be willing to suffer persecution and even be martyred. "In each era, God always finds a person through whom he can render glory to himself, according to the world of his prophet."[78]

Hippolytus corroborates his exhortations with various examples from the Old and New Testaments.[79] He insists that the possibility of martyrdom should not weigh heavily on true Christians, because the faith is a cause worth dying for:

> Let us come to the example of Christ the King of glory, let us talk about the Son of God. Could not God save his Christ so that he would not be handed over to the Jews? Yes! He could. But he let him suffer, so that we may live through his death on the cross.[80]

---

[74] εἰ γὰρ διὰ Θεόν τις ἀποθνῄσκει, χαίρεσθαι ὀφείλει ἐπὶ τούτῳ ζωὴν αἰώνιον εὑρών. *Commentary on Daniel*, III.24.

[75] Tertullian insists that Christians should expect martyrdom as an event preceding full salvation. Tertullian, *Against Marcion*, IV.39.4; Frend, *Rise of Christianity*, 419 n.170.

[76] Δανιὴλ μόνου κατηγόρησαν. *Commentary on Daniel*, III.26.

[77] In this case, "So that the grand works of God might be illumined and that the Babylonians might learn to fear God." *Commentary on Daniel*, II.25.

[78] κατὰ γὰρ καιροὺς Θεῷ ἄνθρωπος οὐ λείπει, ἵνα δι' αὐτῶν δοξασθῇ· ὡς ὁ προφήτης λέγει· ὁ ποιῶν τοὺς κόσμους αὐτοῦ κατὰ τὸν ἕνα ἐπ' ὀνόματι αὐτῶν καλέσει αὐτούς. *Commentary on Daniel*, III.26. Cf. Isaiah 40:26.

[79] *Commentary on Daniel*, II.36.1-8.

[80] ἔλθωμεν δὲ καὶ ἐπ' αὐτὸν τὸν βασιλέα τῆς δόξης καὶ εἴπωμεν περὶ τοῦ υἱοῦ τοῦ Θεοῦ, οὐκ ἠδύνατο ὁ Θεὸς ῥύσασθαι τὸν Χριστὸν αὐτοῦ, ἵνα μὴ Παραδοθῇ τοῖς Ἰουδαίοις; ναί, ἠδύνατο ἀλλ' εἴασεν αὐτὸν παθεῖν, ἵνα ἡμεῖς διὰ τοῦ θανάτου τοῦ σταυροῦ αὐτοῦ ζήσωμεν. *Commentary on Daniel*, II.36.8.

For him, the preeminence of the Christian faith required an *ultimate* service from Christians, and he exhorted his audience to preparedness: "Be firm and steadfast, O man, not stammering in matters of faith, and when you receive a call to become a martyr promptly obey so that your faith will shine forth."[81] This earthly life ought to be subordinated to heavenly purposes; the Christian faith is an act of total self-surrender to God in which everything else is of secondary importance. The Holy Spirit can "show eloquence in grief to the martyrs and exhort them to scorn the death here below to hasten to experience the heavenly benefits."[82] The intensity of this martyrdom exhortation is concluded with two special sayings of Christ in the gospels indicative of a spirit of struggle and sacrifice:

Therefore everyone who comes to the *Logos* must hear what the heavenly King and Master commands: 'He who does not take his cross and follow me is not worthy of me' and 'Whoever does not renounce all that he has cannot be my disciple.'[83]

The Three Youths: A Case Study in Theodicy

Peter Berger explains how religions try to impose order and purpose on wicked and destructive human experience, particularly the phenomena of evil, suffering, and death. He writes that religion provides an explanation that legitimates these confusing events, or to use John Milton's words, give a "justification of the ways of God to man." By casting a higher meaning to the chaos, religion brings life's events under a "sacred canopy" of understanding.[84] Hippolytus uses the story of the three youths to theodicize Christian persecution by Roman society and government. The current absence of miraculous deliverance like those displayed in the scriptures raised questions among Christians. Why did God rescue these (would-be) martyrs in Daniel's day but not save contemporary martyrs? Hippolytus explains this dilemma through a theodicy of the sovereign and unknowable purposes of the Lord that deserves closer examination. Through elaboration of the text and theological explanation, Hippolytus casts logic to their situation so that he might provide encouragement amidst the suffering while ultimately yielding the explanation

---

[81] ἑδραῖος οὖν γενοῦ, ὦ ἄνθρωπε, μήποτε τῇ πίστει βαμβαίνων, ὅτ᾽ ἄν κληθῇς εἰς μαρτύριον προθύμως ἐπάκουσον, ἵνα ἡ πίστις σου φανῇ. *Commentary on Daniel,* II.37.5.

[82] τὸ πνι , τοῦ παρτὸς μελετᾶν τοὺς μάρτυρας διδάσκει προτρεπόμενον αὐτοὺς καὶ παραμυθούμενον καταφρονεῖν μὲν τοῦ θανάτου τούτου, σπεύδειν δὲ ἐπουράνια. *Commentary on Daniel,* II.21.1.

[83] δεῖ οὖν πάντα ἄνθρωπον τῷ λόγῳ προσιόντα ἀκούειν, τί προστάσσει ὁ ἐπουράνιος βασιλεὺς καὶ δεσπότης ὃς ἄν μὴ ἄπῃ τὸν σταυρὸν αὐτοῦ καὶ ἀκολουθήσῃ ὀπίσω μου, οὐκ ἔστιν μου ἄξιος καὶ ὃς μὴ ἀποτάξηται πᾶσιν τοῖς ὑπάρχουσιν αὐτῷ, οὐ δύναται εἶναι μου μαθητής. *Commentary on Daniel,* II.21.3. Cf. Matt. 10:38; Luke 14:33.

[84] Peter Berger, *The Sacred Canopy* (New York: Doubleday, 1967), 53-80.

to the will of a sovereign God.

In Book II.35-37, Hippolytus undertakes the difficult task of explaining why God does not intervene into the numerous acts of persecution against the church. He begins from their perspective, "Someone may say, "So why did God rescue the martyrs in another time and not today?"" He answers by challenging them to think from God's perspective:

> In this era, God saves whom he wanted, so that the works of his magnificence would be revealed to the whole world. But those for whom he desired martyrdom, he crowned them and brought them to himself. If he removed the three young men from the danger, it was so that the boasting of Nebuchadnezzar might appear as nothing, for God wanted to demonstrate that "what is impossible for man is possible for God"... God proved that he is able to remove his servants from danger when he wants.[85]

On the other hand, the readers know that the seven martyrs under Antiochus suffered terrible tortures, and were not rescued from danger. With a pastoral intent, Hippolytus asks:

> Why? Was God not able to punish Antiochus and rescue the seven brothers from danger? Yes, he could do it! But he wanted their martyrdom to serve as an example for us. For if he rescued everyone from danger, who would be a martyr? If all were martyrs and die, the unbelievers would announce that this has happened because God is powerless.[86]

Hippolytus answers with simple logic: If God saved all who were threatened with a martyr's death, who then would have become a real martyr? On the other hand, if all the prospective martyrs died, then the unbelievers would have claimed that the God of martyrs is unable to rescue his faithful servants. In the case of Daniel 3, Daniel and the three youths were saved so that the insolent king would recognize the power of God. In the case of 2 Maccabees 7, the seven heroic youths of the Maccabean revolt died so that they could become a model for believers.[87] In fact, in Hippolytus, we see from Daniel new exhortations to suffer like Shadrach, Meschach, and Abednego *would* have

---

[85] πρόσεχε ὦ ἄνθρωπε ὅτι καὶ τότε οὕς ἤθελεν ἔτι ζῆν ὁ Θεὸς ἐρρύετό ἵνα τὸ μεγαλεῖον τοῦ Θεοῦ ἔργον δειχθῇ καὶ ἐν παντὶ τῷ κόσμῳ ἕως νῦν κηρυχθῇ. οὕς δὲ ἤθελεν μαρτυρεῖν τούτους σεφανώσας προσελάμβανενώστε οὕς μὲν θέλει ρύεται οὕς δὲ θέλει παραλαμβάνει. τοὺς μὲν γὰρ τρεῖς παῖδας ἐρρύσατό ἵνα τὸ τοῦ Ναβουχοδονόσορ καύχημα μηδὲν ὂν φανῇ ἐνδείξασθαι τοῦτο βουλόμενός ὅτι τὰ ἀδύνατα παρὰ ἀνθρώποις δυνατὰ παρὰ Θεῷ. ἔδειξεν αὐτῷ ὁ Θεός. ὅτι δυνατός ἐστιν ρύσασθαι τοὺς ἑαυτοῦ δούλους ἡνίκα ἂν θέλῃ. *Commentary on Daniel*, II.35.3; cf. Luke 18:27.

[86] Τί οὖν; οὐκ ἠδύνατο ὁ Θεὸς πατάξαι τὸν βασιλέα Ἀντίοχον καὶ ρύσασθαι τοὺς ἑπτὰ ἀδελφούς; ἠδύνατο ἀλλ' ἵνα ἡμέτερος οὗτος γένηται ὑπογραμμός. Εἰ γὰρ πάντας ἐρρύετο τίς ἤμελλεν μαρτυρεῖν; εἰ δὲ πάντες ἐμαρτύρουν ἀποθνήσκοντες, ἐλέγετο ἂν ὑπό τινων ἀπίστων. *Commentary on Daniel*, II.35.8-9.

[87] *Commentary on Daniel*, II.35.1-9.

suffered. But for now, his readers should not expect God to intervene.

For Hippolytus, there is something more at work than just immortality for the executed believer, but a divine purpose in martyrdom: to reveal God's glory. God decides how he will bring glory to himself, either through delivering his servants or allowing martyrdom with rewards. In the case of Daniel in the lions' den, God knew both the wicked schemes of the advisors and the simplicity of Daniel's heart that prompted his deliverance. Hippolytus states candidly that God rescues whomever he wants to rescue:

> God saves whom he wants, in order that the works of his magnificence may be revealed to the whole world. But those of whom he desires martyrdom, he crowns them and makes them come up to himself [in heaven]... He rescues whomever he wants; he takes whomever he desires.[88]

The principle that "God so wanted," οὕς θέλει and ὅτε ἠθέλησεν,[89] becomes the defining element for Hippolytus' case in theodicy. All chaos and oppression against his people occurs because the Lord lets it happen—"God so wanted."

Hippolytus quotes scripture for his cause, "What is impossible for man is possible for God" and "If we live, we live unto the Lord; and if we die, we die unto the Lord. Therefore, whether we live or die, we are the Lord's."[90] He likens how God might pull them from the hand of the king as he pulled their ancestor Moses from the hand of Pharaoh and Jonah from the whale.[91] The commentary writer uses these Old Testament saints as examples of how God allowed some to be martyred and some to escape, "So that he may demonstrate that yesterday and today he exists as the one and only God who is able to do as he pleases to his servants."[92] With several Old Testament and Apocryphal examples (Daniel, Susanna, the three youth, Moses, Jonah, the Maccabees), we see proof for Frend's analysis of the commentary, "The martyrs represented a continuance in the church of the righteous examples of the Old Testament."[93]

He also uses the New Testament examples of Peter and Paul, each of whom the Lord rescued at least once for his name's sake (cf. Acts 12:7ff, John 21:18-

---

[88] τότε οὕς ἤθελεν ἔτι ζῆν ὁ Θεὸς ἐρρύετο, ἵνα τὸ μεγαλεῖον τοῦ Θεοῦ ἔργον δειχθῇ καὶ ἐν παντὶ τῷ κόσμῳ ἕως νῦν κηρυχθῇ. Οὕς δὲ ἤθελεν μαρτυρεῖν τούτους σεφανώσας προσελάμβανεν...ὥστε οὕς μὲν θέλει ῥύεται οὕς δὲ θέλει παραλαμβάνει. *Commentary on Daniel*, II.35.

[89] οὕς θέλει is repeated in *Commentary on Daniel* II.35; ὅτε ἠθέλησεν in *Commentary on Daniel*, II.36.

[90] τὰ ἀδύνατα παρὰ ἀνθρώποις, δυνατὰ παρὰ Θεῷ. *Commentary on Daniel*, II.35.5; cf. Luke 18:27, Matt. 19:26. ἐάν τε γὰρ ζῶμεν, τῷ κυρίῳ ζῶμεν. ἐάν τε ἀποθνήσκωμεν, τῷ κυρίῳ ἀποθνήσκωμεν. ἐάν τε ζῶμεν ἐάν τε ἀποθνήσκωμεν, τοῦ κυρίου ἐσμέν. *Commentary on Daniel*, II.36.1; cf. Rom. 14:8.

[91] *Commentary on Daniel*, II.19.

[92] ἵνα εἷς καὶ ὁ αὐτὸς Θεὸς πάλαι καὶ νῦν ὢν ἐπιδεικνύηται, ἐξουσίαν ἔχων ἐκ τῶν δούλων αὐτοῦ ποιεῖν ὅπερ ἂν θέλῃ. *Commentary on Daniel*, II.36.7.

[93] Frend, *Martyrdom and Persecution*, 118.

19; Acts 9:23ff). But when Peter was crucified, and when Paul was beheaded, God did not rescue them—according to his own will. Hippolytus also uses the example of Stephen, whom God did not rescue at all but let the Jews stone. When Stephen had "submitted [to martyrdom], God crowned him."[94] This prompts Hippolytus to use these faithful servants as a test for his readers, "How about you? Would you be a martyr today, if they had not obtained it first, by their martyrdom, their blessedness?"[95] Here, the sovereignty of God is displayed as the defining factor; what happens to his servants is entirely his will. Hippolytus urges his readers to trust that God is working all situations for the best. Christ becomes the ultimate example of willing suffering; he knew the Father's will and declared, "Not my will, but thine, be done" (Luke 22:42).

The will of God guided martyrs in biblical history and also directs the church in Hippolytus' day. He writes: "Which interests you, O man? To suffer martyrdom and to leave this world covered in glory, or to escape, rest here, and continue sinning?" The internal evidence of current persecution lies in statements like this by Hippolytus: "For we know some who, after having made a profession of their faith before the tribunal...."[96] At this point, he introduces the problem of apostasy among the ranks of Christians, revealing the dissatisfaction that comes with yielding one's faith when facing persecution:

> For we know some who, after having made a profession of their faith before the tribunal had been delivered in one fashion or another, according to the design of God. But after having lived for some time, they find themselves in a state of sin. Who does their profession of faith serve? It would have been better for them to leave this world pure, with the heavenly crown, than to remain here and accumulate on their conscience mistakes of which they have realized.[97]

The established theology of martyrdom also helped him to justify the willing sacrifice of the three young men and to transition to similar scenarios. With confidence, Hippolytus declared, "We remain faithful unto death. If one threatens to throw us to the ferocious beasts, before the beasts we will not tremble."[98] That he leaves the furnace of the Daniel text and speaks of wild beasts reveals a concern about contemporary persecutions. This story moves

---

[94] ἀλλὰ ὑπομείναντα τοῦτον ἐστεφάνωσεν. *Commentary on Daniel*, II.36.5.

[95] πῶς σὺ σήμερον ἤμελλες μαρτυρεῖν, εἰ μὴ ἐκεῖνοι πρῶτοι μαρτυρήσαντες ἐμακαρίσθησαν. *Commentary on Daniel*, II.36.6.

[96] πολλοὺς γὰρ ἴσμεν ὁμολογήσαντας πρὸ βήματος. *Commentary on Daniel*, II.37.3.

[97] πολλοὺς γὰρ ἴσμεν ὁμολογήσαντας πρὸ βήματος καὶ δι᾽ ἀφορμῆς τινος κατὰ Θεοῦ πρόνοιαν ἀπολυθέντας καὶ τούτους χρόνον ἐπιβιώσαντας ἱκανὸν καὶ ἐν παραπτώμασιν εὑρεθέντας. τί τούτους ὠφέλησεν ἡ εἰς Θεὸν ὁμολογία συνέφερεν γὰρ αὐτοῖς μᾶλλον, εἰ ἐξεληλύθασιν ἐκ τοῦ κόσμου τούτου καθαροί, ἔχοντες τὸν ἐπουράνιον στέφανον ἢ ἀπομείναντας ἐπισωρεύειν ἑαυτοῖς ἁμαρτίας, περὶ ὧν λόγον ἀποδοῦναι ἔχουσιν. *Commentary on Daniel*, II.37.3-4.

[98] εἰ ἀπειλεῖ τὸν θάνατον ὑπομείνωμεν. εἰ θηρσὶν ἀγρίοις παραβαλεῖν, τοὺς θῆρας μὴ καταπτήξωμεν. *Commentary on Daniel*, II.19.7.

him to twice refer to the tribunal that Christians currently face: "Believers are delivered to the tribunal and make profession of faith according to the design of God," and "If when you are before the tribunal, God wants to take you from there, render glory to God."[99] As part of God's sovereign plan, Hippolytus charges them directly to be willingly to go before the courts, and be willing to die for his name's sake.

> Therefore take courage, O man. Let your faith never tremble. And when you are called to be a martyr, answer willingly to the call so that your faith may be evident. Only God is able thus to prove you, as he proved of old Abraham by asking Isaac of him. If, when you are before the tribunal, God wants to rescue you from there, give back glory to God. Imitate, you also, the three youth and remember their faith. As they answered the king, "God is capable of delivering us, and if he doesn't desire, we are able in him." You respond likewise, "We prefer to die rather than to do what you ask."[100]

Hippolytus elaborates on the influence of the martyrs and their role in the plan of God:

> These things show us what great grace that faith in God obtains for us. Martyrs have rendered glory to God by surrendering themselves unto death; in return, they've not only been glorified by God, but also by the king, and they taught strange nations and barbarians to reverence God.[101]

Their influence extends to many who witness the acts and also endures unto the time of the faith of the church:

> Whenever one of the saints is called to martyrdom and God performs a great miracle through him, henceforth everyone within sight of these marvels is filled

---

[99] πολλοὺς γὰρ ἴσμεν ὁμολογήσαντας πρὸ βήματος καὶ δι' ἀφορμῆς τινος κατὰ Θεοῦ πρόνοιαν. *Commentary on Daniel*, II.37.2. ἐάν σε προσενεχθέντα θελήσῃ ῥύσασθαι, καὶ ἐν τούτῳ τὸν Θεὸν δόξαζε. *Commentary on Daniel*, II.37.5.

[100] ἑδραῖος οὖν γενοῦ, ὦ ἄνθρωπε, μήποτε τῇ πίστει βαμβαίνων, καὶ ὅταν κληθῇς εἰς μαρτύριον προθύμως ἐπάκουσον, ἵνα ἡ πίστις σου φανῇ. τυχὸν δὲ ὁ Θεὸς ἐπείρασέν σε ὡς τὸν Ἀβραάμ, ἡνίκα ᾔτησεν τὸν Ἰσαάκ. ἐάν σε προσενεχθέντα θελήσῃ ῥύσασθαι, καὶ ἐν τούτῳ τὸν Θεὸν δόξαζε. μίμησαι καὶ σὺ τοὺς τρεῖς παῖδας καὶ τὴν τούτων πίστιν κατάόησον εἶπαν γὰρ τῷ βασιλεῖ δυνατὸς ὁ Θεὸς ἐξελέσθαι ἡμᾶς ἐὰν δὲ μὴ θελήσῃ, ἐν τῇ τοῦ Θεοῦ ἐξουσίᾳ ἐσμέν ἡδέως ἀποθύσκομεν ἢ ποιοῦμεν τὸ ὑπό σου προστεταγμένον. *Commentary on Daniel*, II.37.5.

[101] πόσην χάριν πάρεχει ἡ πρὸς τὸν θεὸν πίστις. Ὥσπερ γὰρ αὐτὸν τὸν Θεὸν ἐδόξασαν, ἑαυτοὺς τῷ θανάτῳ παραδόντες, οὕτως πάλιν καὶ αὐτοὶ οὐ μόνον ὑπὸ Θεου, ἀλλὰ καὶ ὑπὸ τοῦ βασιλέως ἐδοξάσθησαν καὶ τὰ ἀλλόφυλα καὶ βάρβαρα ἔθνη τὸν Θεὸν σέβειν ἐδίδαξαν. *Commentary on Daniel*, II.38.3.

with astonishment, and celebrates because of the grandeur of God. And a great number, won to the faith by the martyrs, may also become martyrs of God.[102]

Thus, God's perfect plan is the basis for why some are saved and others are not. The reward for the Christian is not in this world, but in the next, and their death here is requested and used by God. This same guiding principle of sovereignty is underscored in the final book of the commentary, in which Hippolytus examines and analyzes the prophecies of Daniel to illustrate the overarching design of God, even over the kingdoms and rulers of this world when they unjustly persecute his people. This next section examines how this early church presbyter used the eschatological visions of Daniel to explain further how the divine plan of the future relates the current tribulation to God's call to martyrdom.

The Prophecy of the Great Tribulation

Daniel chapters 10-12 contain prophecies of a future foreign ruler who will oppress God's people. This biblical section provides details about a king from the north that will wage war against a competitor in the south. It is a highly apocalyptic section, and the church believed that it detailed in symbolic language how this mysterious tyrant will blaspheme God and torment those faithful to the Lord similar to the prophecies of Revelation.[103] This passage is of particular interest to Hippolytus because it weds persecution with eschatological overtones. Early Christians anticipated a specific persecution because of this prophecy that they paralleled with the Antichrist of the New Testament (2 Thess. 2:3-4, Rev. 13:1-18) and, in turn, they projected onto their Roman authorities.

Hippolytus is no exception. He brought the prophecies about tribulation to the third century church's circumstances, calming fears of the Antichrist's threat, redirecting focus to heaven, and assuring the sovereignty of God over time and events. This section will first examine how Hippolytus relates Rome to the Antichrist, and then compare this interpretation with other church fathers. Given the comment belief that theirs were the last days, many in the church easily believed that the Antichrist was of the current Roman Empire. Hippolytus participates in the trend to consider the period of final events, speculating on the signs of the timing of the Antichrist's coming and cross-referencing his theories with scripture. Yet he especially comments on the prophecies in a way that continues the pastoral encouragement to his persecuted congregations. Our exhorting presbyter offers an optimistic view of this time

---

[102] ἡνίκα γὰρ ἄν τις τῶν ἁγίων ἐπὶ μαρτύριον κληθῇ καὶ μεγαλεῖά τινα ὑπὸ Θεοῦ εἰς αὐτὸν γενηθῇ, εὐθέως πάντες ἰδόντες θαυμάζουσιν, πολλοὶ δὲ δι᾽ αὐτῶν πιστεύσαντες οὕτως καὶ αὐτοὶ μάρτυρες Θεοῦ γίνονται. *Commentary on Daniel*, II.38.4.

[103] For a summary of how Revelation complements Daniel in the mind of the early church, see pp. 71-73 above.

period by (1) identifying the Antichrist and revealing his ultimate defeat, (2) redirecting hopes into the afterlife through eschatological postponement, and (3) positing God's sovereignty over these events. In apocalyptic fashion, Hippolytus uses the text for the urgent task of offering provisional hope to his readers. The prevalence of apocalyptic literature in the early church allows Hippolytus to embellish his application of the Daniel text to contemporary events like no other author. Examining this text in light of inherited apocalyptic spirit will clarify and reinforce the intentions of Hippolytus concerning martyrdom. As the timing of the millennium and the return of Christ in Hippolytus receive attention, they complete the commentary's explanation and exhortation about the church's experiences of suffering.

Early Patristic Notions of Antichrist and Millennium

Early patristic discussion of the millennium often entertained a chronological explanation of end time events with a belief in an Antichrist and a great tribulation. The tribulation of the antichrist immediately precedes Christ's final return in most futurist eschatological theories, including those of early Christian writers, because the parousia involves final judgment and final rewards and punishments. Hippolytus affirmed these popular notions and worked within a similar framework based on scripture's description of future events. Naturally, the parousia became a source of hope and object of longing for persecuted Christians. Jeffrey Siker argues that throughout early Christianity there was "an unresolved tension" between those who expected an imminent return and those who had little expectation of an impending return. In the second and third century Christian writers, we witness this tension:

> In general we see at one end of the spectrum Christians who advanced a thoroughgoing eschatology with the parousia close at hand; on the other end we find Christians who lack any real sense of the parousia. In the middle emerges a centrist position, with various Christians advocating a modern eschatology that looks to an eventual but not imminent parousia—a position that remains a prominent option at the end of the twentieth century. [104]

Works such as *Didache*, the *Epistle of Barnabas*, *1 Clement*, and *Shepherd of Hermas* emphasize an immanent return, while their contemporary Justin Martyr discusses a parousia that seems to lack immanency, but offers hints about its timing. Although Gnostic texts are at times impossible to broad stroke, generally their eschatology is more fully realized, so that the necessity and hope of Christ's return is moot. "Resurrection" is a spiritual resurrection in these

---

[104] Jeffrey S. Siker, "The Parousia of Jesus in Second and Third Century Christianity," in *The Return of Jesus in Early Christianity*, ed. John T. Carroll (Peabody, MA: Hendrickson, 2000), 151.

texts and the parousia is less essential, thus the claim of the Gospel of Mary that "the Son of Man is within you" (8:13-19).[105]

Irenaeus takes the opportunity to refer more specifically to the events surrounding the return of Christ. For him, this return involves justice and rewards, in which believers will receive personal rewards and the satisfaction of judgment against their persecutors. In *Against Heresies*, Irenaeus looks to a time in which Christ will return in glory, calling forth all people from their graves, both "those that have done good to the resurrection of life, and those that have done evil to the resurrection of judgment."[106] He seems to be ordering several components of biblical eschatology in his mind as he tries to process the end of time. Concerning the logic of the parousia, he is certain: "But the advent of the Lord will appear superfluous and useless, if He did indeed come intending to tolerate and to preserve each man's idea regarding God rooted in him from of old."[107]

Irenaeus is the main figure who influences Hippolytus, and here we see that his theological sway extends to eschatology, too. Irenaeus and Hippolytus agree on the following eschatological characteristics: a future Antichrist, a future tribulation, a future resurrection of the saints at the return of Christ, a consequential millennial reign of Christ, and the end of the world 6,000 years after creation.[108] Besides their very comparable eschatological outlooks, both write in a context of anti-Gnostic challenges, with sound biblical exegesis, and with a high view of scripture. Such similarities support a Hippolytan dependence on Irenaeus and thus likely a Western milieu. Concerning the timing of Christ's final return, Irenaeus has a sense of immanency that allows the parousia to be instrumental in the future hope of a Christian's faith.[109] Hippolytus does not share this expectation, and a study in understanding his eschatology begins with the Antichrist.

Threat of the Future Antichrist in the Commentary

Hippolytus ties together the prophecies about the fourth beast (Dan. 7:1-8, 15-28), the seventieth week (Dan. 9:24-27), and the beast of Revelation (Rev. 13:1-18) by identifying the Antichrist as their common referent.[110] He reports that during the last days, one particular impious figure will blaspheme God,

---

[105] For a more detailed theological treatment, see Siker, "The Parousia of Jesus," 145-58.

[106] Irenaeus, *Against Heresies*, V.13.1.

[107] Irenaeus, *Against Heresies*, III.12.6

[108] A summary of their eschatological views can be found in Daley, *The Hope of the Early Church*, 28-32, 38-41; Tsirpanlis, "The Antichrist and the End of the World," 5-17; Carroll, *The Return of Jesus*, 158-59, 161.

[109] For a special study in the chiliastic nature and the timing of Christ's return in Irenaeus' eschatology, see Hill, *Regnum Caelorum*, 11-20.

[110] *Commentary on Daniel*, IV.50.2, IV.54.1; Daley, *The Hope of the Early Church*, 38-41; Dunbar, "The Eschatology of Hippolytus," 103.

disobey him, and pursue his servants to torture them.[111] When this enemy of God, symbolized by the little horn, subdues the ten horns (Dan. 7:19-20) and has fought and persecuted the saints (Dan. 7:21-27, 11:36-45), then will come the parousia of the Lord (Dan. 7:22, 27, 12:1-4). A persecuted early third century church could easily wonder if Emperor Severus' actions were the threat of the biblical Antichrist.

Hippolytus exhorts his readers to consider the scriptures that reveal information about the great tribulation to come, and to pray that it not be in their time. They should look for justice at the coming of the Ancient of Days (Dan. 7:9), for he will give the right of judgment to the saints of the most high, the very object of the Antichrist's wrath. In describing the person of the Antichrist, Hippolytus references Ezekiel 28:2, 28:9, and Isaiah 14:13, passages traditionally interpreted as describing Satan.[112] He further links this activity as Satan-inspired when he appeals to the words of the Apostle Paul in 2 Thessalonians 2:1-9, exhorting his audience to beware apostasy, deceit, lawlessness, exaltation of the Antichrist, and the activities of Satan.[113]

The Jews believed the prophecy in Daniel 10-12 was fulfilled in Antiochus Epiphanes in 167 BCE,[114] but early Christian authors saw its referent in the final days of the world ushering in Christ's final return. Some interpreters, such as Cyprian, would blur the two together: "In Antiochus Antichrist was set forth-sought to pollute the mouths of martyrs, glorious and unconquered in the spirit of confession."[115] Like other patristic writers to follow, Hippolytus also viewed Antiochus' persecution and godless acts during the Maccabean period as the referent of the prophetic material of Daniel 11. With two separate but similar referents, he agrees with both the Jewish, Maccabean interpretation of this text and the Christian reading that anticipated the Antichrist. Thus, for Hippolytus, Antiochus and Antichrist have a continuity that is grounded in the text even before it happens. Such an integrative, two-referent approach is akin to Frances Young's case that patristic exegesis was often "part of an intertextuality of imaginative and creative play" in which the traditional category of "typology" does not suffice.[116] The text serves as an explanation of both the past and the future. Daniel predicted two abominations, one under Antiochus and the other under Antichrist.[117] Hippolytus seems to anticipate Jerome two hundred years later, who sees the sufferings of the Jews under Antiochus, including "fire and sword, slavery and rapine, and even the ultimate penalty of death itself for the sake of guarding the law of God," to parallel and foreshadow future sufferings,

---

[111] *Commentary on Daniel*, IV.12.

[112] *Commentary on Daniel*, IV.12.

[113] *Commentary on Daniel*, IV.21.

[114] C.F. Keil and F. Delitzsch, *Commentary on the Old Testament: Vol. IX, Ezekiel, Daniel*, trans. M.G. Easton (Grand Rapids: Eerdmans Publishing Company, 1978), 450-61.

[115] Cyprian, *Exhortation to Martyrdom, Addressed to Fortunatus*, Treatise XI.11.

[116] Young, *Biblical Exegesis*, 116.

[117] *Commentary on Daniel*, IV.54.

as that seen in Revelation: "But let not one doubt that these things are going to happen under the Antichrist, when many shall resist his authority and flee away in various directions."[118]

The anticipation of the Antichrist raised many logistical questions and anxiety in the minds of his readers about timing of last day events, but Hippolytus insists that regardless of timing it should not draw the believer into fear and anxiety. He rebukes those who live in fear of these events; those who ask when these things will happen are called "unbelievers, people without faith."[119] Instead, he exhorts: "We must not anticipate the will of God, but to know to take patience and pray not to fall in such time."[120] At the end of the world, iniquity will be complete on earth with the coming of the fourth beast, and judgment will come as in the day of Sodom's destruction (Gen. 19:24). These events, although horrible in their time, are a source of hope for Hippolytus who lifts the eyes of his reader just beyond these events to the return of Christ. Hippolytus exhorts them in their tribulation to look to Jesus, "So that one may always hold to what is good, that one may avoid the mumbling of the Spirit, and that one can believe in God with all his heart."[121] Jesus is presently at afar with plans for an eventual return, but Hippolytus hints that his coming is anticipated even in the messenger delivering this vision's explanation to Daniel. Hippolytus brings Christ's presence closer by allegorizing the details of the angels clothed in linen in Daniel 10 to refer to Christ.[122] The effect is the presence of Christ both present and future.

Identifying the Antichrist

Hippolytus is not the first early church writer to harmonize the prophecy with the historical events envisioned by Daniel. According to Eusebius, about the year 200 CE one Judas offered his own exegetical project on Daniel.[123] Noted as the first chronographer, he fit a record of historical events within the

---

[118] Jerome, *Commentary on Daniel*, XI:33, trans. Gleason L. Archer (Grand Rapids: Baker, 1958), 135. Throughout his commentary on Daniel 11, Jerome continually parallels the events of Antiochus with the future events of the Antichrist, with only some exceptions.

[119] ἀπίστων ἐστὶν ἀνθρώπων οὐ πιστευόντων. *Commentary on Daniel*, IV.5.

[120] ὥσπερ οὔτε προλαμβάνειν ἡμᾶς δεῖ τὴν τοῦ Θεοῦ βουλήν, ἀλλὰ μακροθυμεῖν καὶ δέεσθαι, ἵνα μὴ εἰς τοιούτους χρόνους ἐμπέσωμεν. *Commentary on Daniel*, IV.5. Due to the extremely intimidating time, it was common for Christians to pray that the end of the world would not come in their lifetime. Cf. Tertullian, *Apology*, 39.2; Lefèvre, 271, n.b.

[121] ἵνα κατὰ πάντα ἑδραίως ἑστὼς ὁ ἄνθρωπος καὶ ἐν μηδενὶ βαμζαίνων τῷ νοΐ ἐξ ὅλης καρδίας τῷ θεῷ πιστεῦσαι δυνηθῇ. *Commentary on Daniel*, IV.7. Hippolytus here relates this eschatological-based exhortation to "a prior work" thought to be *On Christ and the Antichrist.* Ἐπεὶ οὖν φθάσαντες καὶ ἐν ἑτέρῳ λόγῳ περὶ τούτων ἀποδεδώκαμεν τὸν λόγον; Lefèvre, *Commentary on Daniel*, IV.7, n.a.

[122] *Commentary on Daniel*, IV.37.

[123] Eusebius, *Ecclesiastical History*, VI.7.

framework of Daniel's prophecy of 70 weeks. He proposed the prophecy's final week to end in 202, making it a year of persecution and speculation about the Antichrist. With Judas, we witness how historiography can be seen as an extension of apocalyptic writing and we can witness similarities in Hippolytus' eschatology.[124] Hippolytus' system is more political in content than Judas' project; his apocalyptic exegesis of Daniel is expressed in two ways: the Roman Empire's relationship to this fourth beast with its horns, and the encouragement to endure any oppression in light of the imminent return of Christ.

Hippolytus makes a fine distinction when he outlines the exact relationship between Septimius Severus and the Antichrist. Although some scholars emphasize his interpretation that some symbols in *Daniel* held referent in the current Roman Empire,[125] Dunbar's analysis seems most accrete when he concludes that these interpretations merely "provide a focus and guide" to some future kingdom's persecutions.[126] This issue of timing is important to clarify if we are to fully understand the role of martyrdom in Hippolytus' exhortations to believers in the commentary. Hippolytus identifies the fourth beast with the Roman Empire that now rules, "The beast presently being in place" or the "now ruling beast."[127] This would suggest that the time of the Antichrist is here and that eschatological consummation will soon follow. However, at other times, Hippolytus speaks like the Antichrist is not yet in power, and that this wave of persecutions against the church is not the final one. In his effort to understand the vision, Hippolytus differentiates between the reign of the fourth beast and that of the horn that comes from it; the fourth beast is in power but the horn has not yet emerged and crushed the other horns.[128] The current Roman Empire becomes responsible for fostering the future ruler and persecution, so that Hippolytus "places the Roman state under severe prophetic indictment" even though they are not the final oppressors.[129] His eschatology postpones the great tribulation to a later time—probably almost five hundred years before the Sabbath antitype sets in.

Hippolytus agrees with Irenaeus that the name of the Antichrist has not been declared.[130] Speaking symbolically, Hippolytus prefers the name *Latinus* "Latin man" as most applicable to his political and social circumstances as well as to the number 666.[131] This comment clearly links the Antichrist to the Roman

---

[124] Frend, *Rise of Christianity*, 417.

[125] Simonetti, *Biblical Interpretation*, 28; Hidal, "Apocalypse, Persecution, and Exegesis," 50.

[126] Dunbar, "Eschatological Exegesis," 338. This is the most popular position amongst scholars and best reconciles the sense of already/not yet characterizing his position.

[127] τὸ νῦν κρατοῦν θηρίον. *Commentary on Daniel*, IV.8.7. Cf. *Commentary on Daniel*, IV.10.2., IV.51.1.

[128] *Commentary on Daniel*, IV.13, 26.

[129] Trakatellis, ΛΟΓΟΣ ΑΓΟΝΙΣΤΙΚΟΣ, 542.

[130] Irenaeus, *Against Heresies*, V.30.

[131] Hippolytus, *On Christ and the Antichrist*, V.215.

Empire in a clever way that serves his martyrological purposes. The Antichrist is a distant figure who is also a present reality. Hippolytus uses the biblical description of the tribulation under the Antichrist to serve his understanding of the Roman Empire's present treatment of Christians without calling the emperor the Antichrist. The persecution of Severus and the Roman mobs currently underway are not so different than the ones anticipated in the great tribulation. This is further evidenced by the continuity between the Roman Empire and the Antichrist, especially his remarks about "now ruling beast" and his name being "Latinus."[132] Tsirpanlis recognizes this: "Hippolytus relies on Rev. 17-18 [for his picture of the Antichrist], more strongly stressing Latin or Roman dimensions of the destructive activity of Antichrist (Rome as 'the Mother of Harlots and Abominations of the Earth')."[133] Like Justin Martyr before him, Hippolytus sees the "Antichrist" as "the man of apostasy" who persecutes the Christians of all ages.[134]

Hippolytus provides this treatment of an Antichrist for pastoral reasons, hoping that his readers will understand when these things happen. The real advantage to these prophecies seems not to be the accuracy of prediction, but the way that it informs believers for readiness. To his persecuted churches he says, "Having the mystery of God in our heart, we ought in fear to keep faithfully what has been told us by the blessed prophets, in order that when those things come to pass, we may be prepared for them, and not deceived."[135] This brings us to the other expression of his apocalyptic exegesis: using the text and the timing of the final events to offer pastoral exhortations to his churches.

Despite this delay in the parousia, the overtones of apocalyptic and persecution weigh heavily on Christians. Hippolytus offers encouragement to endure any oppression in light of the ultimate return of Christ. His final conclusion is that the time for the eschatological συντέλια (Dan. 12:13) is not yet ripe, that some signs have yet to come, and that the only appropriate attitude is vigilance and alertness. He knows that the people are anxious and curious, and that they are wondering when all these things will happen—when the Antichrist will be revealed and when the day of the appearance of the Lord will come. He answers that he truly does not know, appealing to the model of faith provided by preceding martyrs:

> Why do you examine the times and search for the day, when the Savior has hidden it from us?....If the martyrs, the one who shed their own blood for Christ, were requested to be patient and wait for a while, why cannot you too wait in

---

[132] *Commentary on Daniel*, IV.52; *On Christ and the Antichrist* V.215.

[133] Tsirpanlis, "The Antichrist and the End of the World," 13.

[134] Justin, *Dialogue with Trypho*, 110-111.

[135] Hippolytus, *On Christ and the Antichrist*, 50.

patience, so that other people would be saved and the number of the called and the saints would be completed?[136]

Delaying Christ's Return

Hippolytus does not imitate Irenaeus with expectations of an imminent return of Christ. With the return of Christ being an ongoing and important hope in early Christianity, Hippolytus expends much energy in the commentary securing a balanced view of the event. He first establishes how it is certainly to be expected, a glorious and triumphant return of the one whose name and people are being oppressed. The church's anticipation of the parousia functioned as a hope in the face of the Antichrist's threat or any hostile persecution that comes against them. Whenever Christ does finally manifest himself, Hippolytus make it clear that all the people of the world will recognize him "King of Kings....and Judge of Judges, in fullness and glory" and "with the strength of the Father."[137] He will come in full glory without any doubt. The reason for contrasting and analyzing the parousia is clear: "These things we say in order to affirm our brothers who believe, so that they do not over anticipate the plans of God and that each knows that the day he leaves this world, he is already judged. For him, everything is accomplished."[138]

His readers were not merely to sit and wait for the judgment of the return of Christ; he challenges them not to become obsessed with the return:

What is the use, then, this inquisitive study about the time and this investigation about the day (of the Lord), when the Savior himself has concealed it from us? Tell me: do you know the day of your death, so as to worry thus about the end of the whole world? If God hadn't patience toward your consideration, in overabundance and of mercy, he would have a long time ago made it end.[139]

---

[136] τί δέ σοι καὶ τοὺς χρόνους περιεργάζεσθαι καὶ τὴν ἡμέραν [τοῦ κυρίου] ἐπιζητεῖν, ὁπότε ἀπέκρυψεν ἀφ᾽ ἡμῶν ταύτην ὁ σωτήρ ... εἰ οὖν τοῖς μάτρυσι προσετάγη μακροθυμεῖν, οἵτινες τὸ ἴδιον αἷμα ὑπὲρ τοῦ Χριστοῦ ἐξέχεαν, διὰ τί καὶ σὺ οὐ μακροθυμεῖς, ἵνα καὶ ἕτεροι σωθῶσιν καὶ ὁ ἀριθμὸς τῶν κλητῶν ἁγίων πληρωθῇ. *Commentary on Daniel*, IV.22.1, 4; cf. Rev. 6:9-11.

[137] ὁ βασιλεὺς τῶν βασιλέων.... καὶ ὁ κριτὴς τῶν κριτῶν μετὰ παρρησίας καὶ δόξης ἐρξόμενος σημανθῇ. *Commentary on Daniel*, IV.24. μετὰ δυνάμεως καὶ δόξης πατρικῆς. *Commentary on Daniel*, IV.18.

[138] ταῦτα δὲ λέγομεν πρὸς στηριγμὸν τῶν πιστῶν ἀδελφῶν, ἵνα μὴ προλαμβάνωσιν τὴν βουλὴν τοῦ Θεοῦ, γινώσκων εἰς ἕκαστος ὅτι ᾗ ἂν ἡμέρᾳ ἐξέλθῃ ἐκ τοῦ κόσμου τούτου ἤδη κέκριται ἔφθασεν γὰρ ἐπ᾽ αὐτὸν ἡ συντέλεια. *Commentary on Daniel*, IV.18.7; cf. John 3:18.

[139] τί δέ σοι καὶ τοὺς χρόνους περιεργάζεσθαι καὶ τὴν ἡμέραν ἐπιζητεῖν, ὁπότε ἀπέκρυψεν ἀφ᾽ ἡμῶν ταύτην ὁ σωτήρ; εἰπέ μοι εἰ γινώσκεις τὴν ἡμέραν τῆς ἐξόδου σου, ἵνα τὴν συντέλειαν τοῦ παντὸς κόσμου πολυπραγμονήσῃς. εἰ μὴ δὲ ἐμακροθύμει ὁ

Giving an example of one who overestimated the immediacy of Christ's return, Hippolytus relates how a leader of a distant church failed to apply himself to the study of the scriptures and did not follow the Lord's words about bewaring rumors of his return. Not understanding the commands of the Lord, this leader persuaded other believers to go to the desert to meet Christ upon his return. In these cases, the governor ignored the matter in order to avoid provoking a general persecution against them.[140]

Instead, Hippolytus strictly warns them that it is not to be fantasized or falsely imagined. Just because they are facing suffering does not guarantee their rescue and they shouldn't hope in the intervention of the parousia alone. Instead, Christians should patiently and bravely face the afflicting duty of martyrdom that confronts them. This eschatological outlook bears even more explicitly on our study when Hippolytus uses the example of the martyred souls in heaven who cry out for vindication as an example of how they, too, should remain patient and faithful for God:

> Hear the world of John in Revelation: "And when He broke the fifth seal, I saw underneath the altar the souls of those who had been slain because of the word of God, and because of the testimony which they had maintained; and they cried out with a loud voice, saying, 'How long, O Lord, holy and true, wilt Thou refrain from judging and avenging our blood on those who dwell on the earth?' And there was given to each of them a white robe; and they were told that they should rest for a little while longer, until *the number of* their fellow servants and their brethren who were to be killed even as they had been, should be completed also." If therefore he has told the martyrs to be patient, to those who have spilt their blood for Christ, why are you not patience, so that other men may be saved and that it may complete the number of elect saints?[141]

He admonishes them to persevere in prayer instead.[142] The apocalyptic genre of Daniel serves his exhortations well here because he redirects his readers to look beyond their suffering to the eternal rewards that await them. Commenting on Daniel 12:8-13, a passage describing the compensation coming to those who

---

Θεὸς ἐφ᾽ ἡμῖν διὰ τὴν ὑπερβάλλουσαν αὐτοῦ εὐσπλαγχνίαν, πάλαι ἄν τὰ πάντα ἐξήλειπτο. *Commentary on Daniel*, IV.22.1-2.

[140] *Commentary on Daniel*, IV.18.

[141] ἀνάγνωθι τὸ εἰρημένον ὑπὸ Ἰωάννου ἐν τῇ Ἀποκαλύψει. καὶ εἶδον τὰς ψυχὰς τῶν πεπελεκισμένων διὰ τὸ ὄνομα Ἰησοῦ ὑποκάτω τοῦ θυσιαστηρίου καὶ ἐβόησαν καὶ εἶπαν πρὸς τὸν Θεόν. ἕως πότε, κύριε ὁ Θεὸς ἡμῶν, οὐ κρίνεις καὶ ἐκδικεῖς τὸ αἷμα ἡμῶν ἀπὸ τῶν κατοικούντων ἐπὶ τῆς γῆς. καὶ ἐδόθησαν αὐτοῖς στολαὶ λευκαὶ καὶ ἐρρέθη αὐτοῖς, ἵνα περιμείνωσιν χρόνον ἔτι μικρόν, ὅπως οἱ σύνδουλοι αὐτῶν πληρώσωσιν τὴν μαρτυρίαν αὐτῶν οἱ μέλλοντες ἀποκτείνεσθαι ὡς καὶ αὐτοί. εἰ οὖν τοῖς μάρτυσι προσετάγη μακροθυμεῖν, οἵτινες τὸ ἴδιον αἷμα ὑπὲρ τοῦ Χριστοῦ ἐξέχεαν, διὰ τί καὶ σὺ μακροθυμεῖς, ἵνα καὶ ἕτεροι σωθῶσιν καὶ ὁ ἀριθμὸς τῶν κλητῶν ἁγίων πληρωθῇ. *Commentary on Daniel*, IV.22.

[142] *Commentary on Daniel*, IV.18.

suffer, he inquires:

> Who are the "chosen ones" except those found worthy of the kingdom? Who are the "white ones" except those believe on the Word of truth in a manner to be purified by him, and to reject the stain of their faults in order to put on the Holy Spirit, pure and enlightening, which comes from heaven, in order to enter immediately with the Bridegroom who will be there? Who are the "purified" by faith, except those who pass through fire and water in the spiritual bath of the new birth and who accomplishes the will of God through the burns that cause the innumerable temptations and tribulations.[143]

He insists to his readers that their suffering will lead to eternal reward. Hippolytus closes the final chapter of his commentary by promising that with the final judgment, God will end all wickedness and restore the righteous to their due reward. It is God who can send us warning about the future, restore us, save us, pardon us, preserve us, guard us from all temptation and all tribulation, in order to make us escape judgment by fire, move us into joy at the coming of his blessed Son and our Lord Jesus Christ.[144]

Rationale for Eschatological Postponement

Although he assures them of the certainty of Christ's return, he tempers this expectation when he clearly postpones the parousia three hundred years into the future. In doing this, Hippolytus does not follow Irenaeus on an imminent return of Christ. Why this similar eschatology for Hippolytus but with a bold desertion of Irenaean millennial hope?

David Dunbar has given three reasons for Hippolytus' unique delay of the parousia, each of which remain grounded in the church father's overall view of eschatology: (1) his philosophy of history, (2) his view of church and state, and

---

[143] τίνες δὲ οἱ ἐκλεγόμενοι ἀλλ᾽ ἢ οἱ ἄξιοι τῆς βασιλείας εὑρισκόμενοι; καὶ τίνες οἱ λευκαινόμενοι ἀλλ᾽ ἢ οἱ τῷ τῆς ἀληθείας λόγῳ πιστεύοντες, ἵνα λευκανθῶσιν δι᾽ αὐτοῦ καὶ ἀποβάλλοντες τὸν τῶν ἁμαρτιῶν ῥύπον ἐνδύσωνται τὸ ἀπ᾽ οὐρανῶν καθαρὸν καὶ διαυγὲς ἅγιον πνεῦμα, ἵνα παρόντος τοῦ νυμφίου εὐθέως συνεισέλθωσιν αὐτῷ; καὶ τίνες οἱ ἐκπυρούμενοι ἢ οἱ διερχόμενοι αὐτῷ διὰ πυρὸς καὶ ὕδατος διὰ τοῦ πνευματικοῦ λουτροῦ τῆς παλιγγενεσίας καὶ τὸ θέλημα τοῦ Θεοῦ διὰ πυρώσεως πολλῶν πειρασμῶν καὶ θλίψεων ποιοῦντες; *Commentary on Daniel*, IV.59.3-5. In this commentary on the text, Hippolytus also quotes 1 Cor. 2:9 to describe the future gifts awaiting the saints, "Eye has not seen, nor ear has heard, neither has entered the heart of man the things that God has prepared for those who love him."

[144] δύναται δὲ ὁ Θεὸς πάντας ἡμᾶς πρὸς τὰ μέλλοντα ἐηρηγόπους ποιῆσαι, καταρτίσαι, σῶσαι, ἐλεῆσαι, φυλάξαι, τηρῆσαι ἀπὸ παντὸς πειρασμοῦ καὶ θλίψεως, ὅπως ἐκφυγόντες τὴν ἐπερχομένην διὰ πυρὸς κρίσιν φθάσωμεν ἀπαντῆσαι μετὰ χαρᾶς εἰς τὴ ἐπιφάνειαν τοῦ ἠγαπημένου παιδὸς αὐτοῦ Ἰησοῦ Χριστοῦ τοῦ κυρίου ἡμῶν. *Commentary on Daniel*, IV.60.3.

(3) his view of ethics.[145] Considering each briefly will assist our study. (1) Chronologically, Hippolytus sees history in a model of seven thousand-year periods. The birth of Christ occurred half way through the sixth thousand-year period, 5500 years after Adam. Writing two hundred years after Christ's birth, Hippolytus calculates another three hundred years before the end of the world and the ushering in of the final thousand years.[146] The Sabbath is "a type and figure" of the future kingdom of peace and rest for the saints who will reign with Christ.[147] He sees Revelation 17:10, "They are also seven kings, five of whom have fallen, one is, the other has not yet come, and when he comes he must remain only a little while," as revealing how the thousand year rest is not yet here. (2) He sees the ongoing friction between an illegal Christianity and the Roman authority structure as negative. It is a necessary evil of an interim period. (3) Ethically, this presbyter had a rigor to be obedient to God whatever the cost. The church is "the holy assembly of those who live in righteousness."[148]

Although Dunbar deduces these three reasons based on Hippolytus' larger, comprehensive eschatological views, I would posit that a martyrdom motive inseparably accompanies this logic. Dunbar recognizes the importance of martyrdom as a factor, but it seems to permeate even deeper, functioning to prevent a false hope that persecution will soon end due to the 1,000-year peace coming on the heels of an immediate parousia.

This postponement removes the element of the imminent rescue and forces his readers to focus on their calling to martyrdom. Hippolytus' eschatology represents a shift in millennial theories in church history. Unlike Irenaeus, Justin, and the Apostolic Fathers, who held to an imminent return of Christ and entertained a chiliastic view of the millennium, Hippolytus postpones the parousia for another three hundred years. He sees Daniel's prophecies about the coming of the Son of Man in a model of seven thousand-year periods.

Further Positing God's Sovereignty

Having already established God's sovereignty in the narrative of the three youths, Hippolytus now applies it over the rulers of this world to further his case for Christian martyrdom. He opens both book III and IV by pointing out how Nebuchadnezzar's arrogance prompted God to make him lose his

---

[145] Dunbar, "The Delay of the *Parousia* in Hippolytus," 313-327.

[146] *Commentary on Daniel*, IV.23. This is the only hint that Hippolytus gives toward a literal millennium, and scholars debate whether he was chiliastic or not. The difficulty lies in the understanding of how literal this thousand year of rest is understood, but its interest to us lies only in its historical timing with Roman rule and her acts martyrdom against the church.

[147] τὸ σάββατον τύπος ἐστὶν καὶ εἰκὼν τῆς μελλούσης βασιλείας τῶν ἁγίων, ἡνίκα συμβασιλεύσουσιν τῷ Χριστῷ. *Commentary on Daniel*, IV.23.5.

[148] *Commentary on Daniel*, I.17.

kingdom.[149] Afterward his humiliating reversion to a beast-like state (Dan. 4), God restored his kingdom to him, Hippolytus points out, thus underlining the Lord's power and his sovereignty even over the powerful rulers of the world.

Part of establishing God's justice among these events is the apocalyptic appeal to look to upcoming judgment for the justice that is longed for. Hippolytus guarantees that God will judge and punish the impious by burning in eternal fire, and give eternal reign to some special categories of Christians: "His servants the prophets, martyrs, and all who believe."[150] All Christians are included in the gift of participating in Christ's eternal reign, but of particular notice is the mention of the martyrs—demonstrating the special desire that Hippolytus has to further the cause of martyrdom.

These things are accomplished because God himself decides such things, raising nations and knocking down leaders. "For all this that God decides, and all this that the prophets announce he accomplishes exactly in his time."[151] This same attitude of justice and judgment is seen in Irenaeus' understanding of religious persecution: "This world is ruled by the providence of one God, who is both endowed with infinite justice to punish the wicked, and with infinite goodness to bless the pious, and impart to them salvation."[152] In the early fifth century, Jerome would realize this from the Daniel text: "It is by the will of God that they [kings and empires] are governed, altered, and terminated. And the cases of individuals are well known to Him who founded all things."[153] This outlook sets the stage for divine justice, as those facing martyrdom could trust that God, in his sovereignty, would give rewards to those faithful and penalty to those faithless.[154]

---

[149] *Commentary on Daniel*, III.1 and IV.2; cf. Dan. 5:21.

[150] *Commentary on Daniel*, IV.14.

[151] ὅσα γὰρ ἤδη παρὰ Θεοῦ προωρίσθη γενέσθαι, καὶ ἀπὸ τῶν προφητῶν προκεκήρυκται, ταῦτα οὕτως καιροῖς ἰδίος πληρωθήσεται. *Commentary on Daniel*, IV.24.

[152] Irenaeus, *Against Heresies*, III.25.

[153] Jerome, *Commentary on Daniel*, II.21.

[154] *Commentary on Daniel*, IV.56.2-7; cf. Dan. 12:2.

CHAPTER 4

Exegetical Method in the *Commentary*

Chapter 3 demonstrated how Hippolytus used the text of Daniel to exhort Christians to be willing to suffer martyrdom under Roman persecution. A closer examination of his exegetical method would serve our understanding of his application of the text to encourage martyrdom. This chapter will demonstrate the novelty of Hippolytus' project, the style in which he crafted the commentary, the exegetical influences on him, the place of scripture as authority, and then the actual exegetical method that shaped his interpretation of scripture. Here, the force of martyrdom and exegesis come together into a powerful motif in his *Commentary on Daniel*.

Hippolytus' Novel Exegetical Task

The early third century saw the beginning of expansive commentaries on scripture by the church. About 170 CE, the Gnostic leader Heracleon wrote a commentary on the Gospel of John and this should be considered the beginning of the era of biblical commentary writing. We can only speculate how the writing of a Gnostic commentary like that of Heracleon or Ptolemy might have been a precedent or model for Hippolytus.[1] He likely knew these commentary materials, but the length and complexity of the *Commentary on Daniel* leads us to imagine that he adapts a certain multifarious agenda of his own to commentary material.

However, because Heracleon's commentary was Gnostic in nature, it was long considered unorthodox and we have no way of knowing the exact popular success of the work. Thus, Hippolytus is often credited with authoring the first continuous Christian commentary on a book of scripture. As orthodox writers persisted in engaging this new genre of writing, Hippolytus' contribution to the growing popularity of this trend becomes more important. By the end of the third century, the study of scripture would never be the same. It was in

---

[1] There is no evidence that the pressure of persecution inspired Heracleon to write a commentary; in fact such a suffering would run contrary to most Gnostic theology. Frend describes the Gnostic mentality: "It was of no avail to confess Christ with one's lips and deny him by one's conduct," so that the martyr's death was of limited importance to Gnostics. Additionally, many Christians in Alexandria showed an aversion to martyrdom. Frend, *Martyrdom and Persecution*, 261.

Jerome's *Lives of Illustrious Men* that we learn that Ambrosius encouraged the great biblical commentator Origen to write commentaries on the scriptures in "emulation of Hippolytus." [2] This Alexandrian in particular would develop the genre of commentary writing into a science as part of his repertoire of authorship projects, and thus become the greatest commentary writer in the early church.

Transforming Patristic Exegesis

As noted in chapter 1, in the development of patristic biblical studies Hippolytus is usually recognized as a transition figure for several reasons that deserve further elaboration here. (1) He created an expansive continuous commentary on a single book of scripture, and scholars believe his *Commentary on Daniel* is the first ever such work by a Christian. He has been called the "inaugurator of the continuous exposition of biblical text within Christianity."[3] He is able to use Daniel for typology, allegory, pastoral and moral exhortation, and constructing theology. Herein lays the distinctive feature of his writing: the extension of the scope of exegesis to never-before explored fields of scripture. Daniélou remarks: "From this point of view he marks not a turning-point, but a decisive step in the history of typology"[4] because Hippolytus build on the exegetical tradition while extending its boundaries to an entire book of scripture.

(2) Exegesis in the first hundred and fifty years of the church dealt mainly with select passages; interest in the Old Testament was almost exclusively in specific prophecies or types that pointed to Christ. Hippolytus breaks this trend so that later Origen could more comfortably move into a wider Christian interpretation of recently neglected scripture. Hippolytus used the Old Testament as a text subject, especially Daniel, Song of Songs, and the Pentateuch, rather than favoring New Testament material as most Christian writers were doing. Unlike the era of apologists, this generation of Christians would expound the entire scriptures for their own people—both the Old and New Testaments.

(3) He demonstrated a theological emphasis on scripture that was more Christological than eschatological or apologetic. The result of his theological transition quality is that he does not always fit neatly into scholar's categories of historical biblical exegesis.[5] His contribution remains clear, however.

---

[2] Jerome, *Lives of Illustrious Men,* LXI.

[3] Daniélou, *Gospel Message,* 259.

[4] Daniélou, *Gospel Message,* 257.

[5] Chronologically, Hippolytus precedes the era of the early great exegetes, which begins with Origen. He is not distinctly Alexandrian or Antiochene in category, yet scholars can not quite squeeze him into the era of the Apologists and Irenaeus. He is probably

Simonetti remarks:

> With Hippolytus, catholic exegesis, restricted so far to controversial, catechetical, or doctrinal purposes, at last frees itself from those fetters and becomes an independent literary genre, with works devoted explicitly to the interpretation, if not yet of an entire book of the Bible, at least of fairly extensive passages.[6]

Thus, in the greater Christian tradition of Daniel hermeneutic, Hippolytus is a pioneer. His accomplishments include using scripture to develop a chronology of time, gleaning its apocalyptic contents to establish a solidly operating sovereignty of God, and enhancing Christological interpretation of Old Testament prophecy so that he can even date the birth of Jesus. This novel hermeneutical spirit also renders the subject of our focus, a martyrdom motif through an exhaustive commentary on Daniel text. From the apostolic fathers to the third century, the church was still systematizing the strong inherited theological milieu of martyrdom and persecution in a way that would explain the sufferings it saw. By the early third century, Christians had written enough theology, understood enough scripture and techniques of typological, apocalyptic, apologetic, and allegorical interpretation that now the church was equipped to interpret the social and political persecutions that were shaking it. These traditions stimulated Hippolytus to move through the biblical text and interpret his contemporary events in light of the text and the hermeneutical framework he inherited. His comments are so thorough and so novel that Hidal remarks, "Nearly all the issues in the patristic exegesis of the Book of Daniel are to be found in this commentary."[7]

Two of the largest unanswered questions surrounding the commentary are why Hippolytus would write a commentary and why he would choice of Daniel as a text for such a pioneering, intensive study. Concerning the first, we know that Heracleon had offered a model of reading scripture that analyzed and systematized the material into a larger Gnostic framework, probably to make a case for its validity in an age of theological and ecclesiological development. The Gnostic writer Heracleon authored what seems to be a complete commentary on the Gospel of John. It comes to us only in Origen's citations in his own John commentary, in which he occasionally takes opportunity to rebut the Gnostic interpretation. Bart Ehrman has argued for a Roman provenance for

---

Western in geography and theology, but still writes in Greek and shows Eastern tendencies. He is usually placed in the chapters of Western exegetes, but remains distinct in style and subject matter from Tertullian, Tyconius, Jerome, and Augustine. As an example of the difficulty of categorizing the unique Hippolytus, Manlio Simonetti places him in chapter 1 among exegetes of the first and second centuries—a time period when he virtually did not even write. Simonetti, *Biblical Interpretation*, 27-31.

[6] Simonetti, *Biblical Interpretation*, 27.

[7] Hidal, "Apocalypse, Persecution, and Exegesis," 51.

the commentary and has made a case for a Western textual source tradition.[8]

Perhaps such a work intrigued Hippolytus. It may be no coincidence that the provenance for the first ever recorded commentary on a book of scripture on record and Hippolytus' new literary enterprise were both of a Roman provenance. Origen's references to Heracleon's exegesis (about fifty in all) offer little about the novelty of his commentary project. There is certainly no evidence that the strain of persecution motivated Heracleon in a way that might parallel Hippolytus' situation as a reason for his commentary. In the case of the John commentary, Heracleon tries to explain a Gnostic interpretation of the events of Jesus' life. These two early church figures seem simply to share a belief that these books are scripture for their faith and worthy of closer commentary.

Concerning the reason for Hippolytus' choice of Daniel as a text for such an intensive study, interpretation, and explanation of scripture, we can insist on one factor and only speculate about others. The work itself does not explicitly state "why a commentary" or "why Daniel among books" as we would like. The prologue to the work does set forth the importance of the witness of the Daniel characters and their contribution to Christian witness. As we have seen in the martyrological data, the significance of a martyrdom motif becomes evident to the reader in the opening lines of the commentary. Hippolytus states the importance of discovering the mysteries of the Book of Daniel "which has produced 'martyrs full of faith' in the world."[9] For an early church presbyter, the witness of the Danielic characters in Babylon become a worthy contribution to the faith of suffering, persecuted church congregations.

The most interesting innovation with this patristic commentary may be that Hippolytus chose an Old Testament book as his subject of study when the church was focusing on the teachings of Christ and their ecclesiastical application in Paul and other New Testament epistles. Often, patristic authors wrote to provide a Christological understanding of the Old Testament. Like much of the early church, Hippolytus desired to offer a Christological explanation of all the prophecies in the book, but it hardly explains the task of a running commentary and is not the primary focus of his exegesis. Simonetti offers an anti-Gnostic concern to the cause of the writing—that the truth of the gospel and the teaching of scripture is the basis for authority of scripture rather than *gnosis*—although the evidence is not predominant in the Daniel

---

[8] For his argument for a Roman milieu, see Bart D. Ehrman, "Heracleon, Origen, and the Text of the Fourth Gospel," *Vigilae Christianae* 47 (1993): 105-18. For his argument for a Western textual milieu, see Ehrman, "Heracleon and the 'Western' Textual Tradition," 161-179. Irenaeus describes this Gnostic commentary on John, *Against Heresies*, I.8.5.

[9] μάρτας πιστοὺς ἐν κόσμῳ προήγαγεν. *Commentary on Daniel*, I.1.

commentary.[10] He also suggests that Daniel might have been part of a larger project in eschatology, evidenced by his *Treatise on the Christ and Antichrist* and his *Commentary on Revelation*.[11] We cannot know exactly what occasioned Hippolytus to write this commentary. However, a partial solution that is posited in this book is certain: the crisis of martyrdom and persecution in the church. Having examined the wealth of martyrdom-related data in the commentary, now we can recognize his attempt to use this martyrdom friendly text to exhort Christians to be willing to suffer for the faith.

This purpose finds expression and exhortation through exegesis of the text. This chapter will attempt to systematize Hippolytus' exegetical methodology to point clearly to his high priority on suffering for the faith. Before defining his exact method, we should highlight some important stylistic features that aid any reader of the commentary to value his exhortations to martyrdom.

Hippolytus' Style of Prose

Hippolytus' transformational affect on patristic exegesis was stimulated by the exegetical methodology he witnessed in the writing of the early church and the scriptural ambiance that Christianity inherited from Judaism. An explanation of his method here will support the ample evidence of a martyrdom motif given in chapter 3.

Hippolytus' style of writing is one that is thoroughly interactive with the text of Daniel, moving through the text of scripture in a general but comprehensive fashion that no Christian scriptural commentator before had done. He engages the text like Eastern fathers would soon after him, and his literary expression and thought is Greek.[12] Hippolytus quotes the biblical text for his theological debate quite extensively. As a result, his commentary is filled with lengthy quotations from the biblical text with comments in between. Often the exchange is only a phrase or two long, but his regular deliberations make for a thoroughly interactive commentary. One scholar took a number of the

---

[10] Simonetti, *Biblical Interpretation*, 27. Additionally, such a theory would link the author of the commentary to the author of the anti-heretical works in the Irenaean tradition—a relationship that Simonetti prefers to deny. Simonetti, *Biblical Interpretation*, 33, n.22. On the other hand, Hippolytus' Song of Solomon commentary does have Gnostic doctrine in view.

[11] Simonetti, *Biblical Interpretation*, 27.

[12] As noted earlier, Johannes Quasten's inspection of the commentary's style suggests that Hippolytus was not native Roman, but an easterner by origin and training. He observes that Hippolytus has a vast familiarity with Greek philosophy and pagan religion, his use of the doctrine of the Logos suggests an Hellenistic training and connection with Alexandria. "His entire mentality, in short, indicates that he came from the East." Quasten, *Patrology*, vol. II, 163. Daniélou denies Alexandrian influence and prefers an influence of Palestinian Judaism or Syrian Judeo-Christianity. Daniélou, *Gospel Message*, 260. See also Cerrato, *Hippolytus between East and West*, 250-258.

commentary pages at random and determined the distribution of biblical texts cited *verbatim* to Hippolytus' own comment was 3 to 2.[13]

Although Hippolytus thoroughly engages the text, he does not systematize scripture as thoroughly as Origen would come to do. He focuses on the text at hand with little allusion to the larger corpus of scripture, and without incorporating the present text into a larger systematic theology as a whole. Scholars have underrated the strength and coherency of his systematic theology expressed in his anti-heretical works, particularly *The Refutation of All Heresies*, and scholarly assessment remains accurate that Origen's systematic foundation of scriptural interpretation would eclipse all before him. Hippolytus' exegetical works are different because his exegetical goal was pastoral and liturgical, while with Origen it was methodical and scientific.[14] The *Commentary on Daniel* particularly demonstrates his pastoral purpose as he encourages his persecuted churches. His pastoral spirit is clearly noted as his exegesis becomes endowed with a martyrdom motif, functioning to boost the spirits of his beleaguered congregations. Hidal confirms this when he states that the commentary has a "paranaetic-typological view of the Book of Daniel."[15]

In the most extensive analysis that has focused on the content and style of Hippolytus' *Commentary on Daniel*, Trakatellis sees Hippolytus' exegetical style in the commentary as similar to the "fighting exegesis" method used by John Chrysostom. In his *Exegesis on the Psalms*, Chrysostom uses the phrase λόγος ἀγωνιστικός as his method of responding to views advanced by his theological opponents, especially heretics, pagans, and Jews. The term entails an attitude of debate, agonistic speech, competition, or dispute with respect to theological issues encountered in a biblical text. Trakatellis says that it "clearly means a full awareness of opponents who must be answered, contradicted, or confuted. It also indicates an evangelistic mentality, an impetus for a positive proclamation of the Gospel which aims beyond the refutation of the opponent's ideas."[16] Although Trakatellis recognizes a pastoral function in the λόγος ἀγωνιστικός theme,[17] he claims that Hippolytus' exegesis of Daniel contains this single agonistic characteristic that he aimed toward a particular multi-faced goal: to battle competitively against other religious ideas, to emphasize the anguishing aspect of political conflict, and to expand evangelism toward conflicting theologies.[18] The theory itself and the particular goals he suggests are insightful.

---

[13] Trakatellis, ΛΟΓΟΣ ΑΓΟΝΙΣΤΙΚΟΣ, 529 n.5.

[14] Daniélou makes the distinction; I offer the reason for it. Daniélou, *Gospel Message*, 259.

[15] Hidal, "Apocalypse, Persecution, and Exegesis," 50.

[16] Trakatellis, ΛΟΓΟΣ ΑΓΟΝΙΣΤΙΚΟΣ, 528.

[17] Trakatellis himself says that there is a pastoral intention in the λόγος ἀγωνιστικός theme. Trakatellis, ΛΟΓΟΣ ΑΓΟΝΙΣΤΙΚΟΣ, 528.

[18] Trakatellis, ΛΟΓΟΣ ΑΓΟΝΙΣΤΙΚΟΣ, 528.

Although Trakatellis' theory identifies part of Hippolytus' writing style, the problem is that he extends this λόγος ἀγωνιστικός intention to so many areas—scripture, Jews, pagans, heretics, the state, oppressors, and eschatological interpretations—that he essentially reduces the goal of the writing theology to mere battle-work by Hippolytus. One is left wondering about the real validity of this sole metanarrative in his writings, and instead we should look to a more pastoral intention accompanying this conflict of competitive theologies. If we do not overextend Trakatellis' paradigm but apply it only to his exhortation and defense of a rigorous Christian lifestyle (against Callistus, toward persecuted believers) plus his passion for orthodox theology (against heresies), then we have a more accurate historical picture of Hippolytus.

Using the theological framework λόγος ἀγωνιστικός, Trakatellis does rightly assess that Hippolytus tries to apply the Daniel text "to be vigilant, to fight and struggle for the faith, and to persevere in persecution." He says this theme functions toward "evangelism, religious propagandas, and conflicts of competitive theologies."[19] Although the prescribed hortatory function is clear, there is little or no evidence of evangelism or resolution of competitive theologies in this commentary. One easily sees that the text is "filled with conflicts, with battles related to faith, and with competitive religious ideas and practices,"[20] but the rhetoric is not of competing theologies as seen in his anti-heretical works, whose nature seems more fitting for Trakatellis' portrayal. Instead the descriptions are of a conflict with the state and with pagan and Jewish people persecuting them. This conflict is grounded in the text of Daniel, with the enemies of God's people exemplified and prophetically typed in Old Testament scripture. Only by modifying Trakatellis, then, can we accurately represent the nature and rhetoric of Hippolytus' prose that aimed to encourage those Christians suffering persecution for their faith.

The Exegetical Influences on Hippolytus

Hippolytus' work had a transforming effect on patristic exegesis when he engaged an entire book of scripture and employed the text for theology, Christology, eschatology, ecclesiology, and practical exhortation. This transformation was stimulated by the exegetical methodology he witnessed in the rich milieu of Jewish and patristic biblical exegesis. An examination of these exegetical influences will give insight into Hippolytus' method of exegesis as he establishes a martyrdom motif in the *Commentary on Daniel.*

Jewish Exegetical Influence

Although Hippolytus may be the first Christian commentator on scripture, the

---

[19] Trakatellis, ΛΟΓΟΣ ΑΓΟΝΙΣΤΙΚΟΣ, 528.
[20] Trakatellis, ΛΟΓΟΣ ΑΓΟΝΙΣΤΙΚΟΣ, 528.

practice was not new to the ancient world. Philo had written continuous commentaries on Genesis and Exodus for the Alexandrian Jewish world. However, most scholars see little evidence of Philonic or Alexandrian influence; the influence of Irenaeus and Justin on Hippolytus stem from a Palestinian Judaism or a Syriac Judeo-Christianity.[21] Simonetti remarks about Hippolytus' commentaries: "On the whole, they resemble less the diffuse commentaries of Philo than the literary commentaries of the pagan world or the Qumran *pesharim* of Judaism." [22]

Hippolytus relies strongly on rabbinical methods of biblical interpretation, as he seems both familiar with Judaism and indebted to its methods. Many of his writings derive their themes from Judaism, including *Benedictions of the Patriarchs, On the Passover, On Song of Songs, On Daniel*, and *On the Antichrist*. Black has argued that Hippolytus even possessed detailed knowledge of the Essenes.[23] Hippolytus' discussions about the dating and computation of Easter are reminiscent of Jewish dialogue over the celebration of Jubilees: "They breathe a Jewish environment."[24] Daniélou maintains that his Old Testament commentaries are highly rabbinical in style, grammar, and theology.[25] Thus, there is a clear Palestinian or Syriac influence on his commentary style, and many essential beliefs about scripture would accompany such an ambiance. In particular, Hippolytus shares a high view of scripture with the rabbinical tradition, their freedom in interpreting and commenting on it, and their overall tendency to interpret the text in a literal fashion. Each of these features deserves clear definition to understand his method.

(1) The Jews based their view of scripture on the belief that it was divinely provided and consequentially was the source legitimizing all of their traditions.[26] In the tannaitic period before Christ's time, Jewish exegesis aimed to improve its understanding of authoritative scriptural claims,[27] and this presupposition had significant influence on the church fathers. The fathers saw

---

[21] Daniélou, *Gospel Message*, 260. Quasten suggests the probability of a connection with Alexandria. Quasten, *Patrology*, 163; cf. Simonetti, *Biblical Interpretation*, 27.

[22] Simonetti, *Biblical Interpretation*, 27.

[23] Matthew Black, "The Account of the Essenes, in Hippolytus and Josephus," in *The Background of the New Testament and Its Eschatology*, ed. W. D. Davies and David Daube (Cambridge: The University Press, 1956), 172-75; Frend, *Rise of Christianity*, 341; Simonetti, *Biblical Interpretation*, 27.

[24] Frend, *Rise of Christianity*, 341.

[25] For a thorough treatment of the rabbinical similarities to Hippolytus' *Commentary on Daniel*, see Daniélou, *Gospel Message*, 257-271.

[26] Greenspahn, *Scripture in the Jewish and Christian Traditions*, 64; Farkasflvy, "Interpretation of the Bible," 466; Longenecker, *Biblical Exegesis*, 19, 48.

[27] Greenspahn, *Scripture in the Jewish and Christian Traditions*, 91; Michael Fishbane, "Jewish Biblical Exegesis: Presuppositions and Principles," in *Scripture in the Jewish and Christian Traditions: Authority, Interpretation, Relevance*, ed. Fredrick E. Greenspahn (Nashville: Abingdon Press, 1982), 92-102.

the Hebrew scriptures as an essential part of their heritage, and like the Jews they believed it to be inspired revelation. Scholars seem to think that some time between the fourth and the second centuries BCE, Jews solidified this belief that "God had revealed his mind and will in a detailed way in scripture."[28] By the time of Christ, they believed that "there was not a word or even a letter found in the Pentateuch, Prophets, and their other sacred books that ought to be looked upon as useless or merely superfluous."[29] Failure to achieve a national identity without foreign occupation catalyzed rabbinical efforts in the tannaitic period to secure scriptural education for every Jew, which in turn prompted a need for a system to apply these important texts. New laws of interpretation, guidelines for living the Jewish life, and the formation of a new class of religious scholars (scribes) all arose during this period and extended into the era of the early church. Jewish exegesis in the first century CE included literal, midrashic, and pesher modes of interpretation, providing a variety of influences on patristic exegesis.[30]

(2) When interpreting scripture, the fathers likewise used these same rabbinical principles while embellishing some and adding their own Christological components. Betrand de Margerie remarks that patristic exegesis employed "a method that transcends that of Jewish exegesis while being in continuity with it."[31] The fathers used the same freedom and innovation that they witnessed in the *midrash* of the rabbis as they sought to find biblical meanings pertinent to the lives of their readers. Although rabbis in the tannaitic period were opposed to allegorical interpretation, they did allow for some embellishment of the text in light of other textual sites. For Christian writers, this was particularly true as they sought to bring the meaning of Old Testament texts to proclaim Christ and the gospel. These scriptures were believed to report prophetic words about Christ, his coming, his function, and his teaching. Likewise, these texts could also contain activities about the end of the world that would prompt Christ's second advent.

(3) In his imitation of rabbinical interpretive freedom, Hippolytus also shares their tendency to interpret the text in a literal fashion. Regardless of what senses the scriptures may hold, the rabbis read scripture like a legal document that needed both an accurate understanding and precise propositions for living.

---

[28] Fredrick G. McLeod, *Image of God in the Antiochene Tradition* (Washington, D.C.: Catholic University of America Press, 1999), 11.

[29] McLeod, *Image of God*, 12.

[30] For a summary of the theological developments in tannaitic Judaism, see Fishbane, "Jewish Biblical Exegesis," 94-102. For even more detail on scripture and interpretation as the center of Jewish and religious life, as well as methods of exegesis, see Michael A. Signer and Susan L. Graham, in "Rabbinic Literature" in *Handbook of Patristic Exegesis: The Bible in Ancient Christianity*, ed. Charles Kannengiesser (Boston: Brill, 2004), 120-144.

[31] Bertrand de Margerie, *An Introduction to the History of Exegesis*, vol. I, *The Greek Fathers* (Petersham, MA: Saint Bede's Publications, 1991), 5.

The rabbinical method of approaching scripture was highly meticulous, gaining the insights of the text in a way that was very faithful to its literal meaning. Predominantly, they practiced a literal approach so that Christians would later coin such an approach "Jewish." The rabbinical traditions of biblical exegesis are mainly associated with the Pharisees, who were the main upholders of this "scribal" tradition in the early church. Their interpretation focused on ritual purity and faithful adherence to the Law, particularly the Midrash concept involving the study of a text for its content and purpose. These rabbis who practiced Midrash believed that scripture *must* be totally consistent with itself, with parts being harmoniously interpreted in light of another parts. Rising interests in different levels of meaning were generally opposed, Bray says, because it suggested that scripture, being essentially a legal document, was ambiguous.[32]

Coming from this Jewish ambiance, the church knew both the Hebrew scriptures and the conventional methods to interpret them. Jewish interpreters varied in hermeneutical methods and applications such as pesher, midrash, hallakah, haggadah, but common principles instructed all their exegesis in ways that bore directly on the biblical writings of Hippolytus.[33] They believed in the divine inspiration of scripture—scripture as they had it originated from God as his very own words. Because of this, the texts were seen as "extremely rich in content and pregnant with many meanings" that were available to the interpreter.[34] The result was the possibilities for literal (plain, obvious) meanings as well as less literal (implied, deduced) meanings. Most importantly, the purpose for any interpretation was to instruct the believer in their life of faith in Yahweh.

We can witness these same principles in Hippolytus' own exegesis, but his methodology contains additional exegetical enhancements. The early church writers preceding him added their own interpretive developments to rabbinical methods, thus creating principles of interpreting scripture that Hippolytus uses when he exhorts his congregation to be willing to suffer in the face of persecution.

---

[32] Gerald Bray, *Biblical Interpretation: Past and Present* (Downers Grove, Ill.: InterVarsity Press, 1996), 57.

[33] The literature Jewish hermeneutics and its influence on Christian interpretation is readily available, but noteworthy surveys include: Longenecker, *Biblical Exegesis in the Apostolic Period*, 19-50; Farkasflvy, "Interpretation of the Bible," in *Encyclopedia of Early Christianity*; and Signer and Graham, "Rabbinic Literature." For a still more in-depth treatment, see the essays in Greenspahn, *Scripture in the Jewish and Christian Traditions.*

[34] Longenecker, *Biblical Exegesis*, 19.

Early Patristic Influence

Besides writing under this rabbinical, Jewish tradition, Hippolytus stands in the tradition of biblical exegesis from Irenaeus and Justin that becomes standard in the West.[35] Like them, he sees the Old Testament as God's divine revelation, its characters and events as historical instruments in the theater of God's plans, and a Christ-centered view of all of its developments. The conviction that scripture is authoritative and that the church can exploit its prophecies and narratives to understand it state of affairs is a sort of first principle of his exegesis. This section compares his exegetical methodology with other patristic figures, especially Irenaeus.

From these hermeneutical principles Hippolytus borrows the idea of Christ as the *Logos* who can be seen in the Old Testament. Justin insisted that Christianity was not a new revelation but a fuller one because Christ was the *Logos*, the consummation of all Judaism, especially its scriptural texts. Justin is unlike Irenaeus and Hippolytus in that the gospel is "not for him the fulfillment of a divine dynamic, growing throughout the economy of salvation…for Justin it presents the concrete and perfect evidence of what has always been the truth for Jewish thinkers as well as for any philosopher."[36] However, his language of mystery and the economy of God working among past civilizations, his use of the Hebrew scriptures for understanding the Christian faith, and his typological interpretations of the events in Genesis and Exodus as prefiguring Christ and the church are preemptive of what Christian writers like Hippolytus would develop further.

Irenaeus deserves special attention due to his proximity to Hippolytus, his relationship with Rome, and Photius' report of Hippolytus' discipleship under Irenaeus. This church father exerted an extremely formative influence on biblical exegesis in the West, in particular his use of scripture and the apostolic tradition in establishing a "rule of faith" that ought to govern theology. Generally speaking, this standard is the tradition of the apostles, evidenced in the church and recorded in an early notion of scripture that was, for Irenaeus and others, handed down to all true churches and her leaders everywhere.[37] To speak more specifically of the rule is the topic of much scholarly debate.[38]

---

[35] For an overview of the exegesis of both Irenaeus and Justin individually, see de Margerie, *An Introduction to the History of Exegesis*, 27-78.

[36] Kannengiesser, *Handbook of Patristic Exegesis*, 434.

[37] This theme can be classified into categories of data from *Against Heresies*. For the rule of faith as found in the apostolic tradition handed down to elders, see I.10.1-2, II.25.1, III.1. Preface, III.2.2, III.3.2-4, III.4.1, IV.26.2, IV.33.6, V.20.1. For the rule of faith as found in the Scriptures, see I.22, II.13.3, III.1.1, III.12.6, IV.33.6, IV.35.4. For the rule of faith as characterizing all the true churches everywhere, see I.9.5, I.10.2, II.27.1, III.3.2-4, IV.1-3, IV.33.6.

[38] Concerning the differences between rules of faith and truth, Osborn explains, "Generally the term rule of faith was preferred for internal use within the church and

Certainly, our understanding of Hippolytus' use of scripture would affirm O'Keefe and Reno who caution against any assumption that the use second-century use of scripture "was nothing more than an exhaustive exercise in proof-texting animated by an anti-intellectual submission to doctrinal authority."[39] Instead, it was an intentional, thoughtful, and faithful effort by church leaders to employ scripture and the apostolic tradition against what they viewed as inferior and dangerous false doctrine. This is the treatment of scripture seen both in Irenaeus and Hippolytus.

Concerning a usage of the Old Testament, Irenaeus saw Christ clearly in the text of Daniel. The stone hewn with hands that smashes the great statue of Nebuchadnezzar's dream in Daniel 2 is Christ, and he establishes an eternal kingdom initiated by the resurrection of the righteous.[40] Jesus is present as the Son of God in the fiery furnace in Daniel 3 and comes in the clouds as the Son of Man in Daniel 7.[41]

Irenaeus designed an understanding of the unfolding plan of God throughout the revelation of the scriptures, informed by the text in Daniel 12:4, "Shut up the words, and seal the book, until the time of the end" when "knowledge shall increase." Until that time, God was preparing his people to be part of a kingdom, "The one who loves God shall arrive at such excellency as even to see God."[42] Christ's suffering on the cross triggered a new era in which these things are now revealed; at his first advent he was rejected (Ps. 118:22) but his second advent will be in glory on the clouds (Dan. 7:13). This divine unfolding finds its way into Irenaeus' exegesis in a methodical and instructive manner based on the parable of the hidden treasure in Matthew 13:44. Christ is the treasure hidden in the field of the Old Testament, and in this new dispensation knowledge of God's plan is abundant in the Old Testament and in the gospel.[43] Hippolytus exploits the principle when he sees the *Logos* present and predicted in the Book of Daniel.

Like Irenaeus and Justin, Hippolytus establishes a Christological fulfillment to Daniel's prophecies. All three fathers distinguish between Old Testament prophecies given in the form of events and figures, *typoi*, from those prophecies given verbally, *logoi*. Yet their focus remains the same: Christ is in the Book of

---

rule of truth was preferred when argument was directed to heretics." Eric Osborn, *Irenaeus of Lyons* (New York: Cambridge University Press, 2001), 145 n.17. Concerning charges of the orthodox abuse of the rule, see Bart D. Ehrman, *The Orthodox Corruption of Scripture: The Effect of Early Christological Controversies on the Text of the New Testament* (New York: Oxford University Press, 1993), especially pp. 3-32, 120-65, and 274-80.

[39] John J. O'Keefe and R.R. Reno, *Sanctified Vision: An Introduction to Early Christian Interpretation of the Bible* (Baltimore: Johns Hopkins University Press, 2005), 126.

[40] Irenaeus, *Against Heresies*, IV.20.11; 5.26.2.

[41] Irenaeus, *Against Heresies*, IV.23.10.

[42] Irenaeus, *Against Heresies*, IV.26.1.

[43] Irenaeus, *Against Heresies*, IV.26.1.

Daniel, and its referents of prophecies are seen in the New Testament and the current dispensation of the church. Daniélou compares Hippolytus with Origen here, saying he "marks the point of transition from an age when oral tradition was the essential element in Christian teaching to the 'age of the Book,' now formally organized into Old and New Testaments."[44]

A clear example of interpreting the Old Testament through the New Testament is Hippolytus' unique theology of the time of Jesus' return. Irenaeus had figured that since God created in six days and then rested, the millennium would begin after six thousand years.[45] According to Daniel 9:27, the Antichrist will reign for three and one half years, sitting in the Temple desecrating its holiness, until the kingdom is given to the saints to rule for a thousand years.[46] Irenaeus understood the evil ruler of Daniel to be the Antichrist, as his interpretation is filtered through the descriptions of the beast in Revelation and the man of lawlessness in II Thessalonians. Hippolytus develops a comparable eschatology based on his own exegesis, interpreting these Daniel passages similarly. Yet, it deviated in his more precise interpretation of the timetable of events and differed by his postponement of any imminent return of Christ.

In terms of exegetical method, the polemical nature of Irenaeus' writings that come to us are not strongly expository; his hermeneutics occur in a context attacking Gnostic writings. Thus, there is nothing in Irenaeus that compares to Hippolytus' commentaries. Still, for Irenaeus "scripture is more of a proof text. It is the matrix of his whole theological discourse."[47] This church father expounds the parable of he vineyard found in Mark 12:1-11 in a way that demonstrates how a literal reading and an allegorical reading both "remain very close in the biblical text."[48] Each step from the vineyard's founding to the appointment of the laborers to the sending of delegates by the landowner represent another component of biblical history: creation or patriarchs or prophets or Christ himself or the coming of the Gentiles.[49] The reading of the Old Testament and gospel letter is the basis for an allegorical understanding in God's greater economy of biblical mysteries. Careful and precise, confident and certain, Irenaeus maintains consistency of all of scripture, especially in the making of parallels and seeing the whole economy of salvation weaving through the texts. Add to this the importance of application in light of new theological errors and troubles in the Christian life, one sees clearly the

---

[44] Daniélou, *Gospel Message*, 259.

[45] Irenaeus, *Against Heresies*, V.28.2-3; 5.25.4, cf. Daniel 7:13.

[46] Irenaeus, *Against Heresies*, V.34.2; cf. Daniel 7:27.

[47] Kannengiesser, *Handbook of Patristic Exegesis*, 477.

[48] Norbert Brox, "Irenaeus and the Bible: A Special Contribution," in *Handbook of Patristic Exegesis: The Bible in Ancient Christianity*, vol. 1, ed. Charles Kannengiesser (Boston: Brill, 2004), 500. For a full treatment of his use of Scripture, see his pp. 483-506.

[49] Irenaeus, *Against Heresies*, IV 36.2.

exegetical influence on Hippolytus. The latter's style and content is remarkably similar to that of Irenaeus, and certainly Irenaeus' formative influence can be seen in Hippolytus' eschatology, hermeneutics, polemical writing, and overall theology.

Authority of Scripture

As expected from an early church father, Hippolytus believes that all of scripture is authoritative because it is divinely provided. He refers to "all scripture" as including "the prophets, the Lord, the apostles, and John in the Apocalypse."[50] Like Justin Martyr before him, there is continuity between the words given to the patriarchs, Moses, and the prophets with the words of Christ and the scriptures developing in the early church. Christ is the source for all revelation in Justin, as he is the preexistent *Logos* who provided all these scriptures. Farkasflvy insists that Irenaeus, Tertullian, and Hippolytus share the same basis of interpretation from both the Old and New Testaments: "They believe that the two are intimately connected and theologically harmonized, affirming at the same time the New Testament's guiding role and supremacy."[51] This allows Hippolytus a clear conscience to craft a commentary on an Old Testament book as a legitimate, authoritative source of divine insight for application in the lives of his congregations, especially when interpreted in a Christological way.

Throughout his exegetical activities, Hippolytus consistently declares the absolute authority of scripture. The anti-heretical and theological treatises attributed to him also share this same premise. He sees the scriptural text as definite truth and uses it profusely to argue his case.[52] Trakatellis notes that scriptural authority was "a basis not merely presupposed and applied, but uncompromisingly advocated as a condition *sine qua non* for any responsible theological debate."[53] The scriptural authority is evidenced in four specific ways in Hippolytus that become a basis for his appeal to martyrdom.

(1) He stands in a long line of historical biblical exegetes that believe the text to be divinely inspired. The fathers virtually unanimously treat the scriptures as provided directly from God, and their writings center on its authoritative application.[54] Hippolytus does not look at the text like a modern

---

[50] Περὶ τούτου πᾶσα γραφὴ οὐκ ἐσιώπησεν, καὶ προφῆται ... καὶ ὁ κύριους... καὶ ἀπόστολοι ... καὶ Ἰωάννης ἐν τῇ Ἀποκαλύψει. *Commentary on Daniel*, IV.49.2.

[51] Farkasflvy, "Interpretation of the Bible," 467.

[52] His more formal, scriptural based cases can be seen in *Commentary on Daniel*, I.29.1, I.30.1, II.28.6, III.12.1-4, IV.1.2, IV.6.2, IV.22.1-2, IV.41.1.

[53] Trakatellis, ΛΟΓΟΣ ΑΓΩΝΙΣΤΙΚΟΣ, 531.

[54] For a small sampling of primary source material evidencing the broad way in which so many fathers viewed inspiration, see Craig D. Allert, *A High View of Scripture? The*

critical scholar, asking questions of authenticity or intentions of the biblical author. But like most early church writers, he simply accepts the text as it is before him, divinely provided and fully authoritative as it stands. D'Alès remarks, "He shows the solid consistency of texture in God's activity.... Scripture is to serve as a touchstone for eliminating every tradition that is of merely human origin."[55]

(2) He quotes scripture quite profusely, as if the power of what is said lies not in the expounding on the text but in the citation itself. Trakatellis describes the commentary's dependence on the text, saying it "is inundated with biblical quotations: lengthy biblical pericopes or short passages constantly are interwoven with his own comments, while on the other hand brief scriptural phrases or terms are so fully and subtly integrated into his own sentences that only a specialist's eye can detect them."[56] His almost constant citation of the biblical text reflects his high view of the scriptures.

(3) Hippolytus deliberately employs and studies scripture because of its function: it is the source for true theology necessary for the life of the church. He writes, "The divine scriptures declare to us nothing irrelevant but what is for our very own instruction, and in order to enhance the prophets and to explain everything that was said by them."[57] He says that church leaders who neglect its study will go astray and lead others to do so: "These things happen to people who are uneducated and unintelligent, who do not pay serious attention to the scriptures, but rather follow human traditions, and their own errors, and their own dreams and mythologies and silly words."[58] As a church leader, he commands his commentary readers to study the scriptures "intensely" and "steadfastly."[59] Already noted, Hippolytus reported on a church leader who failed to apply himself to study of the scriptures and in vain lead his flock to the desert to await Christ's return.[60]

(4) Hippolytus sees a truth claim implied in the text that makes the events and the people there historical and real. He believes Daniel to be the author of

---

Authority of the Bible and the Formation of the New Testament Canon (Grand Rapids: Baker Academic, 2007), 185-188.

[55] "Montrant la solide unite de cette trame divine...l'Écriture servira comme une Pierre de touche, pour éliminer les traditions de provenance humaine." D'Alès, *La théologie de Saint Hippolyte*, 120.

[56] Trakatellis, ΛΟΓΟΣ ΑΓΟΝΙΣΤΙΚΟΣ, 529.

[57] οὐδέν γὰρ ἀργὸν κηρύττουσιν ἡμῖν αἱ θεῖαι γραφαί, ἀλλὰ πρὸς μὲν τὴν ἡμῶν αὐτῶν νουθεσίαν, τῶν δὲ προφητῶν μακαρισμὸν καὶ πάντων τῶν ὑπ' αὐτῶν λελαλημένων ἀπόδειξιν. *Commentary on Daniel*, I.7.2.

[58] ταῦτα συμβαίνει τοῖς ἰδιώταις καὶ ἐλαφροῖς ἀνθρώποις, ὅσοι ταῖς μὲν γραφαῖς ἀκριβῶς οὐ προσέχουσιν, ταῖς δὲ ἀνθρωπίναις παραδόσεσιν καὶ ταῖς ἑαυτῶν πλάναις κιὰ τοῖς ἑαυτῶν ἐνυπνίοις καὶ μυθολογίαις καὶ λόγοις γραψδεσι μᾶλλον πείθονται. *Commentary on Daniel*, IV.20.1.

[59] ἐμπόνως; ἀσφαλῶς. *Commentary on Daniel*, IV.18.2; IV.19.1.

[60] *Commentary on Daniel*, IV.18. His report here could refer to Montantist activities.

the book, a real historical figure born under King Joachim's reign, carried to Babylon according, and performs all the deeds described in the Book of Daniel.[61] He asserts that the Daniel text of Susanna was truly a legitimate story from the time of the Babylonian captivity.[62]

Such a historical reading was common among the fathers, who believed that the divine inspiration that was the basis of its authority necessitated historical authenticity of the biblical report. This enabled them to enhance and empower the application to be drawn from it. The people and events reported in the text were historically real, without being under scrutiny of the critical eye that the pagans would later use on it. In fact, the pagan world rarely even looked at scripture until Porphyry would introduce questions on the historic reliability of the Book of Daniel in the mid-third century.[63] Hippolytus does not even ask the basic critical questions of Jerome, such as which textual version of scripture to use. Hippolytus accepts Theodotian's translation and does not inquire about its varieties, but receives it as the Word of God.

Hippolytus goes to surprising lengths to prove Daniel was a prophet. Hippolytus speaks of the words in the text as predictive prophecy, that these scriptures do not lie, and calls Daniel a prophet.[64] In particular, the fulfilled prophecies from this book "prove the prophecy of Daniel is similar to the others [prophets], that it has the same value, that it differs none from the others, that it reveals the past, present, and future."[65] Thus, as common to the early church, he presents Daniel as a true prophet of God, recipient of the visions and dreams from heaven, possessing the Holy Spirit, and a champion of fidelity, piety, wisdom, and virtue. As a demonstration of his prophecy's divine approval, Hippolytus alleges beyond the text that Daniel's face was transformed like an angel's with a fiery face and burning eyes when he delivered the interpretation of Nebuchadnezzar's dream.[66] Trakatellis argues that "Daniel's eminence as a prophet and as a person of God, and lend more weight to the authority and veracity of his words, which in turn constitute Hippolytus' basis for nearly all

---

[61] *Commentary on Daniel*, I.1. Cf. 2 Kings 24:8, 24:12ff, and Daniel 1:2.

[62] *Commentary on Daniel*, I.14.

[63] Porphyry's critical and polemic study of Daniel is lost, with sections remaining on in Jerome's *Commentary on Daniel*. Hidal compares this critical method to the younger Antiochene School which also critically questioned the text in this fashion. Hidal, "Apocalypse, Persecution, and Exegesis," 50.

[64] That the text contains predictive prophecy, see *Commentary on Daniel*, II.19, 22; IV.5, 12, 13, 18, 23. That these scriptures do not lie, see I.5, 14, 29-32; IV.6, 21, 24. For Hippolytus' explicit references to Daniel as prophet, see I.1, II.22, 26; III.12; IV.15, 24, 25.

[65] ἵνα ἐπιδείξωμεν τὴν προφητείαν τοῦ Δανιὴλ ὁμοίαν τοῖς λοιποῖς καὶ ἴσην, ἐν μηδενὶ διαλλάσσουσαν, πρὸς ἀπόδειξιν τῶν ἤδη μὲν γεγονότων καὶ ὄντων καὶ αὖθις ἐσομένων. *Commentary on Daniel*, III.12.3.

[66] *Commentary on Daniel*, III.7.5-7.

of his arguments."[67] The Book of Daniel contains a wealth of application from God for any suffering group of believers willing to pluck from its storehouse of treasure.

، As to the extent of scripture, Christianity had not yet formally canonized the New Testament scriptures by the time of Hippolytus, but the collection of Hebrew scriptures were fundamental to the fathers' understanding of scripture.[68] In another work, *Contra Gaium*, Hippolytus argues for the genuineness of the Book of Revelation.[69]

Besides recognizing Hippolytus' unique use of the Hebrew scriptures, Goodspeed claims that he demonstrates a broad scriptural familiarity as the first Christian writer to "reflect II Peter, and he must have known James and Jude at least slightly, for he once quotes the first verse of James."[70] For his Old Testament text, Hippolytus uses the prevailing Greek translation of *Daniel*, the Theodotian version, which includes the story of *Susanna*, the *Hymns of the Three Youths*, and the story of *Bel and the Dragon*. These additions are included in the Septuagint and in the Vulgate, but are omitted from the Masoretic text of the Hebrew scriptures.[71] Hippolytus rebukes the Jews for omitting it from scripture and accuses them of not recognizing God's οἰκονομία "administration" of revelation.[72] The motive he ascribes them is their shame

---

[67] Trakatellis, ΛΟΓΟΣ ΑΓΟΝΙΣΤΙΚΟΣ, 531.

[68] For an analysis of the development of the Old Testament and New Testament canons with all the difficulties surrounding their exact dating, see David G. Dunbar, "The Biblical Canon," in *Hermeneutics, Authority, and Canon*, ed. D.A. Carson and John D. Woodbridge (Grand Rapids: Zondervan, 1986), 299-360. Hanson says, "It would indeed be an overstatement to say that Hippolytus when he wrote the *Commentary on Daniel* regarded the New Testament as inspired scripture in the same sense as the Old Testament was." R.P.C. Hanson, *Allegory and Event*, 113.

[69] No longer extant, this work is preserved in the Syriac *Commentary on the Apocalypse, Acts, and Epistles* by Dionysius Barsalibî. John Gwynn, "Hippolytus and His 'Heads Against Gaius,'" *Hermathena* 6 (1888): 397-418. In the early seventh century, Andrew of Caesarea confirms his authorship of such a work. *The Fragments of Papias* 10, in *The Apostolic Fathers: Greek Texts and English Translations*, ed. Michael W. Holmes (Grand Rapids: Baker, 1999).

[70] Goodspeed, *A History of Early Christian Literature*, 150.

[71] The story of *Susanna* is placed before Daniel chapter 1 in the Septuagint and as chapter 13 in the Vulgate. *Bel and the Dragon* is placed as Daniel 14 in the Septuagint. *The Song of the Three Youth*, also called *The Prayer of Azarias*, is inserted by the Septuagint after Daniel 3:23 as a hymn by the three youth after their deliverance by the Lord from the fiery furnace. They are treated as separate books by Old Testament Apocrypha collections. Only Hidal speculates as to Hippolytus' use of the Hebrew text, which he denies; Hippolytus' quotes seem to all be verbatim from the Theodotian text. Hidal, "Apocalypse, Persecution, and Exegesis," 51.

[72] *Commentary on Daniel*, I.14. Hippolytus shares with Origen the belief that Susanna as well as Bel and the Dragon ought to be in canon. The Jews did not treat them as canonical, nor did the West as a whole, but Theodotian's translation contained it. Henry

concerning the behavior of the two Jewish elders who lust after and commit perjury against her. It is a tendency in the West to reject this section as canonical in the early church; Hippolytus shares the belief with Origen, for example, while the position is opposed by Julius Africanus.[73]

The Biblical "Letter," Allegory, and Typology

The divine inspiration of scripture maintained by Jews and early Christians meant that, for them, its words were sacred and thus part of the divine nature of the biblical text. From devotional practice to scholarly study, they gave special attention to the literal reading of the text, *littera*. Charles Kannengiesser remarks, "As God's message to humankind, the Bible made sense by its very *words*...The biblical 'letter' as understood by patristic interpreters had its own status, originating from a divine source in a supernatural way."[74] Reading scripture with this faith perspective was naturally the method of Hippolytus. This literal sense was fastened to the regular reading of the text, taking the meaning from what was naturally conveyed by an original human author through divine direction. However, a higher, deeper, or more distant reading was available to the Christian reader—the "spiritual sense." According to Kannengiesser, "The space of spiritual significance was proper to God's thoughts when authorizing the written, and therefore it transcends the letter of the text."[75]

Ancient Christian exegetes were not always conscious of categories or senses of exegesis, either when imposed on them by prior influences or when practicing them. Although Origen would formulate more distinct categories of literal, moral, and allegorical senses, earlier exegetes like Hippolytus probably would not recognize such clear distinctions and would not be as conscious of their use of scripture at different levels. Still, looking back in history allows us to recognize and distinguish these methods more readily, so a two-fold reading of scripture will be considered for this church father.[76]

Chadwick, *The Early Church*, vol. 1, Pelican History of the Church Series (New York: Penguin Books, 1978), 101-103.

[73] Chadwick describes the correspondence between Origen and Julius on this very point, the latter of whom said that a certain appalling Greek pun in the Susanna text revealed it as an addition to the original book. Chadwick, *Early Church*, 102-103.

[74] Kannengiesser, *Handbook of Patristic Exegesis*, 168.

[75] Kannengiesser, *Handbook of Patristic Exegesis*, 206.

[76] A word of methodological justification is in order here. Early Christian scholars recognize how the distinction of these methods of reading scripture has been oversimplified. Although Frances Young rightly calls for more literary readings and a greater recognition of authorial segments, she seems to do while slighting the use of the traditional categories literal, typological, and allegorical, which she insists "are quite simply inadequate as descriptive tools, let alone analytical tools." Young, *Biblical Exegesis*, 2. While her exploration of literary-critical approaches offer new insights, her

Concerning the sense of scripture, Hippolytus begins with the literal sense and really maintains this position with rare exception. Gustave Bardy distinguishes three methods for Hippolytus' interpretation: the historical, the moral aspect, and the allegorical sense of the text, but most scholars recognize his regular use of moral application and typology with occasional allegory.[77] Hanson describes his scriptural exegesis as the "simple, primitive, literal type. He certainly does allegorize, but not in a very systematic way."[78] On the other hand, Kannengiesser overstates Hippolytus' method of exegetical when he notes in passing, "Allegorism prevailed in Hippolytus' *Commentary on Daniel*."[79] Part of the reason for his statement is his inclusion of typological readings of scripture in the category of allegory, a classification which Hippolytus might not have preferred if he saw typology as a form of prophecy in a more "literal" sense. The allegorical activity of Hippolytus centers mostly on the Susanna story, from which he offers a comprehensive allegorical interpretation of situations of Christian martyrdom and persecution. In what seems to be a blurred distinction between senses, Hippolytus exercises allegory and typology in his exegesis to offer an impressive, comprehensive exhortation to martyrdom.

So, any variation of exegetical method or any methodological imprecision on Hippolytus' part may reflect an exegete not focused on precise method but on the application of scripture towards the present threat against the church. Any parallel in Daniel which he can find to exhort his congregations seems to be appropriate to him. Thus, the authority of scripture that almost any church father would insist on allows Hippolytus to employ the text to bear on the Christian life, sometimes even irrespective of exact methodology. When he deserts a literal reading of the text, then the allegorical reading is still based on a high view of scripture characterizing Jewish and early Christian theory.

Exercising Allegory

Hippolytus identifies the characters and components in Susanna as representative of people and unfriendly external forces in his own third century. The two elders who try to seduce Susanna signify authorities who want to

---

rationale for bypassing the traditional categories is overstated; it is impossible to treat patristic exegesis extensively without at least a fundamental recognition of these categories and methods, as she herself does. Still, her cautions against overuse, misuse, or generalization of these categories are noteworthy, and she admits their usefulness at times. Young, *Biblical Exegesis*, 201.

[77] Bardy, "Introduction," *Commentary on Daniel*, vol. 14, Sources Chrétiennes, trans. Maurice Lefèvre (Paris: Éditions du Cerf, 1947), 19-54.

[78] R.P.C Hanson, *Allegory and Event*, 114.

[79] Kannengiesser, *Handbook of Patristic Exegesis*, 251.

damage God's people in Hippolytus' own day and throughout all time.[80] Specifically, they represent the Jews and the Gentiles who persecute the church socially and politically, "The church is vexed and placed in distress not only by the Jews but also by the Gentiles and by those who call themselves Christians and are not."[81] Hippolytus' use of terminology is odd here, because although he says that the figures function as a "type" (εἰς τύπον δείκνυνται), he evolves his interpretation of them into allegory, blurring the two senses of scripture. Other times, such as his description of the Jewish Sabbath, Hippolytus uses the term "type" more accurately to describe a prophetic image of the final rest of Christians.[82] The two terms are distinguished in most fathers in that the allegory represents a spiritualizing sense whereby the literal meaning of the text is removed, while typology kept the meaning grounded in the text. The original event was historically real while prefiguring an event to come, its antitype, which fulfills the prophetic type. The connection between a type and its antitype is real; there is an "historical connection between the poles."[83] Hippolytus seems to use the word "type" in a representative fashion though, not in a historical sense in which the types prophetically point to future events. He has a fluid use of typology, extending it into a spiritual sense depending on the context and the exact interpretation of the passage's details. Like the rabbis who shared a belief that scripture was divinely inspired, Hippolytus understands any prophetic type and antitype to be foreordained by God.

Susanna is a type προετυποῦτο of the church and the bath into which Susanna descends is a symbol for baptism.[84] Her husband Joachim who stands by her typifies Christ. Whereas the garden represents the community of saints, its place setting Babylon represents the world at large.[85] In this or any case, he

---

[80] οἱ δὲ δύο πρεσβύτεροι εἰς τύπον δείκνυνται τῶν δύο λαῶν τῶν ἐπιβουλευόντων τῇ ἐκκλεσίᾳ, εἰς μὲν ὁ ἐκ περιτομῆς καὶ εἰς ὁ ἐξ ἐθνῶν. *Commentary on Daniel*, I.14. Cf. I.15, τοῦτο ημαίνει; cf. I.21.2, ἡ γὰρ ἐκκλεσία οὐ μόνον ὑπὸ Ἰουδαίων θλίβεται καὶ στενοχωρεῖται, ἀλλὰ καὶ ὑπὸ ἐθνῶν. Bardy translates the expressions "représenter en figure" and "signifier." Hippolytus uses the word "type" here but describes allegory.

[81] ἡ γὰρ ἐκκλεσία οὐ μόνον ὑπὸ Ἰουδαίων θλίβεται καὶ στενοχωρεῖται, ἀλλὰ καὶ ὑπὸ ἐθνῶν. *Commentary on Daniel*, I.21.2; cf. I.29.

[82] τὸ σάββατον τύπος ἐστὶν καὶ εἰκὼν τῆς μελλούσης βασιλείας τῶν ἁγίων, ἡνίκα συμβασιλεύσουσιν τῷ Χριστῷ. *Commentary on Daniel*, IV.23.5 Specifically, he says that the Sabbath is "a type and figure" of the future kingdom of the saints when they will reign with Christ. He sees Revelation 17:10 revealing how the thousand year rest is not yet here.

[83] McLeod makes the distinction in the way that later Antiochenes understood the meaning of scripture, but these principles can apply generally to other rational, historical exegetes. McLeod, *Image of God*, 20. This fluid method of the typological fits the description that Simonetti gives of Hippolytus' method. Simonetti, *Biblical Interpretation*, 28.

[84] *Commentary on Daniel*, I.14; cf. I.16.

[85] *Commentary on Daniel*, I.14, I.17.

does not use the word ἀλληγορέω in any form to describe his own exegetical method; in fact, he uses the term τύπος and goes on to allegorize the text.[86] However, one can certainly contrast his allegory with that of Origen as clearly different in degree and frequency.[87] Goodspeed comments, "He was less atomistic and more historical in his interpretation than his Alexandrian contemporary Origen."[88]

It becomes clear in the commentary that Hippolytus understands the Roman state to be among those who are symbolized by the two elders in the Susanna tale and the satraps in the Danielic lions' den story. They are the ones who currently persecute the church cruelly. Besides the description of the Jews and Gentiles who "harass and bring into agony" the church, there are clear parallels implied between the components of the narrative and present day events.[89] By his use of allegory, Hippolytus makes clear the exact relationship between the events in Daniel and the persecutions against the Christians that plague Hippolytus' own congregations. This is further seen when he allegorizes the details of the angels clothed in linen in Daniel 10 to refer to Christ, bringing together these tribulations by a common heavenly messenger.[90]

Hippolytus saw his contemporary situation with its persecutions of Christians as clearly prefigured in the Book of Daniel. By "prefigure" one should not imagine specific predictive prophecy of third century CE persecutions, but the belief that the Danielic persecutions less specifically foreshadow those of the church. This foreshadowing seems similar enough to contemporary persecutions that early Christian minds could associate them with each other and gain apocalyptic hope from these older models. Hippolytus comes just short of saying that the persecutions witnessed in Daniel are a prophetic type of the persecutions under Severus. Thus, the two elders "show in a type" those who would persecute God's people. Allegory brings out this secret prophetic meaning that prefigured the Roman persecutions that came in his own day. The foreshadowing may apply to the suffering of Christians before Hippolytus' own time, and God's people throughout history, but it has one definite fulfillment in the early third century Roman persecutions.

Exercising Typology

A biblical "type" τύπος is "figure," "image," or "model" between similar features in different parts of scripture. Typology is traditionally as a person, event, or institution that functions as prophecy in one part of scripture and finds fulfillment in a later part of scripture. Kannengiesser suggests that the notion of

---

[86] *Commentary on Daniel*, 1.14.
[87] Trakatellis, ΛΟΓΟΣ ΑΓΩΝΙΣΤΙΚΟΣ, 531, n.13.
[88] Goodspeed, *A History of Early Christian Literature*, 145.
[89] *Commentary on Daniel*, I.14, 15, 16, 20, 21, 29; III.30.
[90] *Commentary on Daniel*, IV.37.

the Law as a "living tradition" between God and his people allowed the Old Testament to interact with the New Testament, like a vision of history with symbolic values.[91] Young emphasizes how "usually types and antitypes contribute to the prophetic understanding of scripture, and so past narrative points to present fulfillment, or present instance is prophetic of future reality."[92] She also recognizes the sense of drama that comes with typology when she remarks: "'Types' usually relate to the Christian sense of a providential history leading to a denouement," in which there is a sense of resolution to the plot.[93]

Hippolytus engages in much typological interpretation to understand the prophecies of the Book of Daniel. Hippolytus specifically uses the phrases εἰς τύπον δείκνυνται "show by a type" and προετυποῦτο "prototype" for his typology. He supposes that this Old Testament book looks beyond itself for fulfillment, as the texts were written with a specific view to the future: Christ himself and his people, the church.

Daniélou recognizes Hippolytus' typology occurring on "three levels": Christ at his first advent (Christological), Christ in his church (ecclesiastical), and Christ in the end of time (eschatological) that deserves further examination. He attributes a "master typology" to Hippolytus, a blueprint that relates all typological events centered on Christ as having an additional referent in Adam and Eve.[94] Susanna walks in a garden both as an allegory for the spiritual life of a Christian and also as an echo of Eve in the Garden of Eden.[95] "As the devil disguised himself of old in Paradise under the form of a serpent, so he hid within the elders in order to destroy Eve a second time."[96]   By presenting Susanna as the church tempted by Satan while alluding to her as a new Eve, Hippolytus can find a referent in the text in both future and past antitypes, an occurrence which Daniélou calls an "extension of typology."[97] The future antitype can be the events surrounding the first or the second advent of Christ, while the past type is a different Christological model.[98] Daniélou describes this

---

[91] Kannengiesser, *Handbook of Patristic Exegesis*, 229.

[92] Young, *Biblical Exegesis*, 153. However, I think Hippolytus would dispute her claim that "it is not its character as historical event which makes a 'type'; what matters is its mimetic quality." Her discussion of typology as ahistorical and instead mythical (pp. 152-61), although intriguing, does not directly correspond to the precedence on the historical seen in patristic thinkers like Hippolytus.

[93] Young, *Biblical Exegesis*, 153.

[94] Daniélou, *Gospel Message*, 267-69.

[95] *Commentary on Daniel*, I.17.

[96] ὥσπερ γὰρ τότε ἐν τῷ παραδείσῳ ἐνεκρύβη ὁ διάβολος ἐν τῷ ὄφει, οὕτω καὶ νῦν ἐν τοῖς πρεσβυτέροις ἐγκρυβεὶς τὴν ἑαυτοῦ ἐνεκίσσησεν ἐπιθυμίαν, ἵνα πάλιν ἐκ δευτέρου διαφθείρῃ τὴν Εὔαν. *Commentary on Daniel*, I.18.4.

[97] Daniélou, *Gospel Message*, 257-71.

[98] This is the phenomenon in Tyconius' rule of part/whole with respect to Christ and his body in which the future antitype can be the events surrounding the first or the second advent of Christ, while the past antitypes are the opportunities for perfection or ideal in

phenomenon: "Hippolytus manages to construct a typological series in which the middle term is not only a type of the full reality revealed in Christ, but it is also a fulfillment of an even earlier type in the history of Israel."[99]

This same occurrence can be recognized in the episode of Daniel in the lion's den. Daniel's practicing of his faith in obedience to God found him at odds with a royal decree and then overnight in the lions' den, yet he remained unharmed. The beasts submitted to Adam in the garden and to Daniel in the den; the rewards or punishments for obedience and disobedience allude to both Eden and heaven. In his use of typology, at times Hippolytus adopts a contrast between partial (μερικῶς) and plenary (καθ᾽ ὅλου) fulfillment, a practice that was fundamental to Justin's writings.[100]

A common point of imagery in early Christian typology is that of deliverance, and Daniel's delivery from the lions' den provides a wealth of typology for Hippolytus. Daniel's rescue from the lions typifies the deliverance accomplished by Christ over sin and death that is available to the believer. The use of Old Testament imagery was common in early Christian reading of the New Testament.[101] In Judaism, the deliverance of Daniel, Noah, Jonah, and the three young men are common examples of deliverance of God's people, and early Christian art and liturgy employ these same images to illustrate the resurrection of Christ, baptism, and the final eschatological resurrection of all believers.[102] Hippolytus relates Daniel's deliverance from the lions with that of Jonah, with the three youths in the furnace, and the crossing of the Red Sea.[103] Of these "long-standing typological traditions," Daniélou recognizes the latter as particularly Irenaean in interpretation. Concerning the "horseman thrown backward" in Genesis 49:17, he remarks: "Returning from the end to the beginning, the Savior raised up and set upon his feet Adam who had fallen," and also, "Jesus is the firstborn of a virgin to make it clear that in him is re-created the first-formed Adam."[104] Thus, the deliverance of Daniel in the lions' den comes to prefigure the deliverance of any believer of God from the clutches of their enemies. So also, the men represent those who secretly watch

---

the history of God's people. In fact, Simonetti suggests that Hippolytus' allegorical interpretations foreshadow Tyconius' fourth rule of interpretation of prophetic texts, *de genere et specie*: sometimes scripture passes from the part to the whole (from species to genus) and vice-versa. Simonetti, *Biblical Interpretation*, 26.

[99] Daniélou, *Gospel Message*, 268.

[100] Daniélou, *Gospel Message*, 268-69.

[101] For example, Christ paralleled his death and resurrection with the sign of Jonah (Matt. 12:39-40); Justin interpreted Psalm 22:21, "Save me from the mouth of the lion," as representing deliverance from the powers of death. Cf. Justin, *Dialogue with Trypho*, CV.3-5.

[102] Daniélou, *Gospel Message*, 269.

[103] *Commentary on Daniel*, II.36; II.35; II.19.

[104] *Commentary on Daniel*, IV.11; Daniélou, *Gospel Message*, 269, n.36.

Christians in order to gather legal evidence against them.[105] Such profound parallels captured the attention of Hippolytus' persecuted churches, and this was a primary goal in Hippolytus' crafting of his *Commentary on Daniel*.

Paraenetic Goal of Exegesis

This typology and allegory presented in the commentary are the basis for Hippolytus' exhortations to his congregations. Their sufferings find validity when they realize that just as God prophesied suffering for their Lord and Savior, he did so for their very own sufferings in the Book of Daniel. The typology and prophecy contained in the text reveal how God's people will experience persecution and even martyrdom. This development of martyrdom into a Christologically minded experience was the exact chord to which Hippolytus appealed. The force of this divine unfolding is not just one of generic fulfillment, however, as if the events merely represent all who suffer at the hands of oppressing enemies of the faith. The fulfillment have a sense that is specific and personal to them in the early third century under Severan rule.

This exegesis with a pastoral goal ought to be recognized as a type of paraenetic exegesis. Paraenesis is an "exhortation, advice, counsel," or "a hortatory composition."[106] In this case, the commentary includes an ongoing exhortation to be willing to suffer martyrdom. This fits with the characterization described by Frances Young: "Paraenetic exegesis drew on scriptural material to foster a certain way of life, applying the text directly to those being addressed." Such an intentional, goal-driven interpretive process allows the exegete a form that "served to delineate and reinforce identity."[107]

Jeffrey Sobosan describes the paraenetic role of a presbyter based on Irenaeus' description in *Against Heresies*.[108] Such an elder was a teacher in the tradition of the apostles, a minister to the congregation but not necessarily a bishop, and a leader in the Christian community with special administrative concerns. As particular communities arose, it would be important to have one person "assigned the task of preserving the faith, teaching it and making sure to defend it against error."[109] Hippolytus would serve in this special capacity, guarding and exhorting his congregations in the faith.

Does this presbyter exegete employ Daniel to explain persecution or does the persecution influence his reading of Daniel? Sten Hidal makes an odd claim about the exegesis constructs the martyrdom motif in the commentary. He

---

[105] *Commentary on Daniel*, I.14, εἰς τύπον δείκνυνται, and I.15, σημαίνει. Bardy translates the expressions "représenter en figure" and "signifier."

[106] *The Oxford English Dictionary*, 2nd ed. (Oxford: Clarendon Press, 1989), 186.

[107] Young, *Biblical Exegesis*, 129.

[108] Sobosan, "The Role of the Presbyter," 129-46. His treatment includes the New Testament standard for presbyter and bishop as well as the historical application of it.

[109] Sobosan, "The Role of the Presbyter," 146.

remarks: "The stress on martyrdom in a way conforms to the apocalyptic character of the Book of Daniel, but is not always supported by the exegesis. Hippolytus has a pastoral aim with the commentary; he wishes to console and strengthen the church against enemies from the outside as well as from the inside."[110] Hidal rightly recognizes that martyrdom is seems to influence Hippolytus' interpretation of Daniel, but consequentially implies that martyrdom governs the reading of text rather than the other way around. Our study shows a more dual-complementary role in which martyrdom does find consistent exegetical support, while the Book of Daniel clearly draws Hippolytus to its paraenetic, martyrological potential.

Although Hippolytus was the first to employ such a comprehensive paraenetic exegetical work, Young explains that with the development of more details commentaries in the years to come, patristic writers normalized their methods: "When more systematic commentary on whole books began, long-established hermeneutical keys, deriving from this initial process of reception and appropriation, were employed." Among the keys she identifies is a prophetic "mind" or intent of the Old Testament that allowed for predictions to be understood as direct, veiled, or mimetic.[111] In the case of the presbyter Hippolytus, the concern was to employ the scriptures in the life and faith of a persecuted church. Here, paraenetic exegesis founds its place: "The Bible's principal function in the patristic period was the generation of a way of life, grounded in the truth about the way things are, as revealed by God's Word. Exegesis served this end."[112]

Apocalyptic overtones of part of Daniel complement the paraenetic purpose of Hippolytus' exegesis. A principle of apocalyptic literature is the important relationship between events in this world and rewards in the next life. Old Testament, intertestamental, and New Testament apocalyptic material call for suffering, sacrifice, and even death for the Lord in this life. As examined above, there is a postponing of the judgment and justice that is due to each member of Christ's kingdom until a time that is both imminent but next-worldly. This interim period proffers persecution and suffering; heaven offers rewards for the faithful and divine justice against the unfaithful and the persecutors. Those "sovereignty explanations" functioned to offer hope to God's people in the absence of theological explanation of chaotic and harmful events, and provided guarantee of final justification through God's judgment. Such a verse occurs at Daniel 11:35, which describes a "refining and purifying" effect that comes from persecution. Collins explains the phenomenon: "The purification bespeaks an interest in individual salvation as distinct (though not opposed to) the

---

[110] Hidal, "Apocalypse, Persecution, and Exegesis," 51. The oddity seems to lie in his precise meaning of "exegesis," in which every application corresponds to a specific verse. Such specificity does not characterize all patristic preaching, however.

[111] Young, *Biblical Exegesis*, 130.

[112] Young, *Biblical Exegesis*, 215.

deliverance of the nation. The death of the martyrs is not vicarious. They are the ones who are purified. The *maskilim* have their effect on the *rabbim* by instructing them."[113] Hippolytus' congregations might suffer now, but their plight guarantees heavenly reward. There is no effort to reform society collectively and often public life is shunned; the concern is primarily with avoiding sin and cleansing oneself through suffering. Hippolytus has a greater spiritual goal for the church that martyrdom serves—to be pure and holy before God, like Christ was the unblemished lamb at his martyr sacrifice.

The stories in Daniel provide a forum for Hippolytus to call for believers to stand firm in the faith. They are to persevere in trials, whether God intervenes to save them or not. The Lord who saved Daniel from the lions and who preserved the three youths in the fiery furnace could certainly protect faithful Christians against their persecutors. Hippolytus does not guarantee their deliverance will be fulfilled in this world, as the Lord may choose for them to suffer and die only to vindicate their sacrifice in the life to come. They are simply to be ready if God calls upon them for martyrdom. Tertullian developed the hope of reward that accompanied this outlook, insisting that Christians should view martyrdom as an event preceding full salvation.[114]

As the inspection of the commentary provenance revealed, a milieu of persecution and martyrdom was almost normative for Christians living in a non-Christian world under pagan rulers. Christian readers of the *Commentary on Daniel* would see this ideal modeled by God's people in Babylon, and they would understand themselves to be God's new people in a new Babylon. The early church's literary allusions to Babylon reflect its self-understanding as a people exiled, prisoners perhaps in paganism's very capitol, and surrounded by hostility against the elect of God. Both cities shared the reputation as the political and religious capitol of world empires with renown for their luxuries and moral corruption. A notion of these cities as the archetypal enemy of the people of God with a pattern of harassing and even martyring their religious enemies is particularly apparent in the references to Babylon in the early church. Daniel 4:30 typifies the concept that Babylon was dedicated not to the glory of God but stood as a monument to ungodly powers of this world: "The king reflected and said, 'Is this not Babylon the great, which I myself have built as a royal residence by the might of my power and for the glory of my majesty?'" Concerning the salutation of 1 Peter, "She who is in Babylon, chosen together with you, sends you greetings" (5:13) Lenski writes: "Those living in this Babylon [Rome] will be the first to suffer, in fact, it seems that their suffering has already begun when Peter writes. This salutation has the sound of: *Morituri salutamus!*"[115]

---

[113] John J. Collins, *Daniel: A Commentary on the Book of Daniel* (Minneapolis: Fortress Press, 1993), 386.

[114] Tertullian, *Against Marcion*, IV.39.4; so Frend, *Rise of Christianity*, 419, n.170.

[115] R.C.H. Lenski, *The Interpretation of the Epistles of St. Peter, St. John and St. Jude*

Close examination of the text clearly reveals a specific goal: to encourage the readers of the commentary that martyrdom is worthwhile because God's sovereignty and rewards supersede the persecution of this world. Hippolytus is a pastor to his congregations, opening God's Word in a way that will encourage their weary and anxious state, all the while furthering the ideals of spiritual development through suffering that this pastor has for the church. Hidal accurately says that Hippolytus takes a "paranaetic-typological view of the Book of Daniel."[116] This specific goal of his exegesis explains why he solidifies the biblical text on the subject of martyrdom, finding typology and moral parallels between Daniel and contemporary events. The apocalyptic genre of Daniel lends itself perfectly to the purpose he has for the text and his readers, as the stories offer hope to the congregations who share the circumstances of being persecuted at the hand of foreign oppressors. His goal of preparing his readers for martyrdom is accomplished by drawing moral exhortations from the narratives of Daniel, employing the apocalyptic genre for encouragement, and providing Christological meanings to the text.

The next feature of our study reinforces this expectation of martyrdom: an anticipation of upcoming eschatological events. Suffering in this life can be inexorably linked to greater eschatological events.

History and Eschatology

Hippolytus' exegesis of Daniel and consequential pastoral exhortations is undergirded by a complex understanding of history and eschatology. His works *Chronicle* and *On Christ and the Antichrist* demonstrate his emphasis on understanding the temporal and reveal to us his exact systematic theology of time.[117] In *Chronicle*, he gives a history of God's interaction with mankind from creation to the year 254. In *On Christ and the Antichrist*, he lays out the manner of the coming of the Antichrist and the chronological relationship between the events at the end of the world based on apocalyptic material in the Old and New Testaments. Additionally, his treatise *Against Plato* explores the logistics of the afterlife, and offers little to our interest except to see the great reward that is due a Christian in the next life. The benefits are not displayed in the traditional millennium but in the final beatitude.[118]

(Minneapolis: Augsburg, 1966), 232. Cf. Revelation 14:8, 16:19, 17:5, 18:2, 18:10, 18:21; *2 Barnabas*, 11:1, 67:7; *Sibyllene Oracles*, 5:143, 159, 434.

[116] Hidal, "Apocalypse, Persecution, and Exegesis," 50. Daniélou specifically contrasts this specific goal in Hippolytus' exegesis with that of Origen. He concludes that Hippolytus was pastoral and liturgical, and Origen's exegesis coming later would be methodical and scientific. Daniélou, *Gospel Message*, 259.

[117] For an overview of his eschatological works, see Daley, *The Hope of the Early Church*, 38-41.

[118] Hippolytus, *Against Plato* 3.

Hippolytus' use of the Old Testament is in line with the belief at the time of Paul when many Jews and Christians believed themselves to be living in the last days. In the first century of Christianity, there is a shift in hermeneutical center of scripture from the Torah to the prophetic messages of the bible. Christians saw the first advent and passion of Christ prophesied in the Old Testament, which secured the text for their own purposes. Then, they applied the prophecies contained in scripture to the final age and the second advent of Christ. For early Christians, the events of Jewish history were seen as prefiguring the events of the end of time, events that began with Christ himself.

The prophetic passages in the Book of Daniel provide an exegetical forum for Hippolytus to discuss eschatological issues and to employ them in the exhortation of suffering Christians. In his *Commentary on Daniel*, he reveals his belief that the reign of the Antichrist and the immediate end of the world will come six thousand years after creation, or approximately the year 500 CE.[119] This will usher in a "Sabbath that is a type and image of the future Kingdom of the saints, when they will reign with Christ" after his coming from heaven, as John narrates in the Apocalypse. The present Sabbath is a type and image of the coming kingdom of the saints.[120]

The apocalyptic overtones of the text complement the martyrdom motif by their otherworldly solutions to Christian suffering. Hippolytus neither develops a full millenarian hope nor an immediate eschatology, postponing final things until the typological six days will expire. His use of futuristic rather than realized eschatology is seen with his unique understanding of the world's empires and the Antichrist. Hippolytus sees world history as a government of evil powers who is granted a brief period of rule by God before the day of final salvation and great judgment. In the vision of Daniel 7, the world empires of apocalyptic history were set in descending order of merit, with that of Rome the last and worst. This was the same worldview the Essenes held, although emphasizing a greater dualism of light and darkness, between good and evil.[121] The Roman Empire currently persecuting them is the climax of these unfriendly world empires, yet is not the one to be led by the Antichrist. For Hippolytus, the Antichrist will come from this Roman womb but is not yet here. He can speak of the adversary's empire as current in that his will be a continuation of the present one. Hippolytus identifies the name of the Antichrist as *Latinus* or "Latin man," most applicable to his political and social circumstances and to the number 666.[122] Expectation of the apocalypse in Hippolytus' Daniel commentary is tempered with sober patience that the time is not yet here. This

---

[119] *Commentary on Daniel*, IV.23.

[120] τὸ σάββατον τύπος ἐστὶν καὶ εἰκὼν τῆς μελλούσης βασιλείας τῶν ἁγίων, ἡνίκα συμβασιλεύσουσιν τῷ Χριστῷ. *Commentary on Daniel*, IV.23.5; cf. IV.37.

[121] Frend, *Rise of Christianity*, 29. For possible Essene influence on Hippolytus, see Black, "The Account of the Essenes," 172-75.

[122] Hippolytus, *On Christ and the Antichrist*, 50.

is what leads Dunbar to remark that these interpretations merely "provide a focus and guide" to some future kingdom's persecutions.[123]

Nevertheless, even this apocalyptic expectation redirects his readers' thoughts from the eschaton to the present events and sufferings of the church. The sufferings of Christians are a revealed type of the suffering Christ portrayed. He is their prototype, and Hippolytus used Daniel and other scripture to assert this. Hippolytus' view of history with a delayed parousia informs his emphatic insistence on accepting suffering as Christ did in a redemptive way. Christians, even the persecuted congregations at the beginning of the third century, should not be so parousia-focused that they should expect to escape the flames by virtue of Christ's personal return. Instead, Hippolytus' eschatology is Christological.[124] It is Christ who will "give us power when all the strength and glory of this life is gone, will give us his hand and raise us, 'as living people from the dead,' from Hades for a resurrection to life."[125] His emphasis is on his readers' response to these things; their moral responsibility is stressed when he declares, "Each one recognizes that on the day when he leaves this world he is already judged, for the consummation has come upon him."[126]

Hippolytus' model of martyrdom combined an apocalyptic spirit and a rigorous courage to suffer at the hands of the world. In the early third century, Montanism was popular and its ethical rigor may have appealed to Hippolytus.[127] However, his eschatology is of a distant future without the Montanist immediacy, and he clearly objects to their withdrawal to the desert to

---

[123] Dunbar, "Eschatological Exegesis," 338. This same eschatology led Simonetti and Hidal to remark how some symbols in Daniel referred to the current Roman Empire for Hippolytus, without explaining the tension between the "already and not yet" applied to the Antichrist. Simonetti, *Biblical Interpretation*, 28; Hidal, "Apocalypse, Persecution, and Exegesis," 50. With this teaching, Bonwetsch remarks that Hippolytus "cut the nerve of expectation of the end in that the Second Coming would come only in the distant future." Bonwetsch, *Studien zu den Kommentaren Hippolyts*, 53; Gammie, "A Journey Through Danielic Spaces," 148, n.11.

[124] Daley, *The Hope of the Early Church*, 39.

[125] τότε ἐνδυναμούμεθα ὑπὸ Χριστοῦ τοῦ ὀρέγοντος χεῖρα καὶ ἐγείροντος ἡμᾶς ὡς ἐκ νεκρῶν ζῶντας καὶ ὡς ἀπὸ ᾅδου εἰς ἀνάστασιν ζωῆς. *Commentary on Daniel*, IV.39.

[126] γινώσκων εἰς ἕκαστος ὅτι ᾖ ἂν ἡμέρᾳ ἐξέλθη ἐκ τοῦ κόσμου τούτου ἤδη κέκριται. *Commentary on Daniel*, IV.18.

[127] Hidal, "Apocalypse, Persecution, and Exegesis," 51. He offers no evidence nor does he speculate further on this provoking thought. There is little scholarship that directly assesses Montanist influence on Hippolytus. It is a project worthy in itself, I think; he shares qualities with and yet is unlike these people. Unlike the Montanists, he clearly lacks an immediate expectation of its fulfillment, as developed above. His negative comments in the *Commentary on Daniel* IV.18-19 affirm his tendency away from Montanism, as do the remarks in Hippolytus, *The Refutation of All Heresies*, 8.12. For a possible response of Hippolytus to the movement in Rome, see Williams, "'Hippolytan' Reactions to Montanism."

await the imminent parousia.[128] In fact, he presents their activities as a source of embarrassment for the church because of their over reactive reading of scripture and misappropriated visions.

---

[128] *Commentary on Daniel*, IV.19.

CHAPTER 5

Conclusive Pastoral Purpose of the *Commentary*

Hippolytus crafted his *Commentary on Daniel* with the hope of encouraging Christians who were suffering persecution and confronted with the threat of martyrdom. This book establishes the presence of a martyrdom motif in the commentary that functioned to bolster the life of the church congregations that received it. As a presbyter, Hippolytus crafted this work with a significant interest in paralleling the Daniel stories and prophecies under Babylonian captivity with the study of the church under Roman rule. The commentary also contains rich insights into theology, exegetical methodology, church history, and the church's perception of itself in the early third century CE, and the work remains ripe for analysis in other areas besides the prominent martyrdom motif. A complex historical and theological milieu is behind the writing of this work, offering a wide variety of issues addressed.

Hippolytus intended for his analysis and theological reflection on Daniel to center on the issue of martyrdom in order to firm up the resolve of his readers who should withstand persecution and persevere even to the point of death. As this early church presbyter comments on the persecution stories contained in the Book of Daniel, the force of his commentary is paraenetic and pedagogical, empathizing with those who suffer for the faith. This fits with the characterization described by Frances Young: "Paraenetic exegesis drew on scriptural material to foster a certain way of life, applying the text directly to those being addressed." Such an intentional, goal-driven interpretive process allows the exegete a form that "served to delineate and reinforce identity."[1] Hippolytus regularly revisits the commentary element of teaching his readers for readiness to suffer for Christ.

This chapter reiterates the significance of a martyrdom motif and reviews how this book unveiled it. As a synthesis chapter, this section summarizes the surrounding historical events and theological traditions that prompted the writing of the commentary, reviews the type of passages in the commentary displaying the theme with specific examples, and analyzes his exegetical method for a complete synthesis of his effort in the commentary. This review will refine our understanding of how Hippolytus endowed his exegesis of Daniel with martyrdom which, in turn, provided a pastoral encouragement to

---

[1] Young, *Biblical Exegesis*, 129.

oppressed and beleaguered Christians. This chapter of synthesis also functions as a quick summary of the entire work for a reader wanting an abbreviated analysis.

Background to the *Commentary*

Hippolytus wrote his *Commentary on Daniel* in a historical milieu of Roman policy and persecution that had spanned several prior generations but that had recently become worse. He had inherited a theology of martyrdom that influenced his interpretation of these events, as well as a tradition of a high view of scripture. This combination allowed for an exegesis that was authoritative and tailored toward bolstering persecuted believers' faiths. His writings reflect a church father that is rigorous in his theological belief systems, including the conviction that Christians should not compromise core Christian beliefs nor yield under religious persecution.

Historical Milieu

The social context of the early third century was one of renewed Roman persecution against the church. In 202, Emperor Severus called for the entire empire to join in the worshipping the Unconquered Sun, *Sol Invictus*. Christian noncompliance prompted the emperor to issue an additional edict that outlawed all new conversions to Christianity. Persecution under Severus was most severe in Africa, but the early church left vivid descriptions of anti-Christian violence in Rome, Corinth, Antioch, and Cappadocia. The result was a large number of martyrs within the Christian church. At times the persecution was sporadic and only local, but at times it was more widespread and severe. Such was the situation in Hippolytus' own day, and as a presbyter he had to shepherd persecuted Christian congregations that were confronted with fear of capture, hardships of secrecy, the temptation toward apostasy, as well as the difficult problem of dealing with apostates. These practical questions were complicated by additional questions about God's apparent inaction during these trials, his ongoing providence, and the divine purposes of their suffering.

A survey of the history of the persecution of Christians prior to the third century CE provides the backdrop to the inimical events in Hippolytus' own day. Three important factors emerge that shaped Hippolytus' understanding of martyrdom and persecution. First, the extensive history and nature of persecution preceding and culminating in the early third century Rome intimidated Christians but also provided a tradition of martyrdom to be cherished and idealized, a tradition that also justified martyrdom and provided ideology for it. Scholars usually classify the historical tendencies of the empire against Christians in three chronological groups: persecution first by the hands of the Jews, then by Roman society, and finally the Roman government—in that order. The greatest nemesis of the early church in the first three centuries was the Roman imperial policy and the crowds of citizens that took liberty to unite against Christians. An examination of the nature of persecution against the church in this era begins to inform us of the nightmare in which Hippolytus found himself, and a brief tracing of imperial policy from Nero to Severus regarding Christians divulges good reason for the church in Hippolytus' day to take seriously the reality of martyrdom and persecution. From Nero to Marcus Aurelius, from sporadic and local persecutions to empire-wide policies, Roman citizens and policy intimidated Christians at regular intervals. In particular, the mass tortures and brutal executions in Lyons and Philadelphia during the reign of Aurelius cast a shadow on the state of Christianity. This is the era into which Hippolytus was born, about 170 CE. The stories of heroes of the faith and the tragedies of former persecutions combined to make a tradition of martyrdom in the third century CE, at the time when Septimius Severus handed down his own legislation of greater severity than his predecessors.

A second important factor shaping Hippolytus' understanding of martyrdom and persecution were the available options for avoiding death that would confront any persecuted believer. He exhorts his congregations to withstand formal persecution, not accepting freedom when it comes with the price of denying the faith. From Trajan's instruction to Pliny in 117, imperial court trials included giving Christians the opportunity to recant their Christian faith and escape with their lives. This policy remained a sort of index for emperors and local administrators to follow. Those Christians that succumbed usually had to offer a sacrifice to the gods or to the emperor as a demonstration of his or her faith. The church identified those who denied the faith as "lapsed Christians" or "apostates," and this option of escape was tempting for many persecuted Christians. Hippolytus knows this temptation and directly urges his readers to stand and suffer like those in Daniel for the sake of their faith and as representatives of Christ.

To those willing to suffer, Hippolytus speaks of a third important factor in the subject of martyrdom that shaped his faith. There was a theologically based optimism available to any candidate for martyrdom who was willing to persevere. This optimism spawned from a theological milieu based on a combination of the important teachings and examples of sacrifice of Christ, the apostles, and early church figures such as Ignatius, Polycarp, and Irenaeus, as well as the Jewish ideologies from the time of the Maccabees. Additionally, apocalyptic literature contributed to the Christian understanding of martyrdom with its notion of rewards in the afterlife and the belief that even suffering is divinely approved. The Book of Daniel embodied specific examples of these beliefs that contributed to this Christian tradition of martyrdom, explaining why Hippolytus chose this text for his commentary. This book offered scriptural justification for the church's suffering.

Growing up in the world of Imperial Rome during the reign of Marcus Aurelius, Hippolytus surely heard stories of the legislations or the social assaults rendered against the church preceding him, and perhaps was witness to some events himself. The reign under Septimius Severus began peacefully in 193, but in 202, the emperor unleashed a shocking and severe persecution against the Christian church. He issued an edict that outlawed all new conversions to Christianity, and local crowds responded with persecution against Jews and Christians who were unwilling to syncretize their own religions with pagan worship. Historical evidence for the decree is found even in the *Commentary on Daniel*, where Hippolytus writes:

> They watch for the favorable day when all [Christians] are praying and singing hymns to God, they enter into the house of the Lord, drag them out, and speak violently through blackmail, threatening to testify against them. When they do not consent, they testify against them before the tribunal, accuse them of acting contrary to the decree of Caesar and condemn them to death.[2]

Hippolytus' martyrological exegesis of Daniel fits perfectly with a situation of persecution against the church. A milieu of suffering and martyrdom prompted the commentary's writing and its exhortations can apply to any situation of persecution in the Roman Empire. In fact, the question of Hippolytan provenance may be answered in part by identifying geographical areas of intense persecution. If we assume a Roman provenance for this work, then Hippolytus' own record demonstrates this principle of willingness to suffer persecution. He was so rigorous in his devotion for suffering for the Lord that he would scrupulously oppose a bishop of greater office than himself if he seemed to be lax on those who deliberately eluded suffering for the Christian faith. Such evidence suggests that the motif suits a Roman provenance, although the writing would fit any situation that has an imminent persecution of the church.

Theological Milieu

From prior generations of social and religious persecution against the church, early Christians developed a theology of martyrdom within the context of their faith. By preserving the legends of martyrs, the church formed its own theology for idealizing martyrdom. Believers' conflict with the "world" was seen as a clash between light and dark, and the persecution that they experienced was

---

[2] παρατηροῦνται ἡμέραν εὐθῆ καὶ ἐπεισελθόντες εἰς τὸν οἶκον τοῦ Θεοῦ προσευχομένων ἐκεῖ πάντων καὶ τὸν Θεὸν ὑμούντων, ἐπιλαβόμενοι ἕλκουσί τινας καὶ κρατοῦσι λέγοντες δεῦτε, συγκατάθεσθε ἡμῖν καὶ τοὺς Θεοὺς θρησκεύσατε, εἰ δὲ μὴ, καταμαρτυρήσομεν καθ᾽ ὑμων. τούτων δὲ μὴ βουλομένων προσάγουσιν αὐτοὺς πρὸς τὸ βῆμα καὶ κατηγοροῦσιν ὡς ἐναντία τοῦ δόγματος Καίσαρος πράσσοντας καὶ θανάτῳ κατακρίνοται. *Commentary on Daniel*, I.20.3. Although Barnes argues that Severus never issued any such decree, most scholars disagree. At the very least, this is clear evidence that Christians in Hippolytus' locale suffered formal persecution by Roman courts. Barnes, "Legislation Against the Christians," 41-43.

considered to be Satanic in origin. The death of the saints at the hands of these worldly powers epitomized this conflict, preparing them to meet their Christ who they imitate in his passion and death. The martyrs became heroes for the people, and Christians idealized those experiencing this noble death. Frend depicts the phenomenon: "Behind their actions lies the whole theology of martyrdom in the early Church. They were seeking by their death to attain to the closest possible imitation of Christ's passion and death. This was at the heart of their attitude."[3]

The concepts of godly suffering preceded the New Testament in the Jewish piety and literature of the Maccabean revolt against the Hellenistic king, Antiochus IV. So significant are these years in the shaping of Christian martyrology, that a Christian theology of martyrdom seems impossible without considering the Maccabees and Daniel. From this Jewish milieu of competing eschatological worldviews—natural and prophetic—the *maskilim* "wise ones" set a tempo of willing suffering as an acceptable sacrifice to God. This is the era that gave birth to two new points of theology that are significant to Hippolytus: a theology of martyrdom and apocalyptic literature.

The image and teachings of Jesus, the apostles, Ignatius, and Polycarp provided and reinforced a theology of martyrdom. From the gospels, Christians recalled how Christ warned his disciples that they would be persecuted for the sake of righteousness and the faith. Jesus' death on the cross for believers became the ultimate example, depicting him as the archetype of persecuted believers. Droge summed up the motivating image, "Behind every description of martyrdom lay the example of Jesus."[4] The spirit of suffering in this world for eternal rewards and the opportunity to die like Christ invigorated Christian martyrs like Ignatius, Polycarp, Irenaeus, and finally Hippolytus himself. Four generations of direct mentoring by teaching and martyrdom embodied the importance of this theological ideal of Christianity.

Suffering earthly martyrdom went hand in hand with apocalyptic literature, which offered otherworldly solutions and retributive returns for such suffering. Certain distinctive features characterize this genre that are associated with martyrdom: conflict between the kingdoms of this world, postponing justice in this life to the afterlife, transcending death here through the resurrection into eternal life, and a resolve that all such events are divinely approved by a sovereign God. These characteristics functioned to offer hope to God's people in the midst of chaotic and harmful events, putting the apocalyptic motif to work for their specific crisis. The apocalyptic literature provided profound theological credibility to the suffering of God's people, and early Christianity gained its own versions seen in the Book of Revelation and the *Shepherd of Hermas*.

These works came to Hippolytus as models for Christian interpretation of

---

[3] Frend, *Martyrdom and Persecution*, 15.
[4] Droge and Tabor, *A Noble Death*, 156.

apocalyptic literature in a way that inspired him in his exegesis of Daniel. The cosmic conflict dimension of the apocalyptic genre made Christian readers feel they were engaged in a greater conflict, that their suffering was part of a greater age old battle between Satan and heaven. Such was one of the established lines of interpretation of the Book of Daniel. Wilken remarks, "The Book of Daniel was seen as a fertile source of prophecies about the coming of Christ and the destruction of the Temple in Jerusalem, a topic which assumed a major role in the early Christian view of history."[5] This book of scripture becomes an ideal text for Hippolytus to craft his commentary.

Hippolytus' Preference for Daniel

Daniel functioned in the Christian community for the special purpose of providing models for suffering for the Lord and for positing the ongoing sovereignty of God over all circumstances. Events, legends, and hermeneutics of the martyrs led to a complex theology of martyrdom in the mind of early Christians that helped them to reconcile their view of God and their sufferings. With such lines of interpretation shaping the church's use of scripture, it becomes easier to hypothesize why Hippolytus would respond to persecution by writing his *Commentary on Daniel*. He surely saw how this Old Testament book provided important principles for Christians living in a context of tribulation, including Roman religious persecution. This presbyter was moved to interpret the biblical text to encourage a harassed and beleaguered church, and to do so in a way that justified their suffering. This brings us to Hippolytus' crafting of his commentary with the burden of a suffering church on his mind.

Synthesis of Martyrological Evidence

The evidence for a martyrdom motif in the commentary lies in its ongoing references, exhortations, and parallels of martyrdom-related events that the Book of Daniel offers. Hippolytus applies these features to the contemporary political situation of his own church congregations. At the core of his application of the Daniel text was a burden to call his congregations to ready themselves for religious persecution, and recurring comments that support this goal assemble to create a martyrdom thesis. This book first evidenced the motif by collecting the many references to martyrdom and suffering, and then reflected on them in light of the exegetical method of Hippolytus for a full understanding of his intentions.

Evidencing a Martyrdom Motif

A theme of martyrdom permeates the entire commentary. Hippolytus reflects

---

[5] Wilken, *The Christians as the Romans Saw Them*, 139.

on the persecutions in the narrative and prophetic material related to persecution and regularly looks to the suffering of Christians in his own day when he reflects on the events in the Book of Daniel. His commentary is broken into four books that individually and generally treat (1) the Susanna story, (2) the three youths in the furnace, (3) Daniel in the lion's den, and (4) visions of a great tribulation, with additional Danielic material treated in each book. These four divisions become the major sections for our analysis of the martyrdom motif after combining the middle two books because of their narrative similarities. We should note that there are other themes in the commentary, even though the focus of this book is the themes of persecution and martyrdom in the work.[6] The martyrdom motif is evident in the narrative stories about specific Jews suffering in Babylon, their function as types prefiguring the persecution of Christians, and the prophecies about future persecutions, all of which becomes springboards for Hippolytus to exhort his congregations to endure persecution and be willing to die for Christ.

SUSANNA STORY

Hippolytus believes strongly that the story of Susanna ought to be included in scripture. The Jews generally did not maintain the stories among their scriptures, even though the Septuagint includes the accounts of *Susanna, the Hymn of the Three Youths*, and *Bel and the Dragon*. In the case of the Susanna episode, Hippolytus accuses them of being "ashamed of what the [Jewish] elders have done" in the story as their motive for omitting the story.[7] The elders' lust and consequential perjury against her result in a demonstration of her faith in God that ought to be a model for persecuted third century CE Christians.

Hippolytus uses several features to accomplish this principle of modeling her faith, including identifying the members and components in the story to represent people and forces in church history who are the antagonists in the ongoing conflict between the world and the church. He centers on his own congregations currently undergoing persecution by using explicit comparison and exhortation to endure martyrdom and thus accomplishes his task of a pastoral-minded exegesis. For example, the two elders represent those who want to damage God's people, while Susanna is a type of the church who is suffering at their hands. She is presented as pure and unadulterated, resisting the temptation to succumb to apostasy.

---

[6] For example, Trakatellis has explored the exegetical style of "agonistic speech" in Hippolytus' use of scripture against the enemies of the faith, and also for eschatology, martyrology, and Christology. Additionally, Dunbar has systematized the eschatology of Hippolytus and the *Commentary on Daniel* provided unique insights towards this end. This book's analysis adds to this collection by suggesting that the pressures of martyrdom provided a lens for Hippolytus to interpret and apply the Book of Daniel.

[7] *Commentary on Daniel*, I.14.

Susanna becomes a paragon to be modeled. "Imitate Susanna" becomes his slogan, peppered with allegorical rhetoric from the Susanna text.[8] Throughout the Susanna story, Hippolytus can find textual material to connect with the issues of persecution and martyrdom surrounding the church of his time. He does not reduce the text to merely curious martryological parallels, but he is able to use prophecy, the character of scripture, God's working in history, and personal holiness in a way that buttresses his call to martyrdom. He has a clear objective in allegorizing the Susanna story to present a heroine in the face of martyrdom. The entire analysis moves toward solid exhortation to the reader to consider martyrdom a justifiable and worthy goal to achieve.

DANIEL AND THE THREE YOUTHS

Daniel's refusal to pray to the king and resultant toss to the lions provides a similar forum for Hippolytus to present an example of enduring persecution. Likewise, the three youth who refused to worship the idol and were thrown into the fiery furnace become model believers who are willing to suffer for Christ. These two episodes of Daniel 3 and 6 get collective treatment in this book because of the similar nature of the material whereby He draws typological-based exhortations from the narrative material. Hippolytus commented on these two books of narrative in three particular ways: by dramatizing the narrative events, by presenting the three youth as models of perseverance, and by positing God's sovereignty even over events of cruelty against his people.

First, he dramatizes the events for his readers using metaphors of athletic competition, and graphic descriptions of suffering. Next, Hippolytus uses the story of the three youths to venerate their courage in the face of martyrdom. Their sagacity, courage, faithfulness, and endurance are noteworthy qualities for a Christian to emulate. For Hippolytus, these sufferings serve an instructive purpose. His rich use of imagery makes for a more dramatic presentation of the suffering of persecuted Christians, which is part of Hippolytus' effort to elevate the martyrs and ready his own churches to the possibility of martyrdom.

The suffering of the Maccabees serves as an enhancement to the distress of the three youths. Hippolytus turns to his readers and urges them "to study the martyrs" who defy death and to focus on the heavenly things because the Spirit of the Father teaches them to do so. Like the Maccabees, the readers of this *Commentary on Daniel* believed their struggle was a personal encounter with Satan, that the adversary was their only remaining obstacle to paradise, and that martyrdom overcame that hurdle. The experience did not defeat their spiritual enemy, and the agonies of persecution did not redirect the evils of the world or God's inevitable judgment on them. However, it personally was victorious for them, as Smith notes, "Death and dying became for the Christian a triple-sign: the reenactment of the folly of Calvary, a bloody but potent proof of the power

---

[8] For example, "Imitate Susanna, and enjoy the delicacies in the garden." τὴν Σουσάνναν μιμήσασθε καὶ τὸν παράδεισον ἐντρυφήσητε. *Commentary on Daniel*, I.33; cf. I.22.

of faith, and a warranty to share with Christ in his glory within the tabernacle of the Lord."[9] The pain of martyrdom may be agonizing, but eternal life was its trade-off—a lucid characteristic of apocalyptic literature.

Besides being exemplars of perseverance, Daniel, Shadrach, Meshach, and Abednego experience and so prove the rescuing hand of a sovereign God, who is able to intervene to deliver his servants as he pleases. Hippolytus says that this is possible because, despite the efforts of any Babylonian ruler, the Lord orders all events according to his will.

THE THREE YOUTHS AS A CASE STUDY IN THEODICY

The story of Shadrach, Meschach, and Abednigo allow Hippolytus to address the theological and logical concerns that surround the drastic difference between the Danielic text and their own day: why contemporary Christians are not being supernaturally rescued. He undertakes the difficult task of explaining why God does not intervene into the numerous acts of persecution against the church by means of a theodicy of the sovereign and sometimes unknowable purposes of the Lord.

Hippolytus first addresses the problem with simple logic: If God saved all who were threatened with a martyr's death, who then would have become a real martyr? On the other hand, if all the prospective martyrs died, then the unbelievers would have claimed that the God of martyrs is unable to rescue his faithful servants. But for Hippolytus, there is something more at work than just a logical explanation for the events with a reward of immortality for the executed believer. There is a divine purpose in martyrdom: to glorify God. Whether God delivers his servants or allows martyrdom with rewards, Hippolytus states candidly that that the prerogative belongs to God for his glory:

> God saves whom he wants, in order that the works of his magnificence may be revealed to the whole world. But those of whom he desires martyrdom, he crowns them and makes them come up to himself [in heaven]… He rescues whomever he wants; he takes whomever he desires.[10]

Through elaboration of the text and by theological explanation, Hippolytus casts a divine logic to their situation in a way that encourages them amidst their suffering. With statements such as, "When he [God] saves one of his servants, he saves them when he wants and as he wants,"[11] this presbyter ultimately yields any understanding of these afflictions to the will of a sovereign God.

---

[9] Smith, *Fools, Martyrs, Traitors*, 92.

[10] τότε οὕς ἤθελεν ἔτι ζῆν ὁ Θεὸς ἐρρύετο, ἵνα τὸ μεγαλεῖον τοῦ Θεοῦ ἔργον δειχθῇ καὶ ἐν παντὶ τῷ κόσμῳ ἕως νῦν κηρυχθῇ. Οὕς δὲ ἤθελεν μαρτυρεῖν τούτους σεφανώσας προσελάμβανεν…ὥστε οὕς μὲν θέλει ῥύεται οὕς δὲ θέλει παραλαμβάνει. *Commentary on Daniel*, II.35.

[11] *Commentary on Daniel*, I.27.

Hippolytus is able to witness this same guiding principle of sovereignty when he examines and analyzes the prophecies of Daniel. God's overarching design extends even over the kingdoms and rulers of this world when they unjustly persecute his people, and the church believed that their own events were, in a special way, prefigured in Daniel.

From the prophecy Daniel 11-12 about a time of great tribulation, the early church anticipated a specific persecution that they paralleled with the Antichrist of the New Testament (2 Thess. 2:3-4, Rev. 13:1-18). In turn, they projected this persecution onto their Roman authorities. Hippolytus supports this trend some, speculating on the signs of the Antichrist's coming and supporting his theories of scripture with apocalyptic cross-references. Our exhorting presbyter offers an optimistic view of this time period by construing the threat of the future Antichrist and his persecution in a soothing way, redirecting hopes into the afterlife through eschatological postponement, and positing God's sovereignty over the events. In an apocalyptic fashion, Hippolytus uses the text for the urgent task of offering provisional hope to his readers.

The anticipation of the Antichrist raised many logistical questions and anxiety in the minds of the readers about timing of last day events, but Hippolytus insists that the uncertainty should not draw the believer into fear and anxiety. He directly rebukes those who live in fear of these distressing events, which although horrible in their time, are a source of hope for Hippolytus who lifts the eyes of his reader just beyond these events to the eschaton in Christ. Hippolytus exhorts them in their tribulation to look to Jesus, "So that one may always hold to what is good, that one may avoid the mumbling of the Spirit, and that one can believe in God with all his heart."[12] The apocalyptic genre of Daniel serves Hippolytus' exhortations well here because he redirects them to look beyond their suffering to the eternal rewards that await them and for the just retribution that is longed for at judgment. Additionally, these things are accomplished because God desires all these things to come to pass, divinely raising nations and knocking down leaders. "For all this that God decides, and all this that the prophets announce he accomplishes exactly in his time."[13]

The return of Christ is an ongoing and important hope in early Christianity, and Hippolytus expends much energy in the commentary securing a balanced view of the return of Christ. Christians were not merely to wait for the

---

[12] ἵνα κατὰ πάντα ἑδραίως ἑστὼς ὁ ἄνθρωπος καὶ ἐν μηδενὶ βαμζαίνων τῷ νοΐ ἐξ ὅλης καρκίας τῷ θεῷ πιστεῦσαι δυνηθῇ. *Commentary on Daniel*, IV.7.1. Hippolytus relates this eschatological-based exhortation to "a prior work" thought to be *On Christ and the Antichrist*. ἐπεὶ οὖν φθάσαντες καὶ ἐν ἑτέρῳ λόγῳ περὶ τούτων ἀποδεδώκαμεν τὸν λόγον; Lefèvre, IV.7.1, n.a.

[13] ὅσα γὰρ ἤδη παρὰ Θεοῦ προωρίσθη γενέσθαι, καὶ ἀπὸ τῶν προφητῶν προκεκήρυκται, ταῦτα οὕτως καιροῖς ἰδίος πληρωθήσεται. *Commentary on Daniel*, IV.24.

judgment of the return of Christ; he challenges them not to become obsessed with the parousia. Instead, Hippolytus strictly warns them that it is not to be fantasized or falsely imagined; facing suffering does not guarantee rescue and they shouldn't hope in the intervention of the parousia to alleviate their circumstances. Instead, Christians should patiently and bravely face the afflicting duty of martyrdom that confronts them.

Although Hippolytus assures them of the certainty of Christ's return, he tempers this expectation when he clearly postpones the parousia three hundred years into the future. His eschatology represents a shift in millennial theories in church history when he significantly postpones the *parousia*. He sees Daniel's prophecies about the coming of the Son of Man in a framework of seven thousand-year periods. Writing two hundred years after Christ's birth, Hippolytus calculates that there must be another three hundred years before the end of the world and the ushering in of the final millennium, fulfilling the symbolic Sabbath of peace and rest for God's people in the seventh millennium since Adam.[14] This postponement removes the element of the imminent and thus forces his readers to focus on their calling to martyrdom.

Hippolytus makes a clear and precise distinction when he outlines the exact relationship between Septimius Severus and the Antichrist. Although some scholars emphasize how Hippolytus interprets symbols in *Daniel* to refer to the current Roman Empire,[15] it seems best to conclude that these interpretations merely "provide a focus and guide" to some future kingdom's persecutions.[16] This would suggest that, for him, the time of the Antichrist is in one sense here and that eschatological consummation will soon follow. At other times, Hippolytus speaks like the Antichrist is not yet in power, and that this wave of persecutions against the church by this generation of Romans is not the final one. The current Roman Empire becomes responsible for fostering the future ruler and persecution, so that Hippolytus "places the Roman state under severe prophetic indictment"[17] even though they are not the final oppressors.

Exegetical Features

Our study of the commentary warranted an examination of how Hippolytus drew out the text's meaning and could apply its truths toward the lives of the believers. Although Hippolytus transformed patristic exegesis when he crafted a thorough commentary on scripture, his basic exegetical method was not so different than his predecessors. A closer examination of his interpretation of scripture provides a final explanation how exegesis and martyrdom go hand in

---

[14] *Commentary on Daniel*, IV.23.
[15] Simonetti, *Biblical Interpretation*, 28; Hidal, "Apocalypse, Persecution, and Exegesis," 50.
[16] Dunbar, "Eschatological Exegesis," 338.
[17] Trakatellis, ΛΟΓΟΣ ΑΓΩΝΙΣΤΙΚΟΣ, 542.

hand in his *Commentary on Daniel*.

In the greater Christian tradition's use of Daniel, as well as in unprecedented ways, Hippolytus uses scripture to develop a chronology of time, whereby he gleans its apocalyptic themes to establish a solidly operating sovereignty of God, and so enhances Christological interpretations of Old Testament prophecies that he can even date the birth of Jesus.[18] This novel hermeneutical spirit also rendered a martyrdom motif through an exhaustive commentary on Daniel text.

The patristic traditions of typological, apocalyptic, and allegorical interpretation motivated Hippolytus to move through the biblical text and interpret his contemporary events in light of it. He seemed to have chosen Daniel because it is a martyrdom friendly text, perfect for exhorting Christians to be willing to suffer for the faith. Prior apostolic and patristic exegetical methods inspired him to recognize how the Old Testament text contained allegorical and typological components that he could use to build up believers' faiths. Likewise, Hippolytus used the examples of suffering believers in Daniel for moral exhortations to endure martyrdom and persecution, challenging Christians to live up to the models of suffering seen in scripture.

The exegetical methodology that stimulated Hippolytus' work was derived from the rich milieu of Jewish and patristic biblical exegesis. He relies strongly on rabbinical methods of biblical interpretation; he seems readily familiar with Judaism and is indebted to its methods. Many of his writings derive their themes from Judaism and his Old Testament commentaries are highly rabbinical in style, grammar, and theology.[19] Hippolytus shares the rabbinical view of scripture, its freedom in interpreting and commenting on it, and its overall tendency to interpret the text in a literal fashion. Like other fathers, he used the same innovation witnessed in the Jewish *midrash* when rabbis sought to find biblical meanings pertinent to the lives of their readers. This was particularly true as the fathers sought to use the Old Testament texts to proclaim Christ and the gospel. Hippolytus shared with Judaism the belief that the scripture was divinely provided and consequentially was the source legitimizing all of their traditions; the text was authoritative and provided by the Lord for the needs of his people.

Hippolytus stands in the particular tradition of biblical exegesis from Irenaeus and Justin that becomes standard in the West. Like them, he sees the Old Testament as God's divine revelation, its characters and events as historical instruments in the theater of God's plans, and its ultimate meaning as Christ-centered. Irenaeus designed an understanding of the unfolding plan of God

---

[18] *Commentary on Daniel*, IV.23.
[19] For a thorough treatment of the rabbinical similarities to Hippolytus' *Commentary on Daniel*, see Daniélou, 257-271.

throughout the revelation of the scriptures, informed by the text in Daniel 12:4, "Shut up the words and seal the book, until the time of the end" when "knowledge shall increase." Hippolytus exploits this exact principle when he sees the *Logos* present and predicted in the Book of Daniel, as well as an anticipation of the current persecutions of Christians. These are both common rabbinical and patristic principles of biblical exegesis that have a direct bearing on the biblical interpretation and writings of Hippolytus.

Like the rabbis, the early church believed in the divine inspiration of scripture, and the purpose of interpretation was to instruct the believer in their faith while in covenant with Yahweh. The conviction that scripture is authoritative and that the church can exploit its prophecies and narratives to understand it state of affairs is a sort of first principle of his exegesis. Any such divinely provided Old Testament book was a legitimate, authoritative source for divine insight and application in the lives of his congregations, especially when performed in a Christological way.

Throughout his exegetical activities, Hippolytus consistently declares the absolute authority of scripture. He sees the scriptural text as definite truth and uses it profusely to argue his case.[20] Trakatellis notes that scriptural authority was "a basis not merely presupposed and applied, but uncompromisingly advocated as a condition *sine qua non* for any responsible theological debate."[21] Hippolytus stands in a long line of historical biblical exegetes that believe the text to be divinely inspired. He quotes scripture quite densely, as if the authority of what is said lies not in the expounding on the text but in the citation itself. He deliberately employs and studies scripture because of its function: it is the source for true theology necessary for the life of the church. Hippolytus writes, "The divine scriptures declare to us nothing irrelevant but what is for our very own instruction, and in order to enhance the prophets and to explain everything that was said by them."[22] He says that church leaders who neglect its study will go astray and lead others to do so, and even provides examples from that day of such spiritual shepherds who ignored the scripture to the detriment of their flocks.

Hippolytus sees a truth claim implied in the text that makes the events and the people there historical and real; the underlying divine inspiration is the

---

[20] His scriptural based cases can be seen in *Commentary on Daniel*, I.29.1, I.30.1, II.28.6, III.12.1-4, IV.1.2, IV.6.2, IV.22.1-2, IV.41.1. In fact, Hippolytus accepts Theodotian's translation and doesn't inquire about its variants, but receives it as the Word of God.

[21] Trakatellis, ΛΟΓΟΣ ΑΓΟΝΙΣΤΙΚΟΣ, 531.

[22] οὐδὲν γὰρ ἀργὸν κηρύττουσιν ἡμῖν αἱ θεῖαι γραφαί, ἀλλὰ πρὸς μὲν τὴν ἡμῶν αὐτῶν νουθεσίαν, τῶν δὲ προφητῶν μακαρισμὸν καὶ πάντων τῶν ὑπ' αὐτῶν λελαλημένων ἀπόδειξιν. *Commentary on Daniel*, I.7.2.

basis for the historical authenticity of the biblical report. This enabled exegetes like Hippolytus to enhance and empower the application to be drawn from it. He goes to surprising lengths to prove that Daniel was a prophet, and that the words in the text were legitimate predictive prophecy. It seems that his effort was to secure his desired interpretations by establishing the authority and veracity of Daniel's words.

TYPOLOGY AND ALLEGORY

Concerning the sense of scripture, Hippolytus begins with the literal sense and really maintains this position with rare exception. The case of his allegorical activity centers mostly on the Susanna story, from which he offers a comprehensive allegorical interpretation of situations of Christian martyrdom and persecution. Hippolytus identifies the characters and components in Susanna as representative of people and forces in his own third century. Hippolytus' use of terminology is odd here, because although he says that the figures function as a "type," εἰς τύπον δείκνυνται, his interpretation evolves into allegory, blurring the two senses of scripture. He seems to use the word "type" in a representative fashion, not in a historical sense in which a type prophetically points to a future event. This vagueness may reflect an exegete not focused on precise method but on the parallel between scripture and the present threat against the church. He has a fluid use of typology, extending it from a historical to a spiritual sense depending on the interpretation in view. In what seems to be a blurred distinction between senses, Hippolytus exercises allegory and typology in his exegesis to offer an impressive, comprehensive exhortation to martyrdom. This study answers Frances Young's call to recognize more literary segments in patristic works that function as interpretive genres, "segments interlinked by connecting threads, issues which keep recurring, and which defy simple organization."[23]

At times, Hippolytus can find a referent in the text in both future and past antitypes, an occurrence which Daniélou calls an "extension of typology." Hippolytus adopts a contrast between partial (μερικῶς) and plenary (καθ᾽ ὅλου) fulfillment in this typology, a practice that was fundamental to Justin's writings.[24] This provided profound parallels that captured the attention of Hippolytus' persecuted churches, and the use of typology and the parallels of allegory are the basis for Hippolytus' exhortations to his congregations. Their sufferings find validity when they realize that God prophesied about their Lord and Savior as well as prefigured their own sufferings in the Book of Daniel. Close examination of the text clearly reveals a specific goal: to encourage the readers of the commentary that martyrdom is justified because God's sovereignty supersedes the persecution of this world. The apocalyptic genre of Daniel lends itself perfectly to the purpose he has for the text and his readers, as

---

[23] Young, *Biblical Exegesis*, 1.
[24] Daniélou, *Gospel Message*, 257-71.

the stories offer hope to the congregations who share the circumstances of being persecuted at the hand of foreign oppressors. The apocalyptic overtones of the text complement the martyrdom motif by their otherworldly solutions to Christian suffering.

The stories in Daniel provide a forum for moral exhortation by Hippolytus to appeal for believers to stand firm in the faith. They are to persevere in trials, whether God intervenes to save them or not. Hippolytus does not guarantee their deliverance will be fulfilled in this world, as the Lord may choose for them to suffer and die only to vindicate their sacrifice in the life to come. They are simply to be ready if God calls them to martyrdom. One gets the sense that the surrounding milieu of persecution and martyrdom was almost normative for Christians living in a non-Christian world under pagan rulers. Christian readers of the *Commentary on Daniel* would see the ideal of perseverance modeled by God's people in Babylon, and they would understand themselves to be God's new people in a new Babylon. It becomes clear in the commentary that Hippolytus understands the Roman state to be among those who are symbolized by the two elders in the Susanna tale and the satraps in the Danielic lion's den story. They represent those who currently persecute the church so cruelly.

A complex understanding of history and eschatology undergirds Hippolytus' exegesis of Daniel. His works demonstrate this emphasis and reveals to us his exact systematic theology of time.[25] He gives a history of God's interaction with mankind; he lays out the manner of the coming of the Antichrist and end of the world, speculates about the return of Christ, and applies the prophecies contained in Old and New Testament passages toward culmination of the ages. The prophetic passages in the Book of Daniel provide an exegetical forum for Hippolytus to discuss eschatological issues and to employ them in the exhortation of suffering Christians. The Roman Empire currently persecuting them is the climax of these unfriendly world empires, yet is not the one to be led by the Antichrist. For Hippolytus, the Antichrist will come from this Roman womb but is not yet here. He sees world history as a government of evil powers who is granted a brief period of rule by God before the day of final salvation and great judgment.

The sufferings of Christians are a revealed type of the suffering Christ portrayed. He is their prototype, and Hippolytus used Daniel and other scripture to assert this. Hippolytus' view of history with a delayed parousia informs his emphatic insistence on willingness to suffer. Christians, even the persecuted congregations at the beginning of the third century, should not be so parousia-focused that they should expect to escape the flames by virtue of Christ's personal return. Instead, Hippolytus' eschatology is Christological,[26] as Christ will "give us power when all the strength and glory of this life is gone, will give

---

[25] For an overview of his eschatological works, see Daley, *The Hope of the Early Church*, 38-41.

[26] Daley, *The Hope of the Early Church*, 39.

us his hand and raise us, 'as living people from the dead,' from Hades for a resurrection to life."[27] His emphasis is on his readers' response to these things; their moral responsibility is stressed when he declares, "Each one recognizes that on the day when he leaves this world he is already judged, for the consummation has come upon him."[28] Thus, the suffering of martyrdom becomes a passageway into the next life where rewards await any sacrificial believer.

Employing Exegesis to Encourage Martyrdom

All of the evidence points to a paraenetic interpretation of Daniel by this church father. Besides a historical context of persecution, Hippolytus was immersed in a theological context from which he could explain and respond to threatening circumstances. He had inherited some impressive notions of martyrdom, and the Book of Daniel provided him a historical, prophetic, prototypical, Christologically-minded reading of the text to which this church presbyter could appeal. From the text of scripture, this pastor encouraged his congregations to be ready for martyrdom as if it were a duty or an obligation that one owed their savior who was martyred for them. In this way, he employed a paraenetic exegesis of Scripture, functioning to encourage suffering for Christ, even to the point of martyrdom.

The stories and prophecies of the book of Daniel naturally had a special appeal to persecuted communities of Jewish and Christian believers. From the time of its writing, God's people have employed the book to encourage and revitalize them, especially in times of systematic harassment and martyrdom. Hippolytus used this book along these same lines for particular application in his beleaguered churches. Of all books of scripture, he chose Daniel to construct the first complete, orthodox commentary on scripture. Careful scrutiny of Hippolytus' *Commentary on Daniel* reveals a distinct martyrdom motif pervading the entire work. The author habitually relates the material in the Book of Daniel to the subject of martyrdom, and empowers his exegesis with an understanding of contemporary events relating to Christian martyrs of that period. The characters in the text and the prophecies of the future recurrently prefigure or point to the martyrs of Hippolytus' own day, and the characters and prophecies also call for them to remain faithful under pressure. It becomes evident that the motif functions to encourage Christians who were suffering persecution and confronted with the possibility of martyrdom. The work contains theological reflection and exhortations to godly living, even a willingness to suffer unto death. Both the surrounding historical milieu and

---

[27] τότε ἐνδυναμούμεθα ὑπὸ Χριστοῦ τοῦ ὀρέγοντος χεῖρα καὶ ἐγείροντος ἡμᾶς ὡς ἐκ νεκρῶν ζῶντας καὶ ὡς ἀπὸ ᾅδου εἰς ἀνάστασιν ζωῆς. *Commentary on Daniel*, IV.39.

[28] γινώσκων εἰς ἕκαστος ὅτι ἡ ἂν ἡμέρᾳ ἐξέλθῃ ἐκ τοῦ κόσμου τούτου ἤδη κέκριται. *Commentary on Daniel*, IV.18.

several Christian theological traditions verify such an intention, and Hippolytus used Daniel to convince and inspire a suffering, beleaguered, persecuted church that martyrdom was a calling well worth its sacrifice.

Bibliography

Primary Sources

Acts of the Martyrs. Herbert Musurillo, Translated by Oxford Early Christian Texts. Oxford: Oxford University Press, 1972.

Augustine. *City of God.* Vol. II, The Nicene and Post-Nicene Fathers, series I. Edited by Philip Schaff. Translated by Marcus Dodd. Grand Rapids: Eerdmans, reprinted 1977.

Clement of Alexandria. *The Stromata.* Vol. II, The Ante-Nicene Fathers. Edited by Alexander Roberts and James Donaldson. Grand Rapids: Eerdmans, reprinted 2001.

Cyprian. *Exhortation to Martyrdom, Addressed to Fortunatus.* Treatise XI, vol. V, The Ante-Nicene Fathers. Edited by Alexander Roberts and James Donaldson. Translated by Ernest Wallis. Edinburgh: T & T Clark, reprinted 1990.

_____. *Letters* (1-81). Translated by Rose Bernard Donna. Vol. 51, The Fathers of the Church. Washington, D.C.: The Catholic University of America Press, 1964.

Epistle of Barnabas. Vol. I, The Ante-Nicene Fathers. Edited by Alexander Roberts and James Donaldson. Grand Rapids: Eerdmans, 1953.

Eusebius. *Ecclesiastical History.* Translated by C.F. Crusé. 2nd Printing. Peabody, Mass.: Hendrickson Publishing, 2000.

Ferrua, A. *Epigrammata Damasiana.* Pontificia Instituto di Archeologia Christiana 35: Rome, 1942.

Hippolytus. *Against Plato.* Translated by S.D.F. Salmond. Vol. V, The Ante-Nicene Fathers. Edited by Alexander Roberts and James Donaldson. Edinburgh: T & T Clark, reprinted 1990.

_____. *Commentaire sur Daniel.* Vol. 14, Sources Chrétiennes. Translated by Maurice Lefèvre. Introduction by Gustave Bardy. Paris: Éditions du Cerf, 1947.

_____. *Commentary on Daniel.* Translated by S.D.F. Salmond. Vol. V, The Ante-Nicene Fathers. Edited by Alexander Roberts and James Donaldson. Edinburgh: T & T Clark, reprinted 1990.

_____. *Commentary on Matthew.* Translated by S.D.F. Salmond. Vol. V, The Ante-Nicene Fathers. Edited by Alexander Roberts and James Donaldson. Edinburgh: T & T Clark, reprinted 1990.

_____. *Contra Noetum.* Robert Butterworth. Translated by Heythrop Monographs. London: Heythrop College, 1977.

_____. *The Extant Works and Fragments of Hippolytus.* Vol. V, The Ante-Nicene Fathers. Edited by Alexander Roberts and James Donaldson. Translated by S.D.F. Salmond. Edinburgh: T & T Clark, reprinted 1990.

_____. *Hippolyte Danielkommentar in Handschrift No. 573 des Meteoronklosters.*
    Edited by Constantin Diobountis. Vol. 37, "Texte und Untersuchungen zur
    Geschichte der altchristlichen Literatur." Leipzig: J. C. Hinrichsche
    Buchhandlung, 1912.
_____. *Kommentar zu Daniel.* Translated by Nathanael Bonswetsch. *Hippolytus Werke*
    I.I. Paleoslavonic Version of the *Commentary on Daniel.* Griechische
    christliche Schriftsteller I. Leipzig (1987): XI-XIII.
_____. *Kommentar zu Daniel.* Translated by Georg Nathanael Bonwetsch. Berlin:
    Akadamie Verlag, 2000.
_____. *The Refutation of All Heresies.* Translated by J. H. MacMahon. Vol. V, The
    Ante-Nicene Fathers. Edited by Alexander Roberts and James Donaldson.
    Grand Rapids: Eerdmans, reprinted 1971.
_____. *Treatise on Christ and the Antichrist.* Translated by S.D.F. Salmond. Vol. V,
    The Ante-Nicene Fathers. Edited by Alexander Roberts and James Donaldson.
    Edinburgh: T & T Clark, reprinted 1990.
_____. *The Treatise on Apostolic Tradition of St. Hippolytus of Rome, Bishop and
    Martyr.* Edited by Gregory Dix and Henry Chadwick. London: The Alban
    Press, 1992.
Ignatius. *To the Philadelphians.* Vol. I, The Ante-Nicene Fathers. Edited by Alexander
    Roberts and James Donaldson. Grand Rapids: Eerdmans, 1953.
_____. *To the Romans.* Vol. I, The Ante-Nicene Fathers. Edited by Alexander Roberts
    and James Donaldson. Grand Rapids: Eerdmans, 1953.
Irenaeus. *Against Heresies.* Vol. I, The Ante-Nicene Fathers. Edited by Alexander
    Roberts and James Donaldson. Grand Rapids: Eerdmans, 1953.
Jerome. *Commentary on Daniel.* Translated by Gleason L. Archer. Grand Rapids: Baker
    Book House, 1958.
_____. *Lives of Illustrious Men.* Vol. III, The Nicene and Post-Nicene Fathers, 2nd
    Series. Grand Rapids: Eerdmans, reprinted 1996.
Josephus. *Jewish Antiquities.* Translated by H. St. J. Thackeray and Ralph Marcus.
    Cambridge, Mass.: Harvard University Press, 1998.
Justin Martyr. *Apology.* Vol. I, The Ante-Nicene Fathers. Edited by Alexander Roberts
    and James Donaldson. Grand Rapids: Eerdmans, 1953.
_____. *Dialogue with Trypho.* Vol. I, The Ante-Nicene Fathers. Edited by Alexander
    Roberts and James Donaldson. Grand Rapids: Eerdmans, 1953.
Martyrdom of Polycarp. Vol. I, The Ante-Nicene Fathers. Edited by Alexander Roberts
    and James Donaldson. Grand Rapids: Eerdmans, 1953.
Migne, J. P. *Patrologia Cursus Completes Accurante. Series graeca.* Vol. X, *Indices
    digessit Ferdinandus Cavallera.* Parisiis: Garnier (1857): 637-697.
Origen. *Commentary on the Gospel According to John.* Books 1-10. Translated by
    Ronald E. Heine. Washington, D.C.: Catholic University of America Press,
    1993.
_____. *Exhortation to Martyrdom. Alexandrian Christianity: Selected Translations of
    Clement and Origen with Introductions and Notes.* Edited by Henry
    Chadwick. Translated by John Ernest Leonard Oulton and Henry Chadwick.

Philadelphia: Westminister Press, 1954.

Papias. *The Fragments of Papias. The Apostolic Fathers: Greek Texts and English Translations.* Edited by Michael W. Holmes. Grand Rapids: Baker, 1999.

Photius. *Bibliotheca.* Translated by N. G. Wilson. London: Duckworth, 1994.

Pitra, J. B. *Analecta sacra* IV. Syriac Fragment Versions on the *Commentary on Daniel.* Parisiis (1883): 47-51, 317-320.

Prudentius. *Crowns of Martyrdom*, vol. XI. Translated by H. J. Thompson. London: William Heinemann, 1969.

Renoux, C. *Hippolyte de Bostra? Le dossier du Galata* 54. Armenian Fragments on the *Commentary on Daniel.* Muséon 92 (1979): 133-158.

The Shepherd of Hermas. The Apostolic Fathers: Greek Texts and English Translations. Edited by Michael W. Holmes. Grand Rapids: Baker, 1999.

Tertullian. *To the Martyrs.* Vol. III, The Ante-Nicene Fathers. Translated by S. Thelwall. Edinburgh: T & T Clark, reprinted 1989.

_____. *Against Marcion.* Vol. III, The Ante-Nicene Fathers. Translated by S. Thelwall. Edinburgh: T & T Clark, reprinted 1989.

_____. *Apology.* Vol. III, The Ante-Nicene Fathers. Translated by S. Thelwall. Edinburgh: T & T Clark, reprinted 1989.

_____. *On Purity.* Vol. 394, Sources Chrétiennes. Translated by Claudio Micaelli. Paris: Éditions du Cerf, 1993.

Secondary Sources

Alexander, James N. S. "The Interpretation of Scripture in the Ante-Nicene Period." *Interpretation* 12 (1958): 272-80.

Allert, Craig D. *A High View of Scripture? The Authority of the Bible and the Formation of the New Testament Canon.* Grand Rapids: Baker Academic, 2007.

Archer, Gleason L. *A Survey of Old Testament Introduction.* Chicago: Moody Press, 1994.

Arndt, William, Walter Bauer, F. Wilbur Gingrich, and Frederick W. Danker. *A Greek-English Lexicon of the New Testament and Other Early Christian Literature.* Chicago: University of Chicago Press, 1979.

Aune, David E. "The Book of Revelation." *Encyclopedia of Early Christianity.* Edited by Everett Ferguson, 1st edition. New York: Garland Publishing, 1990.

Baldovin, John F. "Hippolytus and the *Apostolic Tradition*: Recent Research and Commentary." *Theological Studies* 64 (2003): 520-542.

Baldwin, Joyce G. *Daniel: An Introduction and Commentary.* Tyndale Old Testament Commentaries. Edited by D.J. Wiseman. Downers Grove, Ill.: InterVarsity Press, 1978.

Bardy, Gustave. Introduction to *Commentaire sur Daniel.* Vol. 14, Sources Chrétiennes. Translated by Maurice Lefèvre. Paris: Éditions du Cerf, 1947.

_____. "L'éngime d'Hippolyte." *Mélanges de science religieuse* 5 (1948): 63-88.

Barnes, T. D. "Legislation Against the Christians." *Journal of Religious Studies* 58 (1968): 32-50.

Bercot, David W. *Dictionary of Early Christian Beliefs*. Peabody, Mass.: Hendrickson, 1998.

Berger, Peter. *The Sacred Canopy*. New York: Doubleday, 1967.

Beyschlag, Karlmann. "Kallist und Hippolyt." *Theologische Zeitschrift* 20 (1964): 103-124.

Bibliotheca Hagiographica Graeca. Vol. I. 3rd edition. Edited by François Halkin. Bruxelles: Société des Bollandists, 1957.

Bickerman, Elias. *The God of the Maccabees: Studies on the Meaning and Origin of the Maccabean Revolt*. Vol. 32, Studies in Judaism in Late Antiquity. Edited by Jacob Neuser. Translated by Horst R Moehring. Leiden: E.J. Brill, 1979.

Black, Matthew. "The Account of the Essenes, in Hippolytus and Josephus." *The Background of the New Testament and Its Eschatology*. Edited by W. D. Davies and David Daube. Cambridge: The University Press, 1956.

Bodenmann, Reinhard. *Naissance d'une exégèse: Daniel dans l'eglise ancienne de trois premiers siècles*. Beiträge zur Geschichte der biblischen Exegese 28. Tübingen: Mohr, 1986.

Böhm, Thomas. "Allegory and History." Vol. 1, *Handbook of Patristic Exegesis: The Bible in Ancient Christianity*. Edited by Charles Kannengiesser, Boston: Brill, 2004.

Bonwetsch, G. Nathanael. *Studien zu den Kommentaren Hippolyts zum Buche Daniel und Hohen Liede*. Leipzig: J. C. Hinrichs, 1897.

Botte, Bernard. "Note sur l'auteur du *De universo* attribué à saint Hippolyte." *Recherches de théologie ancienne et médiévale* 18 (1951): 5-18.

Bowersock, Glenn W. *Martyrdom and Rome*. Cambridge: Cambridge University Press, 1995.

Boyarin, Daniel. *Dying for God: Martyrdom and the Making of Christianity and Judaism*. Stanford: Stanford University Press, 1999.

Braverman, Jay. *Jerome's Commentary on Daniel: A Study of Comparative Jewish and Christian Interpretations of the Hebrew Bible*. The Catholic Biblical Quarterly Monograph Series 7. Washington, D.C.: The Catholic Biblical Association of America, 1978.

Bray, Gerald. *Biblical Interpretation: Past and Present*. Downers Grove, Ill.: InterVarsity Press, 1996.

Brent, Allen. *Hippolytus and the Roman Church of the Third Century: Communities in Tension before the Emergence of a Monarch-Bishop*. Vol. XXXI, Texts and Studies of Early Christian Life and Language Series. Edited by J. Den Boeft, R. Van Den Broek, A. F. J. Klijn, G. Quispel, J. C. M. Van Winden. New York: E.J. Brill, 1995.

_____. "Hippolytus' See and Eusebius' Historiography." *Studia Patristica* 24 (1993): 28-37.

_____. "Ligorio's Reconstruction of Hippolytus' Statue and the Recovery of the Hippolytan Corpus." *Medieval Codicology, Iconography, Literature, and Translation: Studies for Keith Val Sinclair*. Edited by Peter Rolfe Monks and D. D. R. Owen. Leiden: E. J. Brill. 1994.

_____. Review of J.A. Cerrato, *Hippolytus between East and West: The Commentaries* and the Provenance of the Corpus. *Journal of Ecclesiastical History* 55 (2004): 342-43.

_____. "St. Hippolytus, Bibilical Exegete, Roman Bishop, and Martyr." *St. Vladimir's Theological Quarterly* 48 (2004): 207-31.

_____. "Was Hippolytus a Schismatic?" *Vigiliae Christianae* 49: (1995) 215-44.

Bromiley, G. W. "The Church Fathers and Holy Scriptures." *Scripture and Truth*. Edited by D. A. Carson and J. Woodbridge. Grand Rapids: Zondervan, 1983.

Brown, Peter. *The World of Late Antiquity AD 150-750*. New York: W. W. Norton and Co., 1989.

Brox, Norbert. "Irenaeus and the Bible: A Special Contribution." Vol. 1, *Handbook of Patristic Exegesis: The Bible in Ancient Christianity*. Edited by Charles Kannengiesser. Boston: Brill, 2004.

Bruce, Fredrick Fyvrie. *The Canon of Scripture*. Downers Grove, Ill.: InterVarsity Press, 1988.

Bynum, Caroline Walker. *The Resurrection of the Body in Western Christianity, 200-1336*. New York: Columbia University Press, 1995.

Campbell, R. Alastair. *The Elders: Seniority within Earliest Christianity*. New York: T&T Clark, 1994.

von Campenhausen, Hans. *The Formation of the Christian Bible*. Translated by J.A. Baker. Mifflintown, Pa.: Sigler Press, 1997.

Capelle, Bernard. "Hippolyte de Rome." *Recherches de théologie ancienne et médiévale* 17 (1950): 145-74.

_____. "Le Logos, Fils de Dieu, dans la théologie d'Hippolyte." *Recherches de théologie ancienne et médiévale* 9 (1939): 109-24.

Carroll, John T, ed. *The Return of Jesus in Early Christianity*. Peabody, Mass.: Hendrickson, 2000.

Carson, D.A. "Understanding Misunderstandings in the Fourth Gospel." *Tyndale Bulletin* 33 (1982): 59-91.

Cerrato, J.A. "The Association of the Name Hippolytus with a Church Order Now Known as *The Apostolic Tradition*." *St. Vladimir's Theological Quarterly* 48 (2004): 179-94.

_____. *Hippolytus between East and West: The Commentaries and the Provenance of the Corpus*. Oxford Theological Monographs Series. Oxford: University Press, 2002.

Chadwick, Henry. *The Early Church*. Vol 1, The Pelican History of the Church. New York: Penguin Books, 1978.

Cherniss, Harold. "The So-Called Fragment of Hippolytus, περὶ ἅδου." *Classical Philosophy* 24 (1929): 346-50.

Collins, John J. *Apocalyptic Imagination: An Introduction to Jewish Apocalyptic Literature*. 2nd edition. Grand Rapids: Eerdmans, 1998.

_____. "Apocalyptic Literature." *Encyclopedia of Early Christianity*. Edited by Everett Ferguson. New York: Garland Publishing, 1990.

_____. *The Apocalyptic Vision of the Book of Daniel*. Harvard Semitic Monongraphs. Edited by Frank Moore Cross. Missoula, Montana: Scholars Press, 1977.

_____. *Daniel: A Commentary on the Book of Daniel*. Minneapolis: Fortress Press, 1993.

_____. *Daniel: With an Introduction to Apocalyptic Literature*. Vol. XX, The Forms of the Old Testament Literature. Edited by Rolg Knierim and Gene M. Tucker. Grand Rapids: Eerdmans, 1984.

Connolly, R. H. "New Attributions to Hippolytus." *Journal of Theological Studies* 46 (1945): 192-200.

Coxe, A. Cleveland. "Introductory Notice to Hippolytus [AD 170-236]." Vol. V, The Ante-Nicene Fathers. Edited by Alexander Roberts and James Donaldson. Edinburgh: T & T Clark, reprinted 1990.

Crouzel, Henri. *Origen*. Translated by A. S. Worrell. San Francisco: Harper & Row, 1989.

D'Alès, Adhémar. *La théologie de Saint Hippolyte*. Paris: G. Beauchesne, 1906.

Daley, Brian E. *The Hope of the Early Church: A Handbook of Patristic Eschatology*. Cambridge: Cambridge University Press, 1991.

Daniélou, Jean. *Gospel Message and Hellenistic Culture*. Vol. 2, A History of Early Christian Doctrine Before the Council of Nicaea. Philadelphia: Westminster Press, 1973.

Davids, Peter H. *First Epistle of Peter*. New International Commentary on the New Testament. Edited by F. F. Bruce. Grand Rapids: Eerdmans, 1990.

DeMar, Gary and Francis X. Gumerlock. *The Early Church and the End of the World* by Gary DeMar and Francis Gumerlock. Powder Springs, Ga.: American Vision, 2006.

Di Lella, Alexander A. *Daniel: A Book for Troubling Times*. Hyde Park, NY: New City Press, 1997.

Dockery, D. S. *Biblical Interpretation Then and Now: Contemporary Hermeneutics in the Light of the Early Church*. Grand Rapids: Baker Books, 1992.

von Döllinger, John J. Ignatius. *Hippolytus and Callistus*. Translated by Alfred Plummer. Edinburgh: T & T Clark, 1876.

Droge, Arthur J., and James D. Tabor. *A Noble Death: Suicide and Martyrdom among Christians and Jews in Antiquity*. San Francisco: HarperSanFrancisco, 1992.

Dunbar, David G. "The Biblical Canon." *Hermeneutics, Authority, and Canon*. Edited by D.A. Carson and John D. Woodbridge. Grand Rapids: Zondervan, 1986.

_____. "The Delay of the Parousia in Hippolytus." *Vigiliae Christianae* 37 (1983): 313-27.

_____. "The Eschatology of Hippolytus of Rome." Ph.D. diss. Drew University, 1979.

_____. "Hippolytus of Rome and the Eschatological Exegesis of the Early Church." *Westminster Theological Journal* 45 (1983): 322-39.

Ehrman, Bart D. "Heracleon and the 'Western' Textual Tradition." *New Testament Studies* 40 (1994): 161-179.

_____. "Heracleon, Origen, and the Text of the Fourth Gospel." *Vigiliae Christianae* 47 (1993): 105-18.

_____. *The Orthodox Corruption of Scripture: The Effect of the Early Christological Controversies on the Text of the New Testament*. New York: Oxford University Press, 1993.

Farmer, David. "Hippolytus." *The Oxford Dictionary of the Saints.* 4th edition. New York: Oxford University Press, 1997.

Farkasflvy, Denis. "Interpretation of the Bible." *Encyclopedia of Early Christianity.* 1st edition. Edited by Everett Ferguson. New York: Garland Publishing, 1990.

Ferch, Arthur J. "Authorship, Theology, and Purpose of Daniel." *Symposium on Daniel: Introductory and Exegetical Studies.* Vol. 2, Daniel and Revelation Committee Series. Edited by Frank B. Holbrook. Washington, D. C.: Biblical Research Institute, 1986.

Ferguson, Everett, ed. *Encyclopedia of Early Christianity.* 1st edition. New York: Garland Publishing, 1990.

_____. "Hippolytus." *Encyclopedia of Early Christianity.* 1st edition. Edited by Everett Ferguson. New York: Garland Publishing, 1990.

_____. "Martyr, Martyrdom." *Encyclopedia of Early Christianity.* 1st edition. Edited by Everett Ferguson. New York: Garland Publishing, 1990.

Fishbane, Michael. "Jewish Biblical Exegesis: Presuppositions and Principles." *Scripture in the Jewish and Christian Traditions: Authority, Interpretation, Revelance.* Edited by Fredrick E. Greenspahn. Nashville: Abingdon Press, 1982): 92-110.

Frend, W. H. C. *The Early Church.* Philadelphia: Fortress Press, 1982.

_____. *Martyrdom and Persecution in the Early Church: A Study of a Conflict from the Maccabees to Donatus.* New York: New York University Press, 1967.

_____. *The Rise of Christianity.* Philadelphia: Fortress Press, 1984.

Frickel, Josef. *Das Dunkel um Hippolyt von Rom Ein Lösungsversuch: die Schriften Elenchos und Conra Nöetum.* Grazer Theologische Studien, 1988.

Froehlich, Karlfried. *Biblical Interpretation in the Early Church.* Philadelphia: Fortress Press, 1984.

Gammie, John G. "A Journal Through Danielic Spaces: The Book of Daniel in the Theology and Piety of the Christian Community." *Interpretation* 39 (1985): 144-56.

Geerard, Mauritius, ed. Vol. 1, *Clavis Patrum Graecorum.* Turnhout: Brepols, 1947-1987.

Goldingay, John E. *Word Biblical Commentary: Daniel.* Vol. 30, Word Books Series. Edited by David A. Hubbard and Glenn W. Barker. Dallas: Word Books, 1989.

Goodspeed, Edgar J. *A History of Early Christian Literature.* Revised and enlarged by Robert M. Grant. Chicago: University of Chicago Press, 1966.

Gould, Graham. Review of J.A. Cerrato, *Hippolytus between East and West: The Commentaries and the Provenance of the Corpus. Journal of Theological Studies* 54 (2003): 312-14.

Grant, Robert. *Augustus to Constantine.* New York: Harper and Row, 1970.

_____. *Early Christianity and Society: Seven Studies.* San Francisco: Harper and Row, 1977.

_____. *Gnosticism and Early Christianity.* New York: Columbia University Press, 1959.

Greenspahn, Fredrick E., ed. *Scripture in the Jewish and Christian Traditions: Authority, Interpretation, and Relevance.* Nashville: Abingdon Press, 1982.

Gregory, Andrew. "Disturbing Trajectories: *1 Clement*, the *Shepherd of Hermas* and the Development of Early Roman Christianity." *Rome in the Bible and the Early Church.* Edited by Peter Oakes. Grand Rapids: Baker Academic, 2002.

Grillmeier, Aloys. *Christ in the Christian Tradition. Vol. 1: From the Apostolic Age to Chalcedon (451).* Translated by John Bowden. 2nd revised edition. London: Mowbrays, 1975.

Gumerlock, Francis X. "The Date of Revelation in the Early Church." *The Early Church and the End of the World* by Gary DeMar and Francis Gumerlock. Powder Springs, Ga.: American Vision, 2006.

Gwynn, John. "Hippolytus and His 'Heads Against Gaius.'" *Hermathena* 6 (1888): 397-418.

_____. "Hippolytus on Matt. xxiv, 15-22." *Hermathena* 8 (1890): 137-50.

Hamell, Patrick J. *Handbook of Patrology: A Concise, Authoritative Guide to the Life and Works of the Fathers of the Church.* New York: Alba House, 1968.

Hanson, Paul D. *The Dawn of Apocalytpic: The Historical and Sociological Roots of Jewish Apocalyptic Eschatology.* Philadelphia: Fortress Press, 1979.

Hanson, R. P. C. *Allegory and Event: A Study of the Sources and Significance of Origen's Interpretation of Scripture.* Richmond: John Knox Press, 1959.

Hanssens, Jean-Michel. *La liturgie d'Hippolyte, ses documents, sen titulaire, ses origins et son caractere.* Orientalia Christiana Analecta 155. Rome: Pont. Institutum Orientalium Studiorum, 1955.

Heine, Ronald E. "Christology of Callistus." *Journal of Theological Studies* 49 (1998): 56-91.

Hidal, Sten. "Apocalypse, Persecution and Exegesis." *In the Last Days: On Jewish and Christian Apocalyptic and its Period.* Aarhus, Denmark: Aarhus University Press, 1994.

Hill, Charles E. *Regnum Caelorum: Patterns of Millennial Thought in Early Christianity.* 2nd edition. Grand Rapids: Eerdmans, 2001.

Hollerich, Michael J. "Religion and Politics in the Writings of Eusebius: Reassessing the First 'Court Theologian.'" *Church History* 59 (1990): 309-25.

Holmes, Michael W., ed. *The Apostolic Fathers: Greek Texts and English Translations.* Grand Rapids: Baker, 1999.

Hultgren, Arland J. and Steven A. Haggmark, eds. *The Earliest Christian Heretics: Readings from their Opponents.* Minneapolis: Fortress Press, 1996.

Kannengiesser, Charles, ed. *Handbook of Patristic Exegesis: The Bible in Ancient Christianity.* 2 vols. Boston: Brill, 2004.

Keil, C.F. and F. Delitzsch. *Commentary on the Old Testament: Vol. IX, Ezekial, Daniel.* Translated by M.G. Easton. Grand Rapids: Eerdmans, 1978.

Kellerman, Ulrich. "Das Danielbuch und die Märtyrertheologie der Auferstehung." *Die Entstehung der Jüdischen Martyrologie.* New York: E. J. Brill, 1989.

Knowles, Louis E. "The Interpretation of the Seventy Weeks of Daniel in the Early Fathers." *Westminster Theological Journal* 7 (1945): 136-60.

Koester, Helmut. "Writings and the Spirit: Authority and Politics in Ancient Christianity." *Harvard Theological Review* 54 (1991): 353-72.

Lampe, G.W.H. *Patristic Greek Lexicon.* Oxford: Clarendon, 1961-68.

Lane Fox, Robin. *Pagans and Christians: Religion and The Religious Life From the Second to the Fourth Century A.D., When the Gods of Olympus Lost Their Dominion and Christianity, with the Conversion of Constantine, Triumphed in the Mediterranean World.* New York: Alfred A. Knopf, 1987.

Lefèvre, Maurice. Translation and commentary. *Commentaire sur Daniel.* Vol. 14, Sources Chrétiennes. Paris: Éditions du Cerf, 1947.

Lenski, R.C.H. *The Interpretation of the Epistles of St. Peter, St. John and St. Jude.* Minneapolis: Augsburg, 1966.

Lesbaupin, Ivo. *Blessed Are the Persecuted: Christian Life in the Roman Empire, A.D. 64-313.* Translated by Robert R. Barr. Maryknoll, NY: Orbis Books, 1987.

Lightfoot, Joseph Barber. *The Apostolic Fathers.* Edited by Michael Holmes. Translated by J.B. Lightfoot and J.R. Harmer. Grand Rapids: Baker Book House, 1989.

Loi, Vincenzo. "La problematica storico-letteraria su Ippolytus di Roma." *Ricerche su Ippolito* 13. Rome: Institutum Patristicum Augustinianum, 1977: 9-16.

Longenecker, Richard. *Biblical Exegesis in the Apostolic Period.* Grand Rapids: Eerdmans, 1975.

Loraux, Nicole. *Tragic Ways of Killing a Woman.* Translated by Anthony Forster. Cambridge, Mass.: Harvard University Press, 1987.

Lynch, E. M. *The Controversy over Patristic Exegesis 1875-1965.* Lauderhill, FL: Atlantic, 1976.

MacMullen, Ramsey. *Christianizing the Roman Empire: AD 100-400.* New Haven: Yale University Press, 1984.

MacRae, Allan A. *The Prophecies of Daniel.* Singapore: Christian Life Publishers, 1991.

Marcovich, Miroslav. "Textual Criticism on Hippolytus' *Refutio.*" *Journal of Theological Studies* 19 (1968): 83-92.

de Margerie, Bertrand. *An Introduction to the History of Exegesis. Vol I, The Greek Fathers.* Petersham, Mass.: Saint Bede's Publications, 1991.

Martin, Ralph P. "Martyr; Martyrology." *The New International Dictionary of the Christian Church.* Edited by J. D. Douglas. Grand Rapids: Zondervan, 1978.

McCollough, C. Thomas. "Daniel." *Encyclopedia of Early Christianity.* Edited by Everett Ferguson. New York: Garland Publishing, 1990.

McLeod, Fredrick G. *Image of God in the Antiochene Tradition.* Washington, D.C.: Catholic University of America Press, 1999.

McKay, Gretchen Kreahling. "The Eastern Christian Exegetical Tradition of Daniel's Vision of the Ancient of Days." *Journal of Early Christian Studies* 7 (1999): 139-161.

McRay, J. "Scripture and Tradition in Irenaeus." *Restoration Quarterly* 10 (1967): 1-11.

Metzger, Bruce M. *The Canon of the New Testament: Its Origin, Development, and Significance.* Oxford: Claredon Press, 1987.

Miller, Fergus. *Emperor in the Roman World 31 BC-337 AD.* Ithaca, NY: Cornell

University Press, 1977.

Mohrmann, Christine. *Liturgical Latin: Its Origins and Characteristics*. Washington, D.C.: Catholic University Press, 1957.

Nautin, Pierre. *Hippolyte et Josipe: Contribution à l'histoire de la littérature chrétienne du troisième siècle*. Paris: Editions du Cerf, 1947.

_____. "Hippolytus." *Encyclopedia of the Early Church*. Edited by Angelo Di Berardino. Translated by Adrian Wolford. 2 vols. New York: Oxford University Press, 1992.

_____. "Notes sur le catolgogue des oeuvres d'Hippolyte." *Recherches de science religieuse* 34 (1947): 99-107.

Neal, Gordon C. "Porphyry." *The New International Dictionary of the Christian Church*. Edited by J. D. Douglas. Grand Rapids: Zondervan Publishing, 1978.

O'Keefe, John J. and R.R. Reno. *Sanctified Vision: An Introduction to Early Christian Interpretation of the Bible*. Baltimore: Johns Hopkins University Press, 2005.

Ogg, George. "The Computist of AD 243 and Hippolytus." *Journal of Theological Studies* 48 (1947): 206-207.

_____. "Hippolytus and the Introduction of the Christian Era." *Vigiliae Christianne* 16 (1962): 2-18.

Osborn, Eric. *Irenaeus of Lyons*. New York: Cambridge University Press, 2001.

Osborne, Catherine. *Rethinking Early Greek Philosophy*. Ithaca, NY: Cornell University Press, 1987.

Pelikan, Jaroslav. *The Christian Tradition: A History of the Development of Doctrine*. Vol. I, *The Emergence of the Catholic Tradition (100-600)*. Chicago: University of Chicago Press, 1971.

Perkins, Judith. *The Suffering Servant*. London: Routledge, 1995.

Plöger, Otto. *Theology and Eschatology*. Translated by S. Rudman. Richmond: John Knox Press, 1978.

Prinzivalli, E. "Statue of Hippolytus." *Encyclopedia of the Early Church*. Edited by Angelo Di Berardino. 2 vols. Translated by Adrian Wolford. New York: Oxford University Press, 1992.

Quasten, Johannes. *Patrology*. 3 vols. Utrecht-Antwerp: Spectrum Publishers, 1966.

Richard, Marcel. "Einleitung." *Kommentar zu Daniel*. Translated by Georg Nathanael Bonwetsch. Berlin: Akadamie Verlag, 2000.

_____. "Hippolyte et Rome." *Dictionnaire de spiritualite* 7 (Paris 1968): 531-71.

_____. "Les difficultés d'une édition du commentaire de saint Hippolyte sur Daniel." *Revue d'histoire des texts, tome 2* (Paris: Centre National de la Recherche Scientifique, 1972): 1-10.

_____. "Pour une nouvelle édition du commentaire de saint Hippolyte sur Daniel." *Kyriakon: Festschrift Johannes Quasten*. Eds. Patrick Granfield and Josef A. Jungmann. Munseter Westfalen: Verlag Aschendorff, 1970.

Ritschl, Dietrich. "Hippolytus' Conception of Deification." *Scottish Journal of Theology* 12 (1959): 388-99.

Rordorf, Willy. "Martyr, Martyrdom." *Encyclopedia of the Early Church*. Edited by Angelo Di Berardino. Translated by Adrian Wolford. 2 vols. New York:

Oxford University Press, 1992.

Ruffin, C. Bernard. *The Days of the Martyrs: A History of the Persecution of Christians from Apostolic Times to the Time of Constantine.* Huntington, IN: Our Sunday Visitor, Inc., 1985.

Russell, David M. *The "New Heavens and New Earth": Hope for the Creation in Jewish Apcocalyptic and the New Testament.* Vol. 1, Studies in Biblical Apocalyptic Literature. Philadelphia: Visionary Press, 1996.

Russell, David S. *Divine Disclosure: An Introduction to Jewish Apocalyptic.* Minneapolis: Fortress Press, 1992.

_____. *The Jews from Alexander to Herod.* Oxford: Oxford University Press, 1967.

_____. *The Method and Message of Jewish Apocalyptic: 200 B.C.-A.D. 100.* Philadelphia: Westminster Press, 1964.

Sadowski, Frank, ed. *The Church Fathers on the Bible: Selected Readings.* New York: Alba House, 1987.

Salisbury, Joyce E. *Perpetua's Passion: The Death and Memory of a Young Roman Woman.* New York: Routledge, 1997.

Salmon, George. "The Commentary of Hippolytus on Daniel." *Hermathena* 8 (1893): 161-190.

_____. "The Commentary of Hippolytus on Daniel." *Hermathena* 14 (1899): 82-128.

Schaff, Philip. *History of the Christian Church.* Vol. II, *Ante-Nicene Christianity AD 100-325.* Grand Rapids: Eerdmans, 1966.

Scholten, Clemens von. "Hippolyt II (von Rom)." *Rivista di archeologia cristiana* 15 (1938): 492-551.

_____. Review of J.A. Cerrato, *Hippolytus between East and West: The Commentaries and the Provenance of the Corpus. Vigiliae Christianae* 59 (2005): 85-92.

Shea, William H. "Early Development of the Antiochus Epiphanes Interpretation." Vol. 2, *Symposium on Daniel: Introductory and Exegetical Studies.* Edited by Frank B. Holbrook. Daniel and Revelation Committee Series. Washington, D.C.: Biblical Research Institute, 1986.

Shelley, Bruce L. *The Cross and the Flame: Chapters in the History of Martyrdom.* Grand Rapids: Eerdmans, 1967.

Shelton, W. Brian. Review of J.A. Cerrato, *Hippolytus between East and West: The Commentaries and the Provenance of the Corpus. Journal of Early Christian Studies* 12 (2004): 361-362.

Signer, Michael A. and Susan L. Graham. "Rabbinic Literature." Vol. 1, *Handbook of Patristic Exegesis: The Bible in Ancient Christianity.* Edited by Charles Kannengiesser. Boston: Brill, 2004.

Siker, Jeffrey S. "The Parousia of Jesus in Second and Third Century Christianity." *The Return of Jesus in Early Christianity.* Edited by John T. Carroll. Peabody, Mass.: Hendrickson, 2000.

Simonetti, Manlio. *Biblical Interpretation in the Early Church: An Historical Introduction to Patristic Exegesis.* Translated by John A. Hughes. Edinburgh: T & T Clark, 1994.

_____. *Ricerche su Ippolito.* Studia Ephemeridis Augustinianum 13. Rome: Institutum

Patristicum Augustinianum, 1977.

Smith, Lacey Baldwin. *Fools, Martyrs, Traitors: The Story of Martyrdom in the Western World.* New York: Alfred A. Knopf, 1997.

Soboson, Jeffrey G. "The Role of the Presbyter." *Scottish Journal of Theology* 27 (1974): 129-46.

Stewart-Sykes, Alistair. "Papyrus Oxyrhynchus 5: A Prophetic Protest from Second Century Rome." *Studia Patristica* 31 (1997): 196-205.

_____. Review of J.A. Cerrato, *Hippolytus between East and West: The Commentaries and the Provenance of the Corpus. St. Vladimir's Theological Quarterly* 49 (2006): 353-355.

Suchla, Beate Regina. "Hippolytus." *Dictionary of Early Christian Literature.* Edited by Siegmar Döpp and Wilhelm Geerlings. Translated by Matthew O' Connell. New York: Crossroad Publishing, 1998.

Thompson, Steven. "Those Who Are Wise: The *Maskilim* in Daniel and the New Testament." *To Understand the Scriptures: Essays in Honor of William H. Shea.* Edited by David Merling. Berrien Springs, Mich.: Institute of Archeology of Andrews University, 1997.

Toon, Peter. "Hippolytus." *The New International Dictionary of the Christian Church.* Edited by J. D. Douglas. Grand Rapids: Zondervan, 1978.

Trakatellis, Demetrios. "ΛΟΓΟΣ ΑΓΟΝΙΣΤΙΚΟΣ: Hippolytus' Commentary on Daniel." *Religious Propaganda and Missionary Competition in the New Testament World: Essays Honoring Dieter Georgi.* Edited by Lukas Bormann, Kelly del Tredici, and Angela Standhartinger. New York: E. J. Brill, 1994.

Tsirpanlis, Constantine. "The Antichrist and the End of the World in Irenaeus, Justin, Hippolytus, and Tertullian." *Patristic and Byzantine Review* 9 (1990): 5-17.

Vallée, Gérard. *A Study in Anti-Gnostic Polemics: Irenaeus, Hippolytus, and Epiphanius.* Vol 1, Studies in Christianity and Judaism. Ontario: Wilfrid Laurier University Press, 1981.

Van Braght, Thieleman J. *The Bloody Theater or Martyrs Mirror of the Defenseless Christians.* Translated by Joseph F. Sohm. 11th edition. Scottdale, PA: Herald Press, 1977.

Vanyó, Laszló. "Daniel: In the Fathers." *Encyclopedia of the Early Church.* Edited by Angelo Di Berardino. Translated by Adrian Wolford. 2 vols. New York: Oxford University Press, 1992.

Violard, E. *Etude sur le commentaire d'Hippolyte sur le Livre de Daniel.* Montbéliard: Imprimerie Montbéliardaise, 1903.

Visser, A. J. "A Bird's-eye View of Ancient Christian Eschatology." *Numen: International Review for the History of Religions* 14 (1967): 4-22.

Young, Frances M. *Biblical Exegesis and the Formation of Christian Culture.* Cambridge: Cambridge University Press, 1997.

Whealey, A. "Pseudo-Justin's *De Resurrectione*: Athenagorus or Hippolytus?" *Vigiliae Christianae* 60 (2006): 420-30.

Williams, Robert Lee. "'Hippolytan' Reactions to Montanism: Tensions in the Churches of Rome in the Early Third Century." *Studia Patristica* 39 (2006): 131-138.

_____. "Persecution." *Encyclopedia of Early Christianity.* 1st edition. Edited by Everett Ferguson. New York: Garland Publishing, 1990.

Wilken, Robert L. *The Christians as the Romans Saw Them.* New Haven, CT: Yale University Press, 1984.

Workman, Herbert B. *Persecution in the Early Church.* Oxford: Oxford University Press, 1980.

_____. *Persecution in the Early Church: A Chapter in the History of Renunciation.* London: Charles H. Kelly, 1906.

Author Index

Scripture Index with Apocrypha

Studies in Christian History and Thought
(All titles uniform with this volume)
Dates in bold are of projected publication

David Bebbington
Holiness in Nineteenth-Century England
David Bebbington stresses the relationship of movements of spirituality to changes in their cultural setting, especially the legacies of the Enlightenment and Romanticism. He shows that these broad shifts in ideological mood had a profound effect on the ways in which piety was conceptualized and practised. Holiness was intimately bound up with the spirit of the age.
2000 / 0-85364-981-2 / viii + 98pp

J. William Black
Reformation Pastors
Richard Baxter and the Ideal of the Reformed Pastor
This work examines Richard Baxter's *Gildas Salvianus, The Reformed Pastor* (1656) and explores each aspect of his pastoral strategy in light of his own concern for 'reformation' and in the broader context of Edwardian, Elizabethan and early Stuart pastoral ideals and practice.
2003 / 1-84227-190-3 / xxii + 308pp

James Bruce
Prophecy, Miracles, Angels, *and* Heavenly Light?
The Eschatology, Pneumatology and Missiology of Adomnán's Life of Columba
This book surveys approaches to the marvellous in hagiography, providing the first critique of Plummer's hypothesis of Irish saga origin. It then analyses the uniquely systematized phenomena in the *Life of Columba* from Adomnán's seventh-century theological perspective, identifying the coming of the eschatological Kingdom as the key to understanding.
2004 / 1-84227-227-6 / xviii + 286pp

Colin J. Bulley
The Priesthood of Some Believers
Developments from the General to the Special Priesthood in the Christian Literature of the First Three Centuries
The first in-depth treatment of early Christian texts on the priesthood of all believers shows that the developing priesthood of the ordained related closely to the division between laity and clergy and had deleterious effects on the practice of the general priesthood.
2000 / 1-84227-034-6 / xii + 336pp

July 2005

Anthony R. Cross (ed.)
Ecumenism and History
Studies in Honour of John H.Y. Briggs
This collection of essays examines the inter-relationships between the two fields in which Professor Briggs has contributed so much: history—particularly Baptist and Nonconformist—and the ecumenical movement. With contributions from colleagues and former research students from Britain, Europe and North America, *Ecumenism and History* provides wide-ranging studies in important aspects of Christian history, theology and ecumenical studies.
2002 / 1-84227-135-0 / xx + 362pp

Maggi Dawn
Confessions of an Inquiring Spirit
Form as Constitutive of Meaning in S.T. Coleridge's Theological Writing
This study of Coleridge's *Confessions* focuses on its confessional, epistolary and fragmentary form, suggesting that attention to these features significantly affects its interpretation. Bringing a close study of these three literary forms, the author suggests ways in which they nuance the text with particular understandings of the Trinity, and of a kenotic christology. Some parallels are drawn between Romantic and postmodern dilemmas concerning the authority of the biblical text.
2006 / 1-84227-255-1 / approx. 224 pp

Ruth Gouldbourne
The Flesh and the Feminine
Gender and Theology in the Writings of Caspar Schwenckfeld
Caspar Schwenckfeld and his movement exemplify one of the radical communities of the sixteenth century. Challenging theological and liturgical norms, they also found themselves challenging social and particularly gender assumptions. In this book, the issues of the relationship between radical theology and the understanding of gender are considered.
2005 / 1-84227-048-6 / approx. 304pp

Crawford Gribben
Puritan Millennialism
Literature and Theology, 1550–1682
Puritan Millennialism surveys the growth, impact and eventual decline of puritan millennialism throughout England, Scotland and Ireland, arguing that it was much more diverse than has frequently been suggested. This Paternoster edition is revised and extended from the original 2000 text.
2007 / 1-84227-372-8 / approx. 320pp

Galen K. Johnson
Prisoner of Conscience
John Bunyan on Self, Community and Christian Faith
This is an interdisciplinary study of John Bunyan's understanding of conscience across his autobiographical, theological and fictional writings, investigating whether conscience always deserves fidelity, and how Bunyan's view of conscience affects his relationship both to modern Western individualism and historic Christianity.

2003 / 1-84227-223-3 / xvi + 236pp

R.T. Kendall
Calvin and English Calvinism to 1649
The author's thesis is that those who formed the Westminster Confession of Faith, which is regarded as Calvinism, in fact departed from John Calvin on two points: (1) the extent of the atonement and (2) the ground of assurance of salvation.

1997 / 0-85364-827-1 / xii + 264pp

Timothy Larsen
Friends of Religious Equality
Nonconformist Politics in Mid-Victorian England
During the middle decades of the nineteenth century the English Nonconformist community developed a coherent political philosophy of its own, of which a central tenet was the principle of religious equality (in contrast to the stereotype of Evangelical Dissenters). The Dissenting community fought for the civil rights of Roman Catholics, non-Christians and even atheists on an issue of principle which had its flowering in the enthusiastic and undivided support which Nonconformity gave to the campaign for Jewish emancipation. This reissued study examines the political efforts and ideas of English Nonconformists during the period, covering the whole range of national issues raised, from state education to the Crimean War. It offers a case study of a theologically conservative group defending religious pluralism in the civic sphere, showing that the concept of religious equality was a grand vision at the centre of the political philosophy of the Dissenters.

2007 / 1-84227-402-3 / x + 300pp

Byung-Ho Moon
Christ the Mediator of the Law
Calvin's Christological Understanding of the Law as the Rule of Living and Life-Giving

This book explores the coherence between Christology and soteriology in Calvin's theology of the law, examining its intellectual origins and his position on the concept and extent of Christ's mediation of the law. A comparative study between Calvin and contemporary Reformers—Luther, Bucer, Melancthon and Bullinger—and his opponent Michael Servetus is made for the purpose of pointing out the unique feature of Calvin's Christological understanding of the law.

2005 / 1-84227-318-3 / approx. 370pp

John Eifion Morgan-Wynne
Holy Spirit and Religious Experience in Christian Writings, c.AD 90–200

This study examines how far Christians in the third to fifth generations (c.AD 90–200) attributed their sense of encounter with the divine presence, their sense of illumination in the truth or guidance in decision-making, and their sense of ethical empowerment to the activity of the Holy Spirit in their lives.

2005 / 1-84227-319-1 / approx. 350pp

James I. Packer
The Redemption and Restoration of Man in the Thought of Richard Baxter

James I. Packer provides a full and sympathetic exposition of Richard Baxter's doctrine of humanity, created and fallen; its redemption by Christ Jesus; and its restoration in the image of God through the obedience of faith by the power of the Holy Spirit.

2002 / 1-84227-147-4 / 432pp

Andrew Partington,
Church and State
*The Contribution of the Church of England Bishops to the House of Lords
during the Thatcher Years*

In *Church and State*, Andrew Partington argues that the contribution of the Church of England bishops to the House of Lords during the Thatcher years was overwhelmingly critical of the government; failed to have a significant influence in the public realm; was inefficient, being undertaken by a minority of those eligible to sit on the Bench of Bishops; and was insufficiently moral and spiritual in its content to be distinctive. On the basis of this, and the likely reduction of the number of places available for Church of England bishops in a fully reformed Second Chamber, the author argues for an evolution in the Church of England's approach to the service of its bishops in the House of Lords. He proposes the Church of England works to overcome the genuine obstacles which hinder busy diocesan bishops from contributing to the debates of the House of Lords and to its life more informally.

2005 / 1-84227-334-5 / approx. 324pp

Michael Pasquarello III
God's Ploughman
Hugh Latimer: A 'Preaching Life' (1490–1555)

This construction of a 'preaching life' situates Hugh Latimer within the larger religious, political and intellectual world of late medieval England. Neither biography, intellectual history, nor analysis of discrete sermon texts, this book is a work of homiletic history which draws from the details of Latimer's milieu to construct an interpretive framework for the preaching performances that formed the core of his identity as a religious reformer. Its goal is to illumine the practical wisdom embodied in the content, form and style of Latimer's preaching, and to recapture a sense of its overarching purpose, movement, and transforming force during the reform of sixteenth-century England.

2006 / 1-84227-336-1 / approx. 250pp

Alan P.F. Sell
Enlightenment, Ecumenism, Evangel
Theological Themes and Thinkers 1550–2000

This book consists of papers in which such interlocking topics as the Enlightenment, the problem of authority, the development of doctrine, spirituality, ecumenism, theological method and the heart of the gospel are discussed. Issues of significance to the church at large are explored with special reference to writers from the Reformed and Dissenting traditions.

2005 / 1-84227-330-2 / xviii + 422pp

Alan P.F. Sell
Hinterland Theology
Some Reformed and Dissenting Adjustments
Many books have been written on theology's 'giants' and significant trends, but what of those lesser-known writers who adjusted to them? In this book some hinterland theologians of the British Reformed and Dissenting traditions, who followed in the wake of toleration, the Evangelical Revival, the rise of modern biblical criticism and Karl Barth, are allowed to have their say. They include Thomas Ridgley, Ralph Wardlaw, T.V. Tymms and N.H.G. Robinson.
2006 / 1-84227-331-0 / approx. 350pp

Alan P.F. Sell and Anthony R. Cross (eds)
Protestant Nonconformity in the Twentieth Century
In this collection of essays scholars representative of a number of Nonconformist traditions reflect thematically on Nonconformists' life and witness during the twentieth century. Among the subjects reviewed are biblical studies, theology, worship, evangelism and spirituality, and ecumenism. Over and above its immediate interest, this collection provides a marker to future scholars and others wishing to know how some of their forebears assessed Nonconformity's contribution to a variety of fields during the century leading up to Christianity's third millennium.
2003 / 1-84227-221-7 / x + 398pp

Mark Smith
Religion in Industrial Society
Oldham and Saddleworth 1740–1865
This book analyses the way British churches sought to meet the challenge of industrialization and urbanization during the period 1740–1865. Working from a case-study of Oldham and Saddleworth, Mark Smith challenges the received view that the Anglican Church in the eighteenth century was characterized by complacency and inertia, and reveals Anglicanism's vigorous and creative response to the new conditions. He reassesses the significance of the centrally directed church reforms of the mid-nineteenth century, and emphasizes the importance of local energy and enthusiasm. Charting the growth of denominational pluralism in Oldham and Saddleworth, Dr Smith compares the strengths and weaknesses of the various Anglican and Nonconformist approaches to promoting church growth. He also demonstrates the extent to which all the churches participated in a common culture shaped by the influence of evangelicalism, and shows that active co-operation between the churches rather than denominational conflict dominated. This revised and updated edition of Dr Smith's challenging and original study makes an important contribution both to the social history of religion and to urban studies.
2006 / 1-84227-335-3 / approx. 300pp

Martin Sutherland
Peace, Toleration and Decay
The Ecclesiology of Later Stuart Dissent
This fresh analysis brings to light the complexity and fragility of the later Stuart Nonconformist consensus. Recent findings on wider seventeenth-century thought are incorporated into a new picture of the dynamics of Dissent and the roots of evangelicalism.
2003 / 1-84227-152-0 / xxii + 216pp

G. Michael Thomas
The Extent of the Atonement
A Dilemma for Reformed Theology from Calvin to the Consensus
A study of the way Reformed theology addressed the question, 'Did Christ die for all, or for the elect only?', commencing with John Calvin, and including debates with Lutheranism, the Synod of Dort and the teaching of Moïse Amyraut.
1997 / 0-85364-828-X / x + 278pp

David M. Thompson
Baptism, Church and Society in Britain from the Evangelical Revival to
Baptism, Eucharist and Ministry
The theology and practice of baptism have not received the attention they deserve. How important is faith? What does baptismal regeneration mean? Is baptism a bond of unity between Christians? This book discusses the theology of baptism and popular belief and practice in England and Wales from the Evangelical Revival to the publication of the World Council of Churches' consensus statement on *Baptism, Eucharist and Ministry* (1982).
2005 / 1-84227-393-0 / approx. 224pp

Mark D. Thompson
A Sure Ground on Which to Stand
The Relation of Authority and Interpretive Method of Luther's Approach to Scripture
The best interpreter of Luther is Luther himself. Unfortunately many modern studies have superimposed contemporary agendas upon this sixteenth-century Reformer's writings. This fresh study examines Luther's own words to find an explanation for his robust confidence in the Scriptures, a confidence that generated the famous 'stand' at Worms in 1521.
2004 / 1-84227-145-8 / xvi + 322pp

Carl R. Trueman and R.S. Clark (eds)
Protestant Scholasticism
Essays in Reassessment
Traditionally Protestant theology, between Luther's early reforming career and the dawn of the Enlightenment, has been seen in terms of decline and fall into the wastelands of rationalism and scholastic speculation. In this volume a number of scholars question such an interpretation. The editors argue that the development of post-Reformation Protestantism can only be understood when a proper historical model of doctrinal change is adopted. This historical concern underlies the subsequent studies of theologians such as Calvin, Beza, Olevian, Baxter, and the two Turrentini. The result is a significantly different reading of the development of Protestant Orthodoxy, one which both challenges the older scholarly interpretations and clichés about the relationship of Protestantism to, among other things, scholasticism and rationalism, and which demonstrates the fruitfulness of the new, historical approach.

1999 / 0-85364-853-0 / xx + 344pp

Shawn D. Wright
Our Sovereign Refuge
The Pastoral Theology of Theodore Beza
Our Sovereign Refuge is a study of the pastoral theology of the Protestant reformer who inherited the mantle of leadership in the Reformed church from John Calvin. Countering a common view of Beza as supremely a 'scholastic' theologian who deviated from Calvin's biblical focus, Wright uncovers a new portrait. He was not a cold and rigid academic theologian obsessed with probing the eternal decrees of God. Rather, by placing him in his pastoral context and by noting his concerns in his pastoral and biblical treatises, Wright shows that Beza was fundamentally a committed Christian who was troubled by the vicissitudes of life in the second half of the sixteenth century. He believed that the biblical truth of the supreme sovereignty of God alone could support Christians on their earthly pilgrimage to heaven. This pastoral and personal portrait forms the heart of Wright's argument.

2004 / 1-84227-252-7 / xviii + 308pp

Paternoster:
thinking faith

Paternoster
9 Holdom Avenue,
Bletchley,
Milton Keynes MK1 1QR,
United Kingdom
Web: www.authenticmedia.co.uk/paternoster

July 2005

www.ingramcontent.com/pod-product-compliance
Lightning Source LLC
Chambersburg PA
CBHW060338100426
42812CB00003B/1044